# STUDIES IN ENGLISH LITERATURE

## Volume XXIX

# THE DUAL HERITAGE

## OF

# JOSEPH CONRAD

*by*

ROBERT R. HODGES

*California State College*
*Fullerton*

1967

MOUTON & CO.

THE HAGUE · PARIS

Printed in The Netherlands by Mouton & Co., Printers, The Hague.

*For my Mother and Father*

# TABLE OF CONTENTS

# INTRODUCTION

In December 1903 Joseph Conrad, self-exiled from both his native Poland and the sea, and only beginning to receive recognition as an English writer, interrupted the composition of *Nostromo* to write a letter to his compatriot in Paris, Kasimir Waliszewski. Unburdening himself in Polish to this fellow Pole, fellow exile, and fellow writer, Conrad confessed: "Homo duplex has in my case more than one meaning." [1] Conrad, a Pole in England and a sailor gone ashore, concluded: "You will understand me. I shall not dwell upon that subject."

Conrad's suggestive phrase, homo duplex, has indeed more than one meaning, but in its most profound sense the phrase points to a basic division in Conrad's mind originating in two contrary influences of his early years. Successively, Conrad's father and then his maternal uncle took responsibility for his education and rearing. Their continuing influence strongly marked his life and writing, illustrating what Joseph Wood Krutch has pointed out about the creation of fiction:

That complicated balance of elements which is necessary for good fiction seems usually to have been achieved by the imagination of a writer whose mind was to some extent divided against itself.[2]

The contrast between the lives and values of his father, Apollo Korzeniowski, and his uncle, Tadeusz Bobrowski, gave Conrad

---

[1] Letter to Kasimir Waliszewski (Dec. 5, 1903), *Conrad's Polish Background, Letters to and from Polish Friends*, ed. Zdislaw Najder (London, Oxford University Press, 1964), p. 240.
[2] Joseph Wood Krutch, *Five Masters* (New York, Jonathan Cape and Harrison Smith, 1930), p. 165.

that mind divided against itself. From his youth he felt that life was double, and in his maturity he dramatized this division in his writing. Even in his last, fragmentary novel written near the end of his life, Conrad has the hero reflect that the world preserves "a mysterious complexity and a dual character".[3]

A glance at Conrad's earliest experiences with the two men reveals the nature of the "mysterious complexity and dual character" of the homo duplex himself. The child saw his father, despite a passionate devotion to ideals, struggle ineffectually against defeat and despair. After his arrest and conviction for conspiracy against the Russian empire, Apollo Korzeniowski and his wife took their four-year old son into exile in Russia. Four years later his wife died, and he was left alone to raise his son. Ultimately he was permitted to bring the boy back to Poland, but, wasted by disease, he then had less than two years to live. When he was only forty-nine, he died; and his eleven year old son followed his coffin to the cemetery. Despite this long sequence of personal and national disasters, Korzeniowski sought first of all to make his son a good Pole, a patriot. After Korzeniowski's death, however, Conrad was taught to disapprove of him. His maternal uncle, a man the antithesis of his father in temperament and career, impressed upon the youth the dangers of his father's weaknesses and the necessities of developing a profession, of avoiding unhealthy introspection, and of following a strict code of moral duty. As a child Conrad could express his loneliness and privation only by repeated severe illnesses. In youth, egotism and sarcasm perhaps represent his reactions to a process of re-education that was too explicit and too late to be carried out successfully.

"Honor thy father" has always been a difficult commandment, but for Conrad, the man with two fathers, the difficulty was compounded. Each father loved him; each had a profound influence upon him. Conrad felt himself torn between his father's impractical idealism and his uncle's practical morality. Both men laid upon

---

[3] *Suspense*, p. 38. All references to Conrad's published writings (with the exception of letters) will be to the Collected Edition of the Works of Joseph Conrad published in London by J. M. Dent between 1948 and 1955. In footnotes I shall simply refer to the title of the book and, if necessary, to the title of the story or essay.

him compelling obligations. The awareness of these antipathies, intensified by Conrad's belief in the claims of heredity upon the individual,[4] made for a life of unrest. All his life Conrad felt the attraction of vigorous revolutionary patriotism and the counter-attraction to something more stable and conservative that was still not ignoble bourgois convention. Encouraged by his uncle in this quest for an honorable conservative bulwark, he sought a number of spiritual fathers, each of whom might initiate him into a profession or craft and thus save him from the ineffectual dilettante-ism pointed out to him as his father's failing. Fidelity to such a craft would compensate for Conrad's patriotic guilt over leaving Poland. In his turn Conrad himself served well as a spiritual father to a number of men, both sailors and writers. Out of these tensions between father and uncle, patriot and cosmopolitan, revolutionist and conservative, romantic and realist, dilettante and craftsman, real father and spiritual father, Conrad created some of his finest fiction.

When these paternal tensions were finally resolved or rather relaxed, largely in favor of Apollo Korzeniowski, Conrad's writing became slack, sentimental, and shallow. And ultimately he had little to write about. His cries of despair filling the letters and reports of his conversation during his last years accompany attempts to re-use old material. When the homo duplex became the homo simplex, his writing suffered accordingly.

The first two chapters of this study discuss the nature of the two influences on Conrad and their direct effect on his mind and his writing. In the last two chapters I shall discuss Conrad's apparent reconciliation of the two influences, his own uncritical acceptance of his father's nationalism, and the unfortunate effects of these inner changes upon his personality and his writing.

The ideas I propose to discuss are, of course, not altogether new. Most critics recognize that Conrad's father and his uncle strongly influenced him and that Conrad felt himself a Pole all his life. They have chiefly emphasized the effect of Conrad's father. E. H. Visiak in *The Mirror of Conrad* speculates that the youthful Conrad saw his father's decline and slow death as the in-

---

[4] "Poland Revisited", *Notes on Life and Letters*, p. 176.

evitable fate of patriotic fanaticism, mental instability, and the failure of self-control.[5] Miss Jerry Allen in the penultimate chapter of her biography of Conrad, *The Thunder and the Sunshine*, points out briefly the fictional results of this experience.

From early years spent with a father extreme in his political and religious beliefs grew Conrad's admiration for the sane view of life and his hostility to political and religious extremists. ... In an echo of his childhood his troubled men of fiction were, like himself, sons deprived of mothers, raised by fathers with fixed ideas. ... .[6]

Irving Howe, in his analysis of Conrad's political novels, discusses both Conrad's relationship to his father's politics and the nature of those politics. Howe defines the revolutionary nationalism that Korzeniowski espoused: "Romantic rather than analytical, it exalts the mystique of the nation rather than the war of the classes, it creates an ambiance of blurred fraternity rather than of social antagonism." [7] He makes three important points concerning Conrad's relation to his father's politics. First he points out, "When the children of revolutionaries revolt, it is against revolution." [8] Second, he brilliantly traces the similarities between anarchism – apparently Conrad's chief target in his political fiction – and revolutionary nationalism.[9] Finally, Howe shows that Conrad's conservatism is rooted in some elements of Polish nationalism.[10]

The most significant of the studies discussing Apollo Korzeniowski and his son is the earliest, Gustav Morf's *The Polish Heritage of Joseph Conrad* (1930).[11] Although Morf's work was for a long time ridiculed for its psychological speculations and has lately been criticized for its factual errors,[12] it nonetheless has

---

[5]  E. H. Visiak, *The Mirror of Conrad* (London, Werner Laurie, 1955), p. 33.
[6]  Jerry Allen, *The Thunder and the Sunshine* (New York, Putnam's, 1958), p. 234.
[7]  Irving Howe, "Conrad, Order and Anarchy", *Politics and the Novel* (New York, Meridian Books, 1957), p. 77.
[8]  *Ibid.*, p. 78.
[9]  *Ibid.*, pp. 83-84.
[10]  *Ibid.*, p. 83.
[11]  Gustav Morf, *The Polish Heritage of Joseph Conrad* (London, Sampson, Low, Marston, 1930).
[12]  Najder, p. 308.

been a pilot study for scholars dealing with Conrad's background. Morf is often too explicit, but his concept that Conrad's fiction repeatedly reflects his guilt over leaving Poland is sound. Recently, Morf's concern for Conrad's relation to his Polish heritage has been taken up in detail. Eloise Knapp Hay prefaces her study of Conrad's political novels (1963) by discussing at length both the romantic political creed of Apollo Korzeniowski as well as Tadeusz Bobrowski's realistic objections to that creed. Furthermore, she indicates the importance of this contrast for Conrad himself. Her book proved extremely useful in completing this study, but where our paths cross we disagree. Mrs. Hay finds no traces in Conrad's work of the central myth of Polish romanticism, national Messianism.[13] I shall try to show that this myth, either disguised or secularized, appears in both the great fiction of his early literary career as well as the weaker fiction and essays of his later years.

Zdzislaw Najder in his introduction to Conrad's letters to and from Polish friends deals succinctly with the Polish background. Drawing on considerable resources, Najder corrects the prevailing hypercritical portrait of Korzeniowski, based too exclusively, he points out, on his brother-in-law's comments. In considering Najder's more accurate image of Conrad's father, we must not forget that it was Bobrowski's view of Korzeniowski, however distorted, which made a profound impression on Conrad. One hesitates to disagree directly with so knowledgeable a Polish critic, yet Najder's description of Bobrowski seems belied by the very letters he has edited. Najder's introduction over-emphasizes Bobrowski's counsels of "resignation", the source he says for Conrad's "deep scepticism, frequently tinged with pessimism".[14] Far more pronounced, rather, in his letters to his nephew are Bobrowski's repeated encouragements of reason, sober self-knowledge, and duty. And these active values, rather than "resignation", constitute Bobrowski's chief influence on his nephew.

Finally, I must comment on my writing this study without

---

[13] Eloise Knapp Hay, *The Political Novels of Joseph Conrad* (Chicago, University of Chicago Press, 1963), p. 79.
[14] Najder, p. 19.

knowing Polish. Had I known where my research and reflection were going to take me, I perhaps would have tried a different approach. Since the substantial completion of this work, however, three important sources of Conradian primary material have appeared only to confirm my conclusions. None of the new Polish material in Jocelyn Baines's detailed biography,[15] Mrs. Hay's study of the political novels, or Najder's edition of letters has suggested that I must abandon my underlying ideas. Thus encouraged, I offer this study of Conrad's dual heritage.

[15] Jocelyn Baines, *Joseph Conrad, A Critical Biography* (New York, McGraw Hill, 1960).

# I

## FATHER AND SON

Of the Korzeniowski and Bobrowski factions warring within Joseph Conrad, surely the Korzeniowski was the more intense, and perhaps ultimately the more important. Of course, fathers often exert a crucial influence upon their sons, but special circumstances made Apollo Korzeniowski's influence upon his only child, Konrad, simply extraordinary. In the first place, as a dedicated poet and patriot, Korzeniowski embodied the ideas of Polish romanticism, ideas which were at the very heart of Polish literary, intellectual, and political life at that time. In the second place, Korzeniowski himself was a vivid, complex man divided by inner conflict, and his impact was always strongly felt. Finally, Korzeniowski's presence must have been overwhelming to the boy because of the strange facts of their life together, especially Korzeniowski's profound religious development. Korzeniowski's influence is clearly reflected in Conrad's work. Korzeniowski's ideas, as one gathers them from the poets who influenced him and from what his own letters and the testimony of his friends suggest, are ideas which recur in Conrad's works; and some of the heroes of Conrad's fiction embody ideals of character and conduct which were extolled in the romantic literature of Poland. This literature, Conrad once claimed, influenced his own writing. Moreover, father and son relationships provide important background to three major Conrad novels: *Chance, Nostromo,* and *Victory.* In each of these novels, Conrad portrays both a father's powerful influence upon a son rendered particularly impressionable by circumstances as well as the son's struggle, often unconscious, to free himself from this essentially negative influence.

I

In order to appreciate Apollo Korzeniowski's impact on Joseph Conrad it is necessary to understand the cultural and political milieu from which he drew his ideas. As poet and patriot Korzeniowski exemplified the romantic movement in Poland. Conrad's Polish friend J. H. Retinger remarks:

Apollo Korzeniowski ... had no other thoughts than those for his country; no life, but the life of a patriot. He was like a sentimental miser, living for self-sacrifice, saving every breath, every atom of personal happiness for his motherland. Wife, child, family were for him details of minor consideration. Such a mentality was far from being uncommon in the generations which preceded mine and Conrad's.[1]

Apollo Korzeniowski particularly resembles other Polish poets of the romantic movement. He shared their patriotic idealism. His career, like theirs, moved from literature to politics to religion, a sequence noted by the literary critic Roman Dyboski in the careers of the three great romantic poets of Poland, Mickiewicz, Slowacki, and Krasinski.[2] Like his greater predecessors, Apollo Korzeniowski spent part of his life in exile, where he suffered great losses for his country's cause.

This common pattern of beliefs and experiences is not surprising. A Polish man of letters between about 1820 and 1860 could be expected to have serious religious and political commitments. There was no trace in Poland of the hostility to organized religion which marked the romanticism and nationalism of western Europe, England, and America. Indeed, the central doctrines expressed in Polish romantic literature unite Roman Catholic Christianity with romantic nationalism. This union characterized both political action in which officials of the church supported the movement for independence, and works of literature, in which Christian doctrines of suffering, sacrifice, and redemption were interpreted in a nationalistic context and the heroes of which act

---

[1]  J. H. Retinger, *Conrad and His Contemporaries* (New York, Roy Publishers, 1943), pp. 18-19.
[2]  Roman Dyboski, *Periods of Polish Literary History* (London, Oxford University Press, 1923), p. 88.

as patriotic messiahs. Poland itself was seen as the Christ of nations, suffering that all mankind might someday enjoy liberty.
Inspired by this profound and moving metaphor which joined
faith to fatherland, the romantic movement in Poland produced a
great literature, but the effects of romanticism on politics, as we
shall see, were less desirable.

One can easily find evidence of the union between Roman
Catholicism and nationalism in political activity. The anti-
clericalism of Italian nationalism was unknown in Poland. Considered elsewhere as oppressor, the Roman Church in Poland was
persecuted while the Eastern Orthodox Church received the official recognition of Russians in Poland who attempted to increase
its sway by absorbing the Uniat Churches.[3] Lay patriots and Roman clerics united in order to throw off Russian tyranny. Roman
Catholic religious processions and rites turned into demonstrations of national sentiment; the Russians feared especially the
funerals of Polish patriots as opportunities for shows of opposition
and even violence.[4] The last words of the archbishop of Warsaw
who died in 1861 were, "Get rid of the Russians".[5]

The clergy not only encouraged the movement for independence but in the previous century had laid the groundwork for the
doctrines of nationalism. Through their influence Poles saw themselves under the special protection of Providence, a chosen people
who had been miraculously delivered from the Protestant Swedes
in the seventeenth century.[6] The partitions, which destroyed
Poland as an independent nation in the late eighteenth century,
forced alterations in this view; Poland was obviously not enjoying

---

[3]   Oscar Halecki, *A History of Poland* (New York, Roy Publishers, 1956),
p. 234. Adam Zoltowski, "Ideological Developments in Polish Catholicism", *Church and Society: Catholic Social and Political Thought and
Movements 1789-1950*, ed. Joseph N. Moody (New York, Arts Inc., 1953),
pp. 578-98.
[4]   H. Sutherland Edwards, *The Private History of a Polish Insurrection*
(London, Saunders, Otley, and Co., 1865), I, pp. 57-60, 272-73.
[5]   G. Jean-Aubry, *The Sea Dreamer*, trans. Helen Sebba (Garden City,
N. Y., Doubleday, 1957), p. 25.
[6]   Robert H. Lord, *The Second Partition of Poland* (Cambridge, Mass.,
Harvard University Press, 1915), p. 24.

the usual benefits of special divine protection. Now Poland's suffering had to be ordained by God.

When Apollo Korzeniowski, his contemporaries, and immediate predecessors thought of themselves as Poles, their Roman
Catholicism made up an important part of their sense of identity
and contributed to their concept of Poland.

Along with Polish Roman Catholicism, the new doctrines of
organic nationalism went into much of nineteenth-century thinking by Poles about their identity and role in history. Growing out
of the romantic conception of organic unity, nationalism was one
of the most powerful ideas of the century.[7] It dominated politics
and found literary expression in all nations of western civilization.
Like the romantic concept of Nature, the idea of nationalism
seemed to many a source of stability and inspiration. Men who
once felt themselves defined as links in metaphysical and social
chains of being now sought in national identity their own identity
and significance. Men transferred their emotional loyalties from
prince and church to the nation, united in language, culture, history, and traditions. The nationality of a people was supposed to
be an eternal natural reality; laws of organic history explained its
inevitable evolution and, usually, its historical world mission.
Each nation claimed a unique depth of mind contrasting with the
superficiality of other cultures; each nation engaged in pseudo-
historical research designed to prove the antiquity and purity of
its people and its customs as well as the justice of its territorial
claims; each nation claimed that its growth represented the fulfill-
ment of history and the climax of civilization. It therefore became
the duty of the citizens of a nation to cherish and foster those
traits distinguishing them from other nations.

Most nations found it fairly easy to adopt and develop the idea
of nationalism. The United States, conscious of her role as a bea-

---

[7]   The history of nationalism is treated extensively by Hans Kohn in three
books: *The Idea of Nationalism: A Study in Its Origins and Background*
(New York, Macmillan, 1944), which covers the idea from its origins in
Israel and Greece to the early nineteenth century; *Pan-Slavism: Its History
and Ideology* (Notre Dame, University of Notre Dame Press, 1953) with
a useful chapter on Polish nationalism; and *Prophets and Peoples: Studies
in Nineteenth Century Nationalism* (New York, Macmillan, 1946).

con light of democracy to all nations, could fulfill her manifest destiny by expanding across the continent and into the Pacific; England could serve as peacemaker of the world, while bringing the blessings of civilization to lesser breeds; Italy, proud of her Renaissance and Roman past, and Germany, confident of the superior creativity of her blood, were able to move steadily toward unification. Russia (which developed a national faith similar to Poland's), growing steadily in power and influence, could assert through Dostoevsky that she was the vessel of the true faith of "the Christ whom we have preserved and whom they [Western Europeans] have never known".[8]

In all these countries national sentiment could gather about political realities or fairly certain hopes. But Poland's field for action was extremely limited and, not satisfied with a purely cultural nationalism as were the Czechs, the nation without a state had to create a destiny out of an unhappy past and an uncertain future. The decline of Poland in the eighteenth century, the partitions, the false hopes raised by Napoleon, the repartition in 1815, the defeat of the revolutions of 1830 rnd 1846, and the failure of Polish expectations from the general European revolution of 1848 as well as from the defeat of Russia in the Crimean War tormented Poles, who were filled with the glory of their past and acutely conscious of their national identity. They needed new support for their image of Poland as civilization's outpost doing battle with barbaric, schismatic, Oriental, despotic Russia and of themselves as a chosen people under divine protection. Neither Old Testament Israel (despite the obvious analogy of the Babylonian captivity) nor the New Testament Church appeared a sufficient model for Poland's concept of herself. In order to explain their role of a chosen people fallen upon evil days, Poles united ideas drawn from their religious faith with the ideas of organic nationalism in a way unique among nations for both its ingenuity and its emotional intensity.

Led by the three major poets of the Polish romantic movement, Mickiewicz, Krasinski, and Slowacki, Poles began in the 1830's to

---

[8] Fyodor Dostoevsky, *The Idiot*, trans. Constance Garnett (New York, Macmillan, 1922), p. 547.

view their repeated disappointments and heavy sufferings in a manner that conferred meaning upon these misfortunes. Poland, like Christ, these poets explained suffered for the sins of the whole world in order to redeem all nations for salvation, and a nation redeemed for salvation is one which has become worthy of freedom. Like Christ, Poland would rise after its bitter innocent sufferings and death. The moment of Poland's resurrection would mark the beginning of world-wide peace, justice and liberty.[9] In *The Books of the Polish Nation*, written to inspire the emigrés after the defeat in 1830, Mickiewicz wrote:

For the Polish Nation did not die: its body lies in the grave, but its soul has descended from the earth, that is, from public life, to the abyss, that is, to the domestic life of nations, who suffer slavery in their country and outside their country, that it may see their sufferings.

But on the third day the soul shall return to the body and the nation shall rise and free all the peoples of Europe from slavery.[10]

Mickiewicz even particularized the three days. The first was the capture of Warsaw in 1794; the second was the re-capture of Warsaw in 1831. The third triumphant day was yet to come. Apollo Korzeniowski and his generation believed that their rebellion would mark its beginning.

Despite what to us are its obviously fanciful characteristics, national Messianism appealed to Poles in the nineteenth century because it had been drawn in part from the strong religious faith

[9]  Halecki, p. 243. Dyboski, pp. 91, 98. Kohn, *Pan-Slavism*, pp. 29-49.

[10]  Quoted by Wiktor Weintraub, *The Poetry of Adam Mickiewicz* (The Hague, Mouton, 1954), p. 196. We may also cite Sigmund Krasinski's patriotic poem "Resurrectis", which begins:

> This world is a graveyard of tears, of blood, and of mire,
> To each one of us an everlasting Golgotha.

It concludes triumphantly:

> And on the third day,
> Over the grave of thy sufferings,
> Out of the gulf of calamities,
> Of the flood of events,
> The unborn shall be born,
> Righteousness shall arise.

Quoted in W. H. Bullock, *Polish Experiences During the Insurrection of 1863-1864* (London, Macmillan, 1864), pp. 246-50.

of a people almost untouched by the enlightenment, because it explained, apparently, the facts of Poland's disaster, and because it agreed with long established ideas and emotions about Poland. Polish Messianism thus appeared an ennobling doctrine of great comfort and inspiration to a suffering people who, faced with adversity, had kept the Faith. It encouraged high ideals: sacrifice, endurance, the solidarity of nations, and liberty.

Polish Messianism, however, contained serious flaws and dangers. A perversion of religious emotion, it fostered uncontrolled egoism in both Poland and in individual Poles. Despite its emphasis on humility, it encouraged pride; despite its emphasis on peace it countenanced war. Conrad's privately expressed dislike of Christianity may in reality be largely an objection to the uses which Polish Messianism made of it. Conrad once explained that he objected to Christianity because in spite of all its dogma and moral formulae, "it lent itself with amazing facility to cruel distortion".[11] He may well have been thinking of his father's national Messianism. Indeed, the particular dangers of Messianism are closely related to Conrad's concern with idealism masking evil.

In Poland the doctrine was dangerous because it encouraged national and individual egoism unchecked by any safe-guards. Although the ethnic emphasis of nationalism would seem to oppose expansion and imperialism, national Messianism usually leads to imperialism. (For individual Poles, of course, circumstances and Christian ethics tempered the implications of national Messianism, but in the twentieth century, National Socialism carried to their logical extremes the doctrines of transcendent national or racial destiny.[12]) In the early nineteenth century, Poles sometimes

[11]   Joseph Conrad, Letter to Edward Garnett (Feb. 23, 1914), *Letters from Joseph Conrad*, ed. Edward Garnett (Indianapolis, Bobbs Merrill, 1928), p. 245. Hereafter cited as *Garnett Letters*.
[12]   A. O. Lovejoy, in his essay "The Meaning of Romanticism for the Historian of Ideas", *Journal of the History of Ideas*, II (1941), pp. 257-78, points out the historical connection between Hitler and Mussolini and the application of three major romantic concepts to the nation: (1) the idea of the whole or the "organismic conception"; (2) the virtue of endless striving; (3) the duty of the individual or people to cherish and intensify their differentness. These played their part, he says, in leading to "the idea of a national State whose members are but instruments to its own vaster ends;

hoped that the faith which supplied the metaphor and emotion basic to the doctrine would also supply the outer check to its excesses. In *The Books of the Polish Pilgrims* (1832), Mickiewicz warns that although the Polish emigrés, the pilgrims, are the soul of Poland, itself a holy land eventually destined for resurrection and freedom, the nation is "not a divinity like Christ, therefore its soul on its pilgrimage over the abyss may go astray", and he concludes with an injunction to the pilgrims to read the gospel of Christ. But to the gospel of Christ he adds "those teachings and parables which the Christian pilgrim [i.e., Mickiewicz himself] hath gathered from the lips and writings of Christian Poles, the martyrs and pilgrims".[13] Thus Mickiewicz has strengthened the identification between Christ and Poland in the very act of attempting to limit it. The Messianic doctrines prophesying an era of universal peace and freedom did not forbid war and violence as a means toward the millenium. One of the petitions in the litany which closes *The Books of the Polish Pilgrims* says, "For a universal war for the freedom of nations, We beseech Thee, Oh, Lord." [14] During the revolution of 1863 the rumor ran through Warsaw that a fiery cross had appeared in the air, and great crowds gathered hoping to see the sign of divine approval.[15]

Polish Messianism not only was applied to the entire nation to explain her misfortunes and to sanction her struggles, but also was frequently projected into the figures of representative men and heroes. "The best developed soul", Mickiewicz said, "is chosen as an instrument of the Godhead. That is the principal dogma of

---

in which, therefore, no internal oppositions or disagreements in individual opinion can be permitted; which, however, is dedicated to perpetual struggle for power and self-enlargement, with no fixed goal or terminus, and is animated by an intense and obsessing sense of the differentness of its own folk, of their duty of *keeping* different and uncorrupted by any alien elements, and by a conviction of the immeasurable value of their supposedly unique characteristics and culture" (p. 278).

[13]   Adam Mickiewicz, *The Books of the Polish Pilgrims*, trans. Dorothea Prall Radin in *Poems by Adam Mickiewicz*, ed. George Rapall Noyes (New York, The Polish Institute of Arts and Sciences in America, 1944), p. 280.

[14]   *Ibid.*, p. 415.

[15]   Edwards, II, pp. 48-49.

Messianism." [16] In "To a Polish Mother" Mickiewicz compares
to the sorrows of Mary, aware of the destiny of her Son, the plight
of the Polish mother who raises her son for patriotic martyrdom.[17]
Krasinski's *Iridion* (1836) and Slowacki's *Anhelli* (1838) present
unhappy youths aspiring to fervent patriotic actions in which they
lead their Christ-like nation to endure its martyrdom or, falling
into gloom, die themselves that the nation may rise again. These
poets associate the romantic virtue of sympathy with Christ's
saving universal love, so that poet, hero, nation, and Christ become one. In a much-quoted passage, the hero of Mickiewicz's
*Forefather's Eve* asserts:

> Now is my soul incarnate in my country
> And in my body dwells her soul;
> My fatherland and I are one great whole.
> My name is million, for I love as millions;
> Their pain and suffering I feel.[18]

One must add that Mickiewicz, along with Krasinski and Slowacki,
did perceive the excesses inherent in the concept. All three found
the correction in the prayers of pure women and the chastisements
of a loving God. But too often these checks, like Mickiewicz's
warning to the Polish pilgrims, ultimately proved to be a further
means of elevating the hero to semi-divine status. Krasinski's hero
Iridion, following his father's plans to destroy foreign oppressors,
sells his soul to the devil, but is then saved by the prayers of a
Christian maiden, and finally goes off to suffering – "the sufferings of thousands will be incarnate in thy one heart" – and long
martyrdom as the Polish Christ. "The unrighteous", God counsels
him, "shall pass away but thou and my words shall not pass
away".[19] After Julius Slowacki's pure, suffering youth Anhelli
(the name means "angel-hero") dies, guarded by the maiden of
pity, the knight of deliverance, set in motion by Anhelli's "sacrifice of the heart", speeds to the rescue of nations in bondage. Thus

[16]   Quoted by Zoltowski, p. 591.
[17]   *Poems by Adam Mickiewicz*, pp. 237-38.
[18]   *Ibid.*, p. 277.
[19]   Sigmund Krasinski, *Iridion*, trans. Florence Noyes (London, Oxford
University Press, 1927), pp. 236-37.

the hero as divinity is a Polish idea too. Although the romantic poets insisted that the excesses of Polish Messianism be curbed by Christian theological concepts of humility versus sinful pride, the doctrines of Messianism nevertheless encouraged feelings of special righteousness and personal Messianism.

National Messianism might appear the one nationalistic doctrine to encourage passivity – evil is exterior, and suffering is neither the punishment for sins nor even the consequence of mistakes. In actuality, it stimulated Poles to intense endeavor. If one's nation is Christ and thus innocent and divine, then the desire to destroy her enemies is innocent, divine, and dutiful. Mickiewicz's *Konrad Wallenrod* (1828) celebrates this kind of extreme nationalism. Konrad, a medieval Pole, joins the order of Teutonic Knights, rises to the head of this enemy force, and then treacherously leads the knights to their death – with the author's approval. This savage story of deceit and national revenge satisfied Mickiewicz's oppressed contemporaries as well as the succeeding generation, which inherited their hopes and hostilities. Poles saw it as a model for their own behavior or used it as an explanation for the underlying motives of Polish leaders who seemed to cooperate too closely with the Russians.[20]

In addition to encouraging uncritical and uncontrolled activities by the national and individual ego, Polish Messianism discouraged thorough rational analysis of contemporary social and political problems. Mickiewicz, for example, warned the emigrés against discussing the future form of government or boundaries of Poland, prophesying grandly that the government "shall be better than all that ye know of" and that the boundaries "shall be greater than they have been at any time". Like a Thoreau turned patriot, he concludes:

And each of you hath in his soul the seed of future laws and the measure of future boundaries.

So far as ye enlarge and better your spirit, so far shall ye better your laws and enlarge your boundaries.[21]

[20]    Edwards, I, pp. 143-44.
[21]    *Poems by Adam Mickiewicz*, p. 409.

Furthermore, Poles rarely had the chance to discover how impractical Messianism was because only during the brief periods of insurrection did they actually govern their own country. Indeed, many Poles in the nineteenth century did not think realistically or constructively about political and social problems. The chief political problem concerned the form that the Polish government should take in the event of a successful revolution. The chief social problem concerned the liberation of the serfs and redistribution of the land. Attempts to solve both these problems were usually liberal in tendency but rather vague in particulars, and in some cases wholly unrealistic. Poles were thus in a peculiar predicament. Messianism simultaneously established patriotism as the highest virtue while making it particularly difficult to translate patriotism into intelligent action.

The political thinking of Conrad's father reflects the inadequacies of Polish nationalism. Intensely loyal to Poland and very active in the revolutionary cause, Apollo Korzeniowski was vague about specific political and social measures beyond underground plotting and obstruction. He could never, for example, make clear to his brother-in-law precisely what, other than opposition to Russian rule, were his political and social ideas. Korzeniowski expressed, wrote Bobrowski, a "nebulous preference for the Republican form of government as delimited by the Constitution of the Third of May".[22] This was a patriotic choice. The third of May is a national holiday in Poland, and a good deal of emotion had gathered about the 1791 constitution, making it a symbol of Poland's power of regeneration at the very moment of dismemberment.[23] However, the positive contributions that the provisions of this constitution could make to political life in the mid-nineteenth century were already obviously too few. The chief provisions – establishing an hereditary monarchy rather than an elective one to avoid foreign influence upon the election of the king, abolishing the *liberum* veto in order to make the Diet efficient, and granting limited legal and political rights to the burghers – did not make

[22]   Bobrowski, *Memoirs*, in Morf, p. 26.
[23]   Dyboski, pp. 81-84.

up a political system adequate for the problems of the 1850's.[24]

The most obvious insufficiency of the Constitution of the Third of May was its position on serfdom. Although the constitution did not abolish serfdom, the government was supposed to take responsibility for the peasantry and to encourage individual contracts between landowners and peasants.[25] Vacillation, half-measures, and overdue reforms marked the movement for Polish independence. Although by Apollo Korzeniowski's day, sentiment for emancipation had grown strong, Korzeniowski himself was unsure about the solution of the most important social question of the time. Bobrowski asked him for his opinion on the question of liberating the serfs and providing them with land. Unable to reply immediately, Korzeniowski finally answered hesitantly that "those who possessed the ground had better decide the question".[26] On another occasion, when he was accused of "socialist" or "communist" leanings, he defended himself virulently. Such terms, he insisted, were foreign, picked from "the garbage heap of Western theories". His own interest in the unfortunate of his land was, he said, "spiritual, moral",[27] not at all part of a social revolution. Clearly, Korzeniowski's nationalism excluded both foreign ideas and ideas pointing out imperfection or division within Poland herself.

The revolutionary movements in Poland throughout the period of the partitions had always tried in some way to unite a solution of the problem of serfdom with their political aims,[28] but because of delay, indecision, and the inability to recognize how strongly many of the peasants distrusted their masters, they generally failed either to work out practical solutions or to gain substantial support from the peasants during the revolt. In 1794, Kosciuszko,

[24]  Halecki, p. 200.
[25]  *Ibid.*
[26]  Bobrowski, *Memoirs*, in Morf, p. 27.
[27]  This comes from Korzeniowski's preface to his translation of Alfred de Vigny's *Chatterton*, 1857, and is quoted by Hay, p. 40. A similar combination of sympathy for the oppressed with only vague views about social reform has been pointed out in the writing of a novelist contemporary with Conrad's father, Joseph Kraszewski, by Julian Krzyzanowski, *Polish Romantic Literature* (New York, E. P. Dutton, 1931), p. 250.
[28]  Halecki, pp. 207-34.

attempting to remedy the constitution of 1791 and to gain the support of the Polish masses, proclaimed the liberty of the peasant; but despite the wide-spread popular support for independence, Prussia and Russia put down the revolt and completed the work of partitioning. Napoleon ended personal serfdom in the Kingdom of Poland in 1807, but he left the peasants without land of their own. The Polish Diet, ruling briefly during the insurrection of 1830-1831, failed to meet the problem of peasant emancipation; and, although the aristocratic leaders of the anti-Austrian revolt of 1846 proclaimed to the peasants freedom and possession of their land, the Austrians convinced large bands of peasants that the leaders of the insurrection planned to enslave them and thus persuaded the peasants to serve as counter-revolutionary forces.

The problem of the serfs in the years preceding the revolt of 1863 was doubly important to Polish patriots. Peasant emancipation represented part of the European liberal movement with which the Polish party of revolution after 1830 was strongly connected, and it also was one of the necessary means for the success of a revolt. In order to drive out the Russians, the revolutionists needed the support of the large peasant population. Most of the peasants, however, were more interested in emancipation and ownership of their land than in national independence. Unfortunately for the leaders of the national revolt, Czar Alexander II, by abolishing serfdom in Russia and Russian Poland in 1861, reduced the appeal of a Polish revolution. His announcement of a nine year delay in emancipation partially returned to the insurrectionists their cause of land reform.[29] This delay as well as the gradualism of Russia's plan, which carefully compensated landowners for loss of property, encouraged some of Korzeniowski's colleagues in the extremist wing of the revolutionary party toward convictions more definite than his. When the revolution broke out fifteen months after his arrest, they proclaimed their clearly liberal policies. This "democratic and revolutionary movement", according to a contemporary British observer in Poland, was made up of ardent and enthusiastic men "who had nothing to lose" by political and social change. "The first public act of its directors,

[29] Allen, p. 3.

after the appeal to arms, was to give the peasants their holdings",
without the payment of a quit rent or compensation to the landowners.[30]

But even this decisive action was unsuccessful in lessening the
hostility of peasants who were not truly Poles. In the three
Ruthenian provinces, Volhynia, Podolia, and the Ukraine (the
home of both the Korzeniowskis and the Bobrowskis) the peasants spoke a Slavic language neither Russian nor Polish and belonged to the Uniat Catholic Churches recently detached from
Rome and forcibly joined to Russian Orthodoxy. In 1863 the
Ruthenian peasants willingly served the Russians as spies, inform-
ers, and village guards hampering all traffic. A group of insurgents
came to a small town in the Polish Ukraine to read the proclamation of the insurrectionary National Government giving the peasants unconditional title to their lands. As soon as the insurgents
laid down their arms, the peasants murdered some of them and
tortured the others, using weapons provided by the Russian
government.[31] In *A Personal Record*, Conrad tells graphically
how a mob of peasants, encouraged by Cossack officers suspicious
of the absence of the aged Nicholas Bobrowski at the opening of
the revolution, looted their master's house.[32] This was a mild if
typical incident. Many Poles in these provinces, even if they were
neither landlords or insurrectionists, had their property destroyed
and were themselves frequently thrown into prison, tortured, or
murdered.[33]

Both the indecisive Korzeniowski and his more decisive fellow
patriots were out of touch with social reality. Neither the future
benevolence of the proprietors nor a sudden bold stroke from the
insurrectionary government could solve the problem of peasant
holdings, convince the Ruthenian peasants that they were Poles,
or unite the nation for effective action. Korzeniowski's attitude
cannot be justified by citing his primary concern with Polish independence, for independence was not attainable without first

[30]  Edwards, I, pp. 162-63.
[31]  Bullock, pp. 159-61.
[32]  *A Personal Record*, pp. 57-63.
[33]  Bullock, pp. 159-65.

solving the problem of peasant emancipation. To leave the question to "those who possessed the ground" was to ignore the most significant social question of the time. Polish nationalism and Messianism stressed the unity of the nation in its sufferings and destiny; the serf question brought out class conflict and opposition of opinions within the nation, indicated the vagueness of the nation's borders, and blurred the distinction between the cause of Poland and the policies of the liberals among the Russian oppressors who had worked for serf emancipation throughout the empire.

The failure of the Polish insurrectionists to meet the problem of serfdom is symptomatic of their illusions and their incompetence. There is no doubt that the Insurrection of 1863 was a terrible mistake. The Russian oppression which immediately preceded the outbreak was brought about by Polish demonstrations. Romantic devotion to the nation blinded Polish patriots to the fact that 10.000 inadequately trained and poorly armed Polish troops were no match for 80.000 Russian regulars. The revolution was followed by mass executions, deportations, and estate confiscations. A modern historian has concluded:

All this [oppression and Russification] was a reversal of Alexander's earlier policies, yet one which circumstances had forced upon him. His wish had been for a slow autonomous evolution of the Kingdom, not for a policy of violent Russification. Similarly he had hoped to work with the moderate nobility and turned to the peasants only as a second choice. As long as was humanly possible, he persevered in the course recommended by Wielopolski [a conservative Polish politician] and Constantine [his brother]. If he had been finally forced to abandon it, this was due almost entirely to the unrealistic dreams and uncompromising line of the Polish patriots and revolutionaries. If the birth of modern Poland ["a predominantly peasant country", p. 117] was the result of Russian tyranny rather than peaceful Polish evolution, the fault lies not with Alexander but with the Polish nobles who, like the Bourbons, could neither learn nor forget.[34]

Polish romanticism was not solely responsible for Korzeniowski's political confusion. His own character discouraged clear thinking; he was excitable, passionate, and disturbed by inner conflict. The

[34] W. E. Mosse, *Alexander II and the Modernization of Russia* (New York, Macmillan, 1958), pp. 109-10.

fact that he suffered from inner conflict is evident in the mixed motives behind some of his political positions. Tadeusz Bobrowski, aware of Korzeniowski's wavering social views and of the disparity between his uncertainty about specific contemporary problems and the unmistakeable positions of his revolutionary colleagues, perceived a contradiction within his brother-in-law's politics.

Though he considered himself a sincere democrat, and others called him a "revolutionist", a "Red", he was a greater aristocrat than myself, as I showed him many a time, whom nobody suspected of democratical convictions.[35]

Deeper than this conflict between democratic ideals and a conservative temperament was the conflict which raged between his genuine sympathy for mankind and his strong egoism. Apollo Korzeniowski was at once a warm, deeply sympathetic person and an extremely proud, even haughty one. Bobrowski pays tribute to Korzeniowski's genuine sympathy for suffering that seemed to account for his radical ideas. "He had a soft sensitive heart and much compassion for the poor and oppressed." [36] This sympathy for the under-privileged was, however, accompanied by a scorn for the rich and proud which found such vehement expression in his verse plays that their violent diatribes against the propertied class still please Polish Marxist critics.[37] Bobrowski warned Conrad that his father had "loved mankind and wished them well, but he had two standards for judging them. He was indulgent to the poor and very hard on the rich." [38] Such a double standard of judgment reveals that more than simple observation, analysis, and sympathy produced Korzeniowski's social views. They seem rather the response to a personal dilemma than the reaction of the rational citizen to present problems.

The personal dilemma which Korzeniowski projected into his public views and which helped to make those views both vehement

---

[35] *Memoirs*, in Morf, p. 26.

[36] *Ibid.*

[37] Czeslaw Milosz, "Joseph Conrad in Polish Eyes", *Atlantic Monthly*, CC (November, 1957), p. 219.

[38] Letter (July 30, 1891), quoted in G. Jean-Aubry, *Joseph Conrad, Life and Letters* (Garden City, N. Y., Doubleday, 1928), I, p. 146.

and confused arose from his frustrated pride. 'He was implacable in thought and expression", Bobrowski said, "because indulgent in everyday life." [39] This indulgence had brought about two financial disasters in the first few years of his marriage which were, of course, very damaging to his pride. Korzeniowski's attacks on the propertied class – deserved as they probably were in semi-feudal Poland – were partly motivated by his frustrated efforts to maintain his status in that class. (The reluctance of the gentry of the border provinces to support the revolution further reinforced his criticism of them.) Both his literary and political activities, then, seem to have been motivated partly by his impracticality in everyday life.

Korzeniowski's compensatory implacability in thought and expression was easily put to rout by the intrusion of genuine political and social problems demanding solution. Bobrowski commented:

I am not at all surprised at this, for it is a fact that poets, who are men of imagination and ideals, are incapable of formulating clearly their views on practical questions, and do better, therefore, not to occupy themselves with such questions, but to leave them to those who, are perhaps no idealists, but are familiar with the struggles and necessities of everyday life.[40]

So long as Korzeniowski could define his positions for himself, he was firm and clear; but when political realities such as serf emancipation, the real power of Russia, precise provisions of a constitution, and Poland's lack of foreign friends interrupted his hopeful dream made of pride and sympathy, he became indecisive and confused.

If during his years of activity in Poland, Apollo Korzeniowski had demonstrated the impractical, muddled political thinking typical of Polish nationalism, during his years of exile he demonstrated the gloom and religious mysticism that also characterized it. Before his arrest, trial, and deportation, Korzeniowski had been a witty and excitable man who loved social gatherings, who had managed to avoid the results of his improvidence, and who was just beginning to receive recognition in the theater and in revolu-

---

[39] *Memoirs*, in Morf, p. 26.
[40] *Ibid.*, p. 27.

tionary literary journalism. Now, in exile, he became in the face of illness, poverty, and defeat, a desperately unhappy man who sought self-control through religious faith. But in his religious experiences there was more of terror and anguish than of serenity and comfort. These years are especially significant since during most of them he was his son's only companion.

His father's unpredictable behavior must have troubled the child. There were happy hours of tender companionship during which Apollo Korzeniowski taught Conrad to read aloud the poetry of Mickiewicz or permitted him to help read proofs of his translations of Victor Hugo. But there were also long silent hours in which Korzeniowski withdrew not merely to write but to brood uncontrollably on his fate or to remain immobilized by a vision of terror.

Korzeniowski's exile and the defeat of the January Insurrection turned his political hopes to despair. He did not abandon the cause he knew to be hopeless, but whereas he had once seen social and personal ills corrigible by satire or an appeal to idealism, now evil, in the form of Russian "barbarity", appeared almost inevitable in its triumph. In *Poland and Russia*, a study written during the exile and smuggled out to be published in a Polish paper in Leipzig, he wrote:

Such as Muscovy is, from fear of her own annihilation she is forced to fight outside her borders. Although Europe may avoid the struggle for a long time yet, the moment will come when it will be no longer possible to escape it; but then the time will have been chosen by Muscovy. Thus will Europe be robbed of half its strength.[41]

Even in this pessimism he remained faithful to Polish Messianism's belief in the universal importance of the cause of Polish independence; he considered the failure of the insurrection an important loss to all western Christian civilization.[42]

As the exile continued, Korzeniowski's religion grew more intense, and his pessimism threatened to overwhelm him. Conrad himself commented that his father during this period was a man "of strong religious feeling degenerating after the loss of his wife

[41]  Quoted by Milosz, p. 200.
[42]  *Ibid.*

into mysticism touched with despair".[43] Conrad's suggestive phrase, "mysticism touched with despair", is borne out by evidence. He was undergoing a spiritual crisis; he was struggling desperately to achieve self-control. The year 1865 was probably the worst of Korzeniowski's life. Just the year before, the revolution had been defeated. Then his wife, who had been arrested, tried, and exiled under sentence with him, died after a long illness which had been aggravated by the damp, the cold, and the lack of medical care in Russia. He was left to raise and educate a seven year old boy. He was torn between his desire to keep his son with him and his knowledge that it would be better for the boy to go back to Poland, either to his grandmother and Uncle Tadeusz or to the home of one of his own friends. For himself, Korzeniowski could see no end to exile.

A letter written to a cousin in this year reveals the growing intensity of his religious feelings.[44] Because the letter is rich with the ideas, emotions, and half-conscious assumptions of the Polish romantics and because it is a profound revelation of the state of Apollo Korzeniowski's mind during a crucial period, it is well worth intensive analysis. In this letter Korzeniowski describes three attacks of acute despair and his three attempts to withstand the attacks. Calling on the resources of religious faith and national Messianism, he succeeded in resisting only the first two attacks. Despite his strong-willed attempt to meet the third, he was not able to overcome his feeling that his exile was a form of damnation. From the opening of the letter it is evident that his religious faith grew powerfully under the trials of exile and widowhood. He thanks God for the strength to survive his misfortune. Like Job he seeks their meaning: "I have passed through heavy and even terrible days of brooding on God's blessings and if I survive, it will not be thanks to my own, but God's strength." The pattern, though a familiar Christian one, follows the semi-autobiographical experiences chronicled by the Polish romantics in the lives of their tragic heroes. No longer presuming to be God's instrument for the redemption of nations, Korzeniowski now ponders the meaning of

[43]  *Garnett Letters* (Jan. 20, 1900), p. 168.
[44]  Letter (1865), *Joseph Conrad, Life and Letters*, I, p. 16.

God's terribly ambiguous "blessings". But as he continues to meditate upon his own life, he seems to cross over the thin line that divides the imitation of Christ from the identification with Christ.

I know that I have not suffered and never could suffer like our Savior, but then I am only a human being. I have kept my eyes fixed on the Cross and by that means fortified my fainting soul and reeling brain. The sacred days of agony have passed.

The old habits of Polish Messianism are still with him; and, although he specifically rejects the tempting comparison of himself with Christ, he is actually asserting that once one has allowed for the differences between a man and God, Apollo Korzeniowski, a martyr for the Polish cause, has suffered like Christ; and with the words, "the sacred days of agony", he clearly establishes an identification of himself with Christ.

Two more times he wrestles with despair. He is unhappy that he can give nothing to his son, and now worries that he is also unable to sacrifice. He interprets this inability either to "sacrifice or give anything" as a sign of the will of Providence and, in some sense, it would seem, the withdrawal of divine grace. "It is sad indeed", he continues, "for a man to see the two doors [of giving and sacrificing] through which alone he can approach the presence of God shut against him." During this second experience of meeting the onrush of despair, he explains that he regained his composure by rereading letters from Poland, instead of fixing his eyes on the Cross as he had done before. The sense of his inability to approach God had come over him. "When my bitterness chokes me, I read your second dear letter and the pride of despair changes into divine sadness. My tears flow, but their fount is reason."

His serenity is short lived and for a third time his equilibrium is upset. Horror or despair comes over him as he now considers the likeness of the place of exile to a monastic cell. Both father and son share this experience. "For the *memento mori* we have the grave of our dear one, and every letter which reaches us is the equivalent of a day of fasting, a hair shirt or a discipline." A devout Roman Catholic would not compare his misfortunes to monastic life merely to emphasize their harshness and rigor; the image of a severe prison would serve that simple purpose much better. Rather, Korzeniowski is giving meaning to their exile, and that meaning is that illogical mixture of patriotism and religion which makes up Polish Messianism. Just below the surface of the letter's prose lurks the notion of Poland as the promised land, the lost paradise, even Heaven, whose messages both discipline and comfort the true believer, like a means of grace. But even the idea of Poland seems insufficient to calm his mind, and he is again disturbed by the problem of egoism. "We are overwhelmed by the destitution of our fellowmen, our brothers, but prayer remains to us, and in our prayers I call God to witness there is scarce a word about ourselves."

Feeling himself abandoned by God and no longer supported by the idea of his fatherland, Korzeniowski becomes obsessed with the idea that there is no escape from their place of exile, and a climactic metaphorical description of it concludes his letter.

Should I describe this place I would say that on one side it is bounded by locked doors behind which the being dearest to me breathed her last, without my being able to wipe even the death sweat from her brow, while on the other, though there the doors are open, I may not cross the threshold, and I see, what Dante did *not* describe, for his soul, appalled though it was with terror, was too Christian to harbour inhuman visions. Such is our life.

Again he expresses the horror of the withdrawal of divine grace; the imagery is reminiscent of the "two doors" through which man approaches God. Now of course, these doors lead away from God.

This letter, then, recounts a spiritual crisis which is difficult to translate into conceptual language. But Korzeniowski seems to be saying something like this: The modes of self-transcendence which he had sought in mystical religio-politics failed because they encouraged egoism and self-assertion. Now divested of illusions of transcendence and also of a significant social role, he has been thrust back upon himself. In a moment of vision, the naked self perceived that it stands near the hellish abyss of downward self-transcendence.

The circumstances of his life, the conflicts of his mind, and the contradictions of his political and religious philosophy worked to make Apollo Korzeniowski an ill-integrated personality. His sensitive heart was at war with his pride; practical ineptitude frustrated his attempts to become a country gentleman; his liberal beliefs conflicted with his aristocratic ego; the political realities of the mid-nineteenth century broke in rudely on his flaming poetic idealism; and his messianic mysticism revealed to him visions of hell rather than of heaven. He is an example of the romantic personality: impetuous, contradictory, irrational, by turns generous and selfish, withal attractive.

His effect upon his son was powerful and enduring. Although for most of his life Conrad agreed with the principles behind his uncle's criticism of his father, his uncle's objective analysis and calm consistent attitude were not possible for him. The force of Korzeniowski's personality, the support given to his ideas by an entire culture, and the circumstances of Conrad's childhood had made it impossible for Conrad simply to leave behind him after a time his father's faults and opinions. They were too deeply embedded in his own character. The power of political idealism fascinated Conrad all his life although he was aware of its strong tendency to perversion and deception.

Conrad was involved in a similar way with his father's religion, although to a lesser extent. Despite his early loss of religious faith he could never regard Christianity as negligible sentimental piety or a mask of superstition behind which Jesuitical Machievels plotted for power. In some sense he regarded himself a Roman Catholic all his life. When his agent J. B. Pinker and Mrs. Conrad were parodying a Catholic processional chant, Conrad suddenly and icily interrupted: "Yes, and I'm a Catholic aren't I." [45] And, of course, he was buried a Roman Catholic. He rarely presents Roman Catholicism or Christianity in his novels, but his early experiences with his father gave rise to both his criticism of the perversion of Christian virtues and his strong moral drive.

Not long before his death Korzeniowski wrote a friend about his aims in raising his son. Here as elsewhere Apollo Korzeniow-

---

[45] Jessie Conrad, *Joseph Conrad and His Circle* (New York, E. P. Dutton, 1935), p. 228.

ski refers to the boy simply as Conrad, a name rich in patriotic associations because of Mickiewicz's continued use of it.[46] "My main purpose", Korzeniowski wrote, "is to bring Conrad up to be neither a democrat, aristocrat, demagogue, republican, monarchist – or a servant or lackey of any of those parties – but only to be a Pole." [47] Although this assertion of aims for his son's education seems to express a disillusionment with practical politics, Korzeniowski's rejection of all specific political programs is to be expected from a romantic nationalist. The affirmation, "only to be a Pole", seems on the surface simple and proper. Yet contradictions lie beneath the conventional patriotic formula; and the young Conrad had already experienced vividly the results of his father's fidelity to the principle, "only to be a Pole". Apollo Korzeniowski's program for his son implies impossible obligations toward the fatherland while, paradoxically, it warns against any action. It created for Conrad important psychological tensions which he expressed in his fiction.

II

Apollo Korzeniowski's influence on his son's mind is reflected in his son's writing where, however, it usually appears indirectly. Conrad avoided writing about his father in his autobiographical volume, *A Personal Record*, and, although he based a good deal of his fiction directly upon his own experiences, he wrote nothing about his childhood that portrays episodes from his own life in the manner that "Heart of Darkness" directly reflects his journey to Africa. Nevertheless, the effect of Apollo Korzeniowski does appear in Conrad's fiction and in two ways. First, the doctrines of Polish Messianism are criticized in Conrad's portrayal of the heroes of several novels as well as, perhaps, in Conrad's dislike of an ethic of sympathy and anti-authoritarianism. Second, in several novels Conrad portrayed father-son relationships which have something in common with his own relationship with his father.

[46] Morf, p. 45.
[47] Letter to Stefan Buszczynski, quoted by Allen, p. 49.

Both Conrad's reticence about his father in his autobiographical writing and the oblique reflection of him in Conrad's fiction stem from Conrad's mixed and doubtless painful feelings about his father. Loyal to his family and to Poland, Conrad could portray only by indirect means the qualities he regarded as unstable and egoistic in his father and in himself.

Conrad's concern with the presuming hero who seeks to redeem or reform his world – Kurtz, Lord Jim, Victor Haldin – recalls the hero ideal of Polish romanticism. The romantic poets of Poland had only tentatively criticized their Messianic heroes and had found remedies for their shortcomings available in religious faith and human sympathy. Conrad often portrays his romantic heroes with a good deal of affection, but he criticizes them deeply and often despairs of finding a remedy for their faults.

Conrad most thoroughly criticizes Messianic egoism in "Heart of Darkness". In depicting Kurtz's impossibly exalted view of human nature and destiny and his assumption of divinity, the novel recalls Polish Messianism. Proud of his idealism, Kurtz imagines himself a Messiah to African tribesmen. In reality he becomes at once a voracious tyrant and a debased devotee of their devilish cults. His tendency to idealize, to see himself regenerating the dark continent, has made him capable of far worse evils than the petty hypocrites and efficiency-minded materialists also portrayed in the story. In addition to this overt criticism of the romantic ego, "Heart of Darkness" contains interesting resemblances to the experiences of Apollo Korzeniowski during his exile. Conrad seems to be recalling his own and his father's Russian experiences when he portrays in the novel exile, moral isolation, and a vision of hell. Even Conrad's allusions to Dante's *Inferno* recall his father's letter to his cousin as well as the literature of Polish Messianism which frequently alluded to Dante to project a vision of Poland's suffering. One hesitates to make very much of these resemblances, yet at the least they suggest that Apollo Korzeniowski's religious experiences had a deep and lasting effect on the boy who witnessed them and that the character of Kurtz owes as much to introspection and memory as it does to Kurtz's model in life.

The portrayal of the hero in *Lord Jim* also recalls the heroes of

Polish romanticism. Their romantic egoism and Messianic pre-
sumptions are reflected in Jim's concept of himself as a savior and
martyr as well as the mistaken belief of his native followers in his
divine sanction and strength. Like Kurtz, Jim succumbs to the
temptation to be a god to superstitious primitives, and legends
spread among his people about his miraculous appearance in
Patusan. When he fails to protect his people from invasion, he
goes to what he regards as an expiatory death. It distinctly recalls
the crucifixion. Jim says that he has taken the responsibility "upon my head" and announces his arrival to his executioners in ar-
chaic Biblical language: "I am come in sorrow ... I am come
ready and unarmed." [48] Conrad reveals Jim's Messianic complex
as romantic egoism, not as an ideal of service. His death is not a
sacrifice of the heart bringing about the liberty of the nations.
Rather his death is accompanied by chaos and tyranny. We can
regard the novel, partly at least, as a criticism of the hero ideal of
Polish romanticism.

Victor Haldin, the Russian revolutionist in *Under Western
Eyes*, also presumes to be a Messiah. He looks forward to sacri-
ficing his life, forgives his enemies in advance for his death, pre-
dicts that after his death his immortal soul will continue to work
for freedom, and describes his work as an underground propa-
gandist in terms drawn from Christ's parable of the great supper.[49]
Conrad criticizes such idealistic presumption not only by showing
the fatal consequences of Haldin's assassinating a tyrannical po-
lice official but also by simply describing Haldin's inhuman enact-
ment of the political murder. Haldin throws a bomb into a street
crowd in order to kill one man. Unlike "Heart of Darkness" and
*Lord Jim*, *Under Western Eyes* directly reflects Polish Messianism. Both Haldin and his revolutionary colleagues as well as the
defenders of autocracy express the sentiments of Messianic nationalism. Because the characters are Russian, these ideas may
remind the reader of Dostoevsky, to whose work Conrad once
feared the novel would be compared. Nevertheless, Conrad's in-

---

[48]  *Lord Jim*, p. 415.
[49]  *Cf. Under Western Eyes*, p. 56 and Luke 14 : 23.

sight into Slavic nationalism and its heroes arose from early personal experience.

In his fiction Conrad presents the idea of national or personal Messianism after a process of secularization had been completed and the religious safe-guards to its excesses had disappeared. God and good women had saved Mickiewicz's presumptuous Konrad; there was no God to save or punish Kurtz, for example, and the good women were either foolish like his aunt or egoistic like his fiancee. Even Lord Jim's faithful Jewel was powerless to save him from self-destruction.

Although Conrad's disapproval of humanitarian sympathy when it is combined with resentment of authority does not represent a reaction to ideas peculiar to Polish Messianism, it may well stem partially from his uncle's analysis of the relation between his father's social views and his personality. *The Nigger of the "Narcissus"* dramatizes this disapproval. The crew's self-indulgent sympathy for the tubercular Negro sailor, encouraged by the lazy Donkin, a self-styled defender of the working man's "rights", leads them to attempt mutiny. When the helmsman leaves the wheel to join the mutiny, the ship is nearly wrecked. "It was as if an invisible hand had given the ship an angry shake to recall the men that peopled her decks to the sense of reality, vigilance, and duty." [50]

Suspicion of humanitarian sympathy and criticism of the romantic hero are fairly central to Conrad's work. Less important in the body of his work but more obviously related to his Polish background is a recurrent presentation of a father-son relationship in which a father's attitudes toward life prove detrimental in the life of his son. This theme was announced tentatively in *Lord Jim*, and in subsequent novels received fuller development. Jim is the son of a simple country clergyman whose own life is safely bounded by small blessings and smaller difficulties. Jim, living in a more perilous world, has drawn his standards from his father's strict moral code. And in a work often considered a reflection of Conrad's own guilt over deserting Poland, one of the protagonist's most painful feelings is that he can never return home to face his

[50] *The Nigger of the "Narcissus"*, p. 124.

father. In this book Conrad avoids saying whether or not Jim's fatal illusion of being a Christian hero comes from his father's influence. However, in three works in which the protagonist is not so directly and deeply an author-projection, Conrad takes up the nature and extent of a father's influence upon his son. It always proves an unfortunate influence. In *Chance*, *Nostromo*, and *Victory*, we can discern a pattern in the relationships of fathers and sons. From his father a son receives an inheritance – temperament, property, or attitude – which he misunderstands to his own peril and the danger of those about him. The father's death usually strengthens the son's loyalty. If the son fails to recognize the nature of his fatal inheritance or recognizes it too late, he brings disaster upon his own head. Although the characters in these three novels differ a good deal from Apollo Korzeniowski and his son, they all reflect Conrad's recognition of the dangers of his father's influence.

In *Chance* Conrad presented a father-son relationship with the least success. Despite considerable attention paid the relationship in the novel, it is neither convincing nor necessary, and exists largely in the narrator's comments. In *Nostromo* and *Victory* Conrad presented this relationship far more effectively. In each of these novels the son's relation to his dead father remains dynamic throughout the book, a basic part of the son's mind. The hero of *Nostromo* constantly attempts to adjust his actions to his dead father's outlook, but because the two are incompatible he must indulge in complicated and revealing rationalization. In *Victory* the relationship between father and son is much less complex. The son's departure from his father's philosophy results simply in a rueful awareness of his apostasy and ultimately in a recognition that his father's philosophy was destructive. But this very lack of complexity makes *Victory* an unequivocal dramatization of the perils of paternal influence.

In *Chance*, Captain Roderick Anthony inherits from his father an idealizing temperament which compels him to try to live up to an unreal standard of conduct. He is thus easily convinced by a hostile relative that he is taking unfair advantage of his fiancée who, the relative persuasively insists, is forced to marry Anthony for material reasons. Excessively chivalrous, Anthony decides that it would be cruel and selfish to consummate his marriage. Ultimately this misunderstanding is cleared up, but not until tragedy has almost destroyed the couple. Conrad thus shows that a father's values have proved false guides for his son's conduct.

A superficial reading of *Chance* might suggest that the novel is autobiographical. The similarities between the father and son in the novel and Apollo Korzeniowski and Joseph Conrad are rather striking upon first consideration. The father in the novel, Carleon Anthony, is a romantic poet whose work reflects the mistaken idealism of his times. The narrator once comments on the poet in terms reminiscent of Tadeusz Bobrowski's criticism of Conrad's father: "Poets not being generally foresighted in practical affairs, no vision of consequences would restrain him." [51] Carleon Anthony's wife dies when his son Roderick is young. The son, a sensitive young man, goes to sea and eventually becomes a ship's captain. At the age of thirty-five, he impulsively marries a girl a good deal younger than he. All of this roughly follows the facts of Conrad's biography, and to some extent Captain Anthony seems to be a self-portrait although Conrad himself was far from simple and unsophisticated. But the differences between Conrad's own father and Carleon Anthony are too profound to permit any meaningful comparison. Apollo Korzeniowski, like many of his contemporaries and the greater nationalistic poets of the previous generation, was willing to sacrifice for his ideas. Not so Conrad's Carleon Anthony. A brute in his domestic life, he wore out two wives and lived wholly for himself. In his private life his idealism was only a demand that the world come up to the "supra-refined standard of the delicacy which is so perceptible in his verses". [52] Furthermore, Anthony's idealism has nothing in common with the passionate revolt and mysticism of the Polish romantics. His views are genteel, conventional, and complacent. His poetry glibly reconciles the conflicts of serious thinkers and glosses over the dark side of human experience.

---

[51]   *Chance*, p. 62.
[52]   *Ibid.*, p. 328.

The late Carleon Anthony, the poet, sang in his time, of the domestic and social amenities of our age with a most felicitous versification, his object being, in his own words, "to glorify the result of six thousand years' evolution towards the refinement of thought, manners, and feelings". Why he fixed the term at six thousand years I don't know. His poems read like sentimental novels told in verse of a really superior quality. You felt as if you were being taken out for a delightful country drive by a charming lady in a pony carriage.[53]

The passage reveals that the poet combined middle-class gentility with belief in progress, and an optimistic view of evolution which he prudently reconciled with the conventional Christian idea about the age of the earth. Obviously not a satirical portrait of Apollo Korzeniowski and Polish Messianism, the description of Carleon Anthony and his verses is part of the novel's attack on Victorianism.[54]

Despite the effective portrait of a popular Victorian poet, the father-son relationship is neither plausible nor meaningful. One can, in fact, imagine *Chance* without it. Anthony's character and motivations would be comprehensible if his father were never mentioned. Anthony's excessive chivalry does not evolve out of his relationship to his father. Conrad merely asserts unconvincingly that Anthony inherited this temperament and takes care to eliminate other explanations of paternal influence. He says nothing of Anthony's childhood with his father; he tells the reader that Anthony ran away to sea early in his life; and he insists that Anthony had never read his father's poetry embodying the delicate ideals that played havoc with Anthony's marriage.

We are told twice that Captain Anthony's idealizing temperament is a direct inheritance from his father. With the first announcement Conrad explains the genetic theory accounting for this transmission of temperament.

---

[53] *Ibid.*, p. 38.
[54] As a satirical attack on a Victorian poet, the portrait of Carleon Anthony takes its place with the other attacks which the novel makes on Victorian shams: behind the militant feminism of Anthony's sister lies conventional and selfish class prejudice; behind the prim decorum of the heroine's governess lies sexual viciousness; and behind the grandiose investment schemes and confidence-inspiring slogans of a banker lie folly and chicanery.

I imagined to myself Captain Anthony as simple and romantic. It was much more pleasant. Genius is not hereditary but temperament may be. And he was the son of a poet with an admirable gift of individualizing, of etherealizing the common-place; of making touching, delicate, fascinating the most hopeless conventions of the so-called refined existence.[55]

Even if temperament can be inherited, Conrad does not show that Captain Anthony's simple and romantic temperament comes from his father; in fact, he makes it clear that the shy and generous son has little in common with his brutal and selfish father.

In his second explanation of Anthony's inheritance of a chivalrous temperament, Conrad attempts also to take into account the differences between father and son.

All the supremely refined delicacy of tenderness, expressed in so many fine lines of verse by Carleon Anthony, grew to the size of a passion filling with inward sobs the big frame of the man who had never in his life read a single one of those famous sonnets singing of the most highly civilized, chivalrous love, of those sonnets which. . . . You know there's a volume of them. My edition has the portrait of the author at thirty, and when I showed it to Mr. Powell the other day he exclaimed: "Wonderful! One would think this the portrait of Captain Anthony himself if . . ." I wanted to know what that if was. But Powell could not say. There was something – a difference. No doubt there was – in fineness perhaps. The father, fastidious, cerebral, morbidly shrinking from all contacts, could only sing in harmonious numbers of what the son felt with a dumb and reckless sincerity.[56]

In view of the enormous differences between father and son, this explanation seems inadequate. Furthermore Conrad seems, in this paragraph, to have altered his conception of Carleon Anthony in order to lessen these differences. The poet's "shrinking from all contact" is inconsistent with Conrad's portrayal of his brutality elsewhere in the book.

We may ask why Conrad has gone to the trouble of presenting this tenuous theory unnecessary for psychological motivation. The answer seems to lie in Conrad's desire to unify the book. The theme of the book is the triumph of the normal over the abnormal.

---

[55]  *Chance*, p. 193.
[56]  *Ibid.*, p. 332.

The abnormal is largely found in the shams and hypocrisies of society. The heroine in her marriage triumphs over various social ills which have deceived and injured her. Her chief triumph, however, is over her husband's mistaken restraint. Clearly, this too should be a victory over one of society's ills. In order to make it so and unify his novel, Conrad also associates Anthony's reserve with the false idealism of society. And furthermore, since Flora is menaced by her father – an ex-convict with an incestuous attraction to her – so Conrad portrays Captain Anthony as also menaced by his father. The delayed consummation of their marriage is supposed to represent for Anthony as well as for Flora a triumphal escape from the selfish and inhibiting hand of the father.

Conrad's portrait of a father's influence upon his son in *Nostromo* does not suffer from such implausibility and forced relevance. It is carefully and convincingly presented and plays a significant part in the story. It motivates the initial deed from which arises the action of the novel and illustrates the novel's themes of idealism, materialism, and self-deception.

Charles Gould's relationship to his father releases forces which change many lives. When Gould disobeys the wishes of his dead father by re-opening the silver mine which he has inherited, he brings tumultuous political and social change to a sleepy South American country whose semi-feudal peace had hitherto been disturbed only by rapid changes of government, and brings to himself and others deep personal failure and disappointment. Conrad demonstrates ironically that orderly and legal handing of property from father to son, a mark of stability and tradition in every society, can lead despite good intentions to bloodshed, cruelty, the weakening of human ties, and the corruption of upright natures.

Conrad devotes a great part of an early chapter to the history of the silver mine and the way in which Charles Gould takes up his inheritance. Not merely mechanical exposition, the chapter characterizes Charles Gould by revealing his deepest motives.

Even before a corrupt government forces the mine concession on Gould's father, it is a source of evil in Costaguana. In the days of Spanish rule, the mine was worked primitively with slaves until "it had ceased to make a profitable return, no matter how many corpses were thrown into its maw".[57] During the long peaceful rule of a native dictator who rose to power after the rebellion against the Spanish, an English company works the mine; but during the revolution following the dictator's death, the native miners murder their English chiefs and wreck the equipment. The new government in a burst of patriotic and moral rhetoric reclaims the mine.

The decree of confiscation ... began with the words: "Justly incensed at the grinding oppression of foreigners, actuated by sordid motives of gain rather than by love for a country where they come impoverished to seek their fortunes, the mining population of San Tomé, etc...." and ended with the declaration: "The chief of the State has resolved to exercise to the full his power of clemency. The mine, which by every law, international, human, and divine, reverts now to the Government as national property, shall remain closed till the sword drawn for the sacred defense of liberal principles has accomplished its mission of securing the happiness of our beloved country."[58]

This crude and defensive claim for the mine foreshadows Charles Gould's more subtle self-deceiving justifications.

The mine enters the lives of the principal characters when one of the many successive governments of the republic forces it as a perpetual concession upon Gould's father, a second-generation British emigrant to Costaguana. "The third and most important clause stipulated that the concession-holder should pay at once to the Government five years' royalties on the estimated output of the mine." [59] This payment as well as further assessments for non-working of the ruined and abandoned mine take a large part of Gould's fortune. The legal form of the robbery particularly distresses the English merchant.

He became at once mine-ridden, and as he was well read in light literature it took to his mind the form of the Old Man of the Sea fastened upon his shoulders. He also began to dream of vampires. Mr. Gould exaggerated to himself the disadvantages of his new position, because he viewed it emotionally. His position in Costaguana was no worse than before. But man is a desperately conservative

[57]  *Nostromo*, p. 52.
[58]  *Ibid.*, pp. 52-53.
[59]  *Ibid.*, p. 53.

creature, and the extravagant novelty of this outrage upon his purse distressed his sensibilities.[60]

Gould's only relief is to write to his son Charles whom he has sent to school in England. Every month for almost ten years he violently pours out his troubles and frustrations to the impressionable youth. The natural bond between father and son becomes almost wholly entangled with the mine. In his letters Gould senior repeatedly advises his son to renounce his inheritance and make his living in Europe, away from Costaguana. The elder Gould's advice is objectively sound, but he gives it emotionally and irrationally. In effect it is an appeal for loyalty. The passion with which he advises his son to abandon the mine makes that advice a call for revenge.

Profoundly affected by his father's letters, Charles Gould also begins to view the mine emotionally and simple renunciation seems an inadequate response to his father's plea.

By the time he was twenty Charles Gould had, in his turn, fallen under the spell of the San Tomé mine. But it was another form of enchantment, more suitable to his youth, into whose magic formula there entered hope, vigour, and self-confidence, instead of weary indignation and despair.[61]

Conrad's presentation of Charles Gould's disobedience of his father makes *Nostromo* a major study of rationalization and self-deception. Before his father dies, Charles Gould obeys him only to the extent of staying away from Costaguana; but in Europe studying mining engineering, he is surely preparing to return to open the mine. His studies are not purely practical or professional. The European mines that he visits appeal to his emotions. Conrad describes this appeal as a form of the impulse which he often criticizes: the desire to rescue an unfortunate victim.

Abandoned workings had for him strong fascination. Their desolation appealed to him like the sight of human misery, whose causes are varied and profound. They might have been worthless, but also they might have been misunderstood. His future wife was the first, and perhaps the only person to detect this secret mood which gov-

---

[60]   *Ibid.*, pp. 55-56.
[61]   *Ibid.*, p. 55.

erned the profoundly sensible, almost voiceless attitude of this man towards the world of material things.[62]

When his father dies, Gould knows that he will return immediately to re-open the silver mine. Conrad examines the tangle of conscious and unconscious thoughts and feelings by which Gould convinces himself that he must work the mine.

That irreparable change a death makes in the course of our daily thoughts can be felt in a vague and poignant discomfort of mind. It hurt Charles Gould to feel that never more, by no effort of will, would he be able to think of his father in the same way he used to think of him when the poor man was alive. His breathing image was no longer in his power. This consideration, closely affecting his own identity, filled his breast with a mournful and angry desire for action. In this his instinct was unerring. Action is consolatory. It is the enemy of thought and the friend of flattering illusions. Only in the conduct of our action can we find the sense of mastery over the Fates. For his action the mine was obviously the only field. It was imperative sometimes to know how to disobey the solemn wishes of the dead. He resolved firmly to make his disobedience as thorough (by way of atonement) as it well could be. The mine had been the cause of an absurd moral disaster; its working must be made a serious and moral success. He owed it to the dead man's memory. Such were the – properly speaking – emotions of Charles Gould. His thoughts ran upon the means of raising a large amount of capital in San Francisco or elsewhere; and incidentally there occured to him also the general reflection that the counsel of the departed must be an unsound guide. Not one of them could be aware beforehand what enormous change the death of any given individual may produce in the very aspect of the world.[63]

After Gould returns to Costaguana, he continues to rationalize his disobedience. The material success of the mine, he insists, will be moral success. His father in despair over owning the ruinous mine had written that there seemed to be no ray of hope for the country; the son interprets the coming success of the mine as that ray of hope. He explains to his wife, who has begun to doubt the wisdom of opening the mine, that the development of material interests will inevitably bring secure prosperity and lawful order:

[62]   *Ibid.*, p. 59.
[63]   *Ibid.*, pp. 65-66.

"And who knows whether in that sense even the San Tomé mine may not become that little rift in the darkness which poor father despaired of ever seeing." [64] Having obtained American capital to finance his project, Gould rationalizes that this justifies disobeying his father and, in fact, makes his action essentially obedient.

Poor father did not understand. He was afraid I would hang on to the ruinous thing, waiting for just some such chance to sell the rights, and waste my life miserably. That was the true sense of his prohibition, which we have deliberately set aside.[65]

Only once does he feel that he has made a mistake, but his remorse is short lived.

For a moment he felt as if the silver mine, which had killed his father, had decoyed him further than he meant to go; and with the round-about logic of emotions, he felt that the worthiness of his life was bound up with success. There was no going back.[66]

Under all circumstances Gould is able to invoke his father's wishes to sanction what he is going to do with the mine. When it is in danger of confiscation by the bandit-politicians whom it has drawn to the Occidental Province, Gould takes his father's advice literally for the first time. Rather than have the mine taken from him, he will have the entire operation dynamited. "The Gould Concession could not be resumed. His father had not desired it. The son would never surrender it." [67]

Desiring further family sanction for disobeying his father's wishes, Gould justifies his romantic desire for action and success by invoking his Uncle Harry, who had entered Costaguana politics only to be shot by the succeeding revolutionary government. His uncle, Gould insists, "went to work in his own way because it seemed right, just as I feel I must lay hold of that mine".[68]

Gould like his father becomes the slave of the mine; it becomes a fixed idea estranging him from his wife. "The mine had got hold of Charles Gould with a grip as deadly as ever it had laid up-

[64] *Ibid.*, p. 24.
[65] *Ibid.*, p. 73.
[66] *Ibid.*, p. 85.
[67] *Ibid.*, p. 402.
[68] *Ibid.*, p. 11.

on his father." [69] To outside eyes, the elder Gould had been defeated, and Charles Gould had triumphed. In reality both are defeated, but Charles Gould does not know it. "He was like his father. He had no ironic eye." [70] At the conclusion of the novel Charles Gould is hurrying back to the mine after the briefest of visits to his home. His wife, who had once shared his naive idealism about the development of material interests and had commented enthusiastically, "you are splendidly disobedient",[71] at last sits alone musing on the bitter lessons she has learned.

She saw clearly the San Tomé mine possessing, consuming, burning up the life of the last of the Costaguana Goulds: mastering the energetic spirit of the son as it had mastered the lamentable weakness of the father. A terrible success for the last of the Goulds.[72]

*Nostromo* is hardly an autobiographical novel. Yet the story of Charles Gould and his father does seem to have significant affinities with Conrad's own experience. In telling the story of the young man who returns home to take up a ruined inheritance and to redress the wrongs done to his father, Conrad may well be dramatizing obliquely his own imaginative fears about what could have happened to him if he returned to Poland to take up his father's cause. The fact that Gould's success is worse than his possible failure shows how deeply Conrad criticized and feared the unexamined inheritance.

In *Victory* Conrad also made a significant and credible presentation of the disastrous influence of a father upon his son. For the novel Conrad created an articulate intellectual who is acutely conscious of his father's philosophy. He made the father's influence credible by having the son live for several years with his father, who impresses upon the young man his views. This situation in outline resembles Conrad's own childhood experiences. However, the philosopher-father in the novel bears no similarities at all to Apollo Korzeniowski; his philosophy is neither religious nor patriotic, it is cynical and materialistic. Its pessimism, how-

[69]  *Ibid.*, p. 400.
[70]  *Ibid.*, p. 378.
[71]  *Ibid.*, p. 84.
[72]  *Ibid.*, p. 522.

ever, probably does reflect the gloom surrounding Conrad's child-hood, as well as, of course, his own adult experiences and reflec-tions.

*Victory* is Conrad's most completely realized working out of the theme of the fatal inheritance and must be considered his final statement about the question: shall I be faithful to my father's ideas? Of course, Conrad answers this question negatively, but far more explicitly than he had done in *Nostromo* where the father had not elaborated his opinions into a formal philosophy.

Between the ages of eighteen and twenty-one, Heyst lives alone in London with his father where the older man impresses his phi-losophy of negativism on his son. According to that philosophy, the universe is devoid of meaning; and all human action, neces-sarily based on the illusion of meaning, leads to disaster and self-contempt. Most people, the elder Heyst insists, have some intima-tion of this truth, but refuse to face it. Unable or unwilling to express such a bleak insight, they draw back from it, saying, "Anything but this".[73] Usually they prefer their servitude as vic-tims of life's traps, masking the cruelty of life with religion – the "Great Joke" according to Heyst – or the illusion of progress.

The philosopher himself feels that he has attained a complete moral and intellectual freedom unavailable to the mass of man-kind, but he is not certain his son has done so. When the youthful Heyst asks his father, "Is there no guidance", the father inter-prets the question as evidence of a lingering remnant of faith or idealism or a tendency toward involvement.

"You still believe in something, then?" he said in a clear voice, which had been growing feeble of late. "You believe in flesh and blood, perhaps? A full and equable contempt would soon do away with that, too. But since you have not attained to it, I advise you to cultivate that form of contempt which is called pity. It is perhaps the least difficult – always remembering that you, too, if you are any-thing, are as pitiful as the rest, yet never expecting any pity for yourself."

But this is not definite enough for the son, and he wants it trans-

[73]   *Ibid.*, p. 219.

lated into a code of conduct. His father then advises him, 'Look on – make no sound." [74]

Heyst attempts to put this advice into practice. He drifts, becoming merely a spectator, because, as he explains, "Intelligent observation of the facts was the best way of cheating the time allotted to us whether we want it or not." [75] Above all, he avoids creating ties. But this turns out to be impossible for him because 'No decent feeling was ever scorned by Heyst".[76] Pity, which his father had advised him to cultivate as an easy form of contempt, leads Heyst inevitably to deeper involvements. By pity, the elder Heyst had meant simply an attitude arising from a philosophical contemplation of mankind. Heyst reads in his father's writings: "Man alone can give one the disgust of pity; yet I find it easier to believe in the misfortune of mankind than in its wickedness." [77] His father would undoubtedly have approved of Heyst's buying drinks for casual acquaintances, especially when he ironically offers to quench the thirst of a well-known alcoholic.[78] But he would not have approved of his son's first major venture into pity, an episode which seems to prove to Heyst the accuracy of his father's ideas.

His sense of pity is touched by the plight of Morrison, a ship's captain about to lose his ship, and he rescues him with a loan. Then, in order to avoid the embarrassing emotional involvement of Morrison's gratitude, he lets himself get more deeply involved by going into business with him. Not engaging in an ordinary scheme, Heyst and Morrison plan to take advantage of the imminent shift from sail to steam by mining and selling coal on the islands of the east. The venture tempts Heyst far into action and illusion. He rushes about making arrangements and although far too sophisticated and disillusioned to believe in the theory of progress, he nevertheless talks of their plans principally in terms of a "great stride forward for these regions", a phrase which moves the narrator to suggest that Heyst is concerned chiefly for

[74]   *Ibid.*, pp. 174-75.
[75]   *Ibid.*, p. 54.
[76]   *Ibid.*, p. 18.
[77]   *Ibid.*, p. 220.
[78]   *Ibid.*, p. 8.

a "stride forward ... in the general organization of the universe".[79]

The results are disastrous. When Morrison goes to England on business, he catches cold in the damp climate and dies. Heyst blames himself for Morrison's death. The Tropical Belt Coal Company collapses, and the rumor spreads that Heyst had exploited Morrison and then sent him home to die. Retiring to his island filled with the decaying remains of the coal company, Heyst is convinced that his father had accurately perceived the "infamous" character of the scheme of life.

I had allowed myself to be tempted into action. It seemed innocent enough, but all action is bound to be harmful. It is devilish. That is why this world is evil upon the whole. But I have done with it! I shall never lift a little finger again.[80]

Heyst's second departure from the life of aloof detachment proves his father wrong. Belatedly falling in love, he learns that human ties give value to life and that years of following his father's ideas have enfeebled his will and attenuated his powers of communication.  He cannot defend himself and Lena, the woman he loves, from evil intruders; and before he commits suicide, he repudiates his long lasting distrust of hope, of love, and of life itself.

Such an outline of the action makes *Victory* seem too simple a book, in part an obvious case of a bad influence turning out to be a bad influence, or worse, an exemplary tale about the evils of mis-education. At best, one might see Conrad's attention to the ideas of Heyst's father as only a convenient way of accounting for the motivation of his unusual protagonist. What saves *Victory* from being a simple tale of cause and effect is a series of ironic contradictions: first, a contradiction between the origin and content of the philosophy of Heyst's father; then, obvious differences between that philosophy and the elder Heyst's conduct of his own life; finally and most significantly, a profound irony in the relationship between Heyst and his father; that is, in the way in which the counsels of non-involvement took hold of Heyst's mind. These ironic contradictions are intensified by the fact that Heyst is par-

[79]  *Ibid.*, p. 6.
[80]  *Ibid.*, p. 54.

tially aware of some of them and yet not sufficiently aware to free
himself from the destructive influence of his dead father.

The basis of the philosophical thought of the elder Heyst is not
a rational analysis of the conditions of life, but the emotions of
disillusionment and fear.

Thinker, stylist, and man of the world in his time, the elder Heyst
had begun by coveting all the joys, those of the great and those of
the humble, those of the fools and those of the sages. For more than
sixty years he had dragged on this painful earth of ours the most
weary, the most uneasy soul that civilisation had ever fashioned to
its ends of disillusion and regret. One could not refuse him a measure of greatness, for he was unhappy in a way unknown to mediocre
souls.[81]

The elder Heyst, then, began as a romantic – optimistic, eager for
all experience, confident in the vast possibilities of his own spirit.
When life did not meet his extravagant demands, he swung violently in the other direction to declare it evil and corrupting.
Heyst, unfortunately, has only a little understanding that his
father's views were almost entirely psychological in origin. Explaining to Lena that his father is responsible for his existence, he
mainly shows the limitations of his insight.

I don't know much of his history. I suppose he began like other
people; took fine words for good, ringing coin and noble ideals for
valuable banknotes. ... Later he discovered – how am I to explain
it to you? Suppose the world were a factory and all mankind work-
men in it. Well, he discovered that the wages were not good enough.
That they were paid in counterfeit money.[82]

Heyst speaks as though his father's radical disillusionment were a
fairly common experience – "he began like other people" – but
the admission that he did not know much about his father's history and the phrase, "I suppose", accurately reveal Heyst's limitations in understanding his father's ideas. Heyst has greater insight into the fear motivating his father's thought, but again he is
unable to use this understanding critically. Reading one of his
father's books, Heyst inwardly comments:

[81]   *Ibid.*, p. 91.
[82]   *Ibid.*, pp. 195-96.

With what strange serenity, mingled with terrors, had that man considered the universal nothingness! He had plunged into it headlong, perhaps to render death the answer that faced one at every inquiry, more supportable.[83] Heyst feels that his father's mind had given him a "special insight into its mastery of despair".[84] Like his father, Heyst does not fear death, but he does not consider, until far too late, that not valuing life may be too a high a price for his freedom.

Just as his thought was based on contradictions largely unperceived by his son, so is there an ironic gap between the elder Heyst's theory about the conduct of life, which his son practices, and the actual conduct of his own life. He successfully impresses upon his son's mind a theory of non-involvement, mere observation, emotional apathy. And the son goes through life regularly exhibiting an attitude of playful aloofness. But the elder Heyst's life was marked by emotional turmoil. He quarreled with his family; he exiled himself from Sweden; and his writing, violent and filled with contempt, greatly angered his readers. Following his father's counsels, the son takes a tepid interest in the world of "hard facts". But this slowly dying interest hardly matches his father's opinionated reactions to the world:

The elder Heyst had written of everything in many books – of space and of time, of animals and of stars, analyzing ideas and actions, the laughter and the frowns of men, and the grimaces of their agony.[85]

Conrad emphasizes this contradiction between the elder Heyst's theory and practice in the incisive ironic sentence immediately following the young Heyst's request for guidance, "What is one to do then?"

"Look on – make no sound", were the last words of the man who had spent his life in blowing blasts upon a terrible trumpet which had filled heaven and earth with ruins, while mankind went on its way unheeding.[86]

Although Heyst is aware of humanity's response to his father, he cannot use this knowledge to free himself from his father's in-

[83] *Ibid.*, p. 219.
[84] *Ibid.*, p. 196.
[85] *Ibid.*, p. 218.
[86] *Ibid.*, p. 175.

fluence. He reads the obituary notices, "generally insignificant and some grossly abusive", but he dismisses them by saying to himself, "This is the hate and rage of their fear ... and also of wounded vanity."[87]

Why, one might ask, should Heyst, intelligent and skeptical, remain so imperceptive about his own father and his father's influence upon him? The answer comes in the ironic inconsistency between what Heyst's father has taught him about human relationships and their own relationship. Heyst, of course, has had impressed upon him the notion that human relationships, like all other involvement in life, are a snare and worthless. But this notion has gripped Heyst so firmly only because of the strong natural bond between father and son. Furthermore, since Heyst had faithfully avoided all human entanglements, just as his father had advised, his tie to his dead father grew more strong. Thus the philosophy which condemned love makes its claim on one man by means of love. This irony, which goes as unperceived by Heyst as those in his father's thought and life, involves him in some elaborate self-deception. When his father dies, Heyst tries to deny to himself his genuine filial affection. Momentarily he even attempts to tell himself that he ought to hate his father like so many others. But the possibility of this improbable sentiment suddenly disappears as the young man begins to weep. Still faithful to his father's ideas Heyst tries to explain away his grief.

He became aware of his eyes being wet. It was not that the man was his father. For him it was purely a matter of hearsay which could not in itself cause this emotion. No! It was because he had looked at him so long that he missed him so much.[88]

And so, loving his father, too proud to join ordinary humanity in the pursuits of life he has learned to despise, he remains aloof. Even his later insight that his father had dominated him easily because he was not a "heartless man" or "without pity"[89] and that he himself was flattered to be taken into his father's confidence does nothing to shake his belief in his father's views. In-

[87]  *Ibid.*
[88]  *Ibid.*
[89]  *Ibid.*, p. 196.

deed, Heyst follows this oblique admission of his father's feeling for him with a defense of his ideas.

The longer he remains aloof and skeptical, the stronger grows his attachment to his dead father. Because he is faithful to his father's outlook the world becomes unreal to him a place of shadows and appearances, something quite distant and unimportant to Heyst living "too long within myself watching the mere shadows and shades of life".[90] In the midst of this shadowy unreality that Heyst presently finds impossible to deal with, one thing retains force and solidity, Heyst's memory of his father. For many years he dutifully has his father's house and possessions cared for – everything in its place just as Heyst recalls it, but regularly aired as though awaiting the owner's imminent return. Heyst often thinks of these possessions during his wanderings.

It seemed as if in his conception of a world not worth touching, and perhaps not substantial enough to grasp, these objects familiar to his childhood and his youth and associated with the memory of an old man, were the only realities, something having an absolute existence.[91]

When the house is to be demolished, he finds himself "surprisingly distressed".[92] His emotion surprises him, of course, because he cherishes the illusion of total indifference. Later as proprietor of the short-lived coal company, he has these possessions shipped to Samburan, and after the business fails he remains on the island attached to it chiefly by their presence. He hangs his father's portrait in the principal room of his bungalow, and he sits beneath it, shrinking under his father's eye, reading his father's books, and thinking of his apostasy from his father's teachings. Even when he is groping toward an understanding of Lena and still confused by her physical existence, his father's reality remains strong. While he reads in one of his father's volumes, he permits his sense of his father's existence to overcome him.

It seemed to him that he was hearing his father's voice, speaking and ceasing to speak again. Startled, at first, he ended by finding a charm in the illusion. He abandoned himself to the half-belief that some-

[90]  *Ibid.*, p. 318.
[91]  *Ibid.*, p. 176.
[92]  *Ibid.*

thing of his father dwelt yet on earth – a ghostly voice, audible to the ear of his own flesh and blood.[93]

Again the impact of his father surprises Heyst, but he yields to it only too readily.

In the final sequence of action in the novel, where Heyst demonstrates his incapacity again and again, Conrad effectively reminds the reader of Heyst's father, the strongest reality his son has known as well as the source of his paralysis of will, by at least four references to his portrait. By combining these allusions to the portrait with references to Lena, Conrad suggests the forces of negation and affirmation contending within Heyst. Slowly, in this section of the novel, his father's possessions and what they symbolize weaken before the superior force of Lena. In the first of these passages a glance at the portrait almost stifles what Heyst is saying to Lena.

He glanced at the portrait of his father, exactly above the head of the girl, and as it were ignoring her in its painted austerity of feeling. He did not finish the sentence . . . .[94]

Twice more Conrad juxtaposes the portrait and Lena. The inclusion also of the villainous Ricardo in these two passages allies Heyst's father with evil, despite the portrait's apparent irrelevance to the scene.

She had come out after Heyst's departure, and had sat down under the portrait to wait for the return of the man of violence and death [Ricardo].[95]

Unheard by them both [Lena and Ricardo], the thunder growled distantly with angry modulations of its tremendous voice, while the world outside shuddered incessantly around the dead stillness of the room where the framed profile of Heyst's father looked severely into space.[96]

Although Lena cannot gain a victory over the villains on the scene, she gains one over Heyst's father. When Heyst's inability to disarm one of the villains results in Lena's being shot, his father's possessions lose their force for him.

[93]  *Ibid.*, p. 219.
[94]  *Ibid.*, p. 359.
[95]  *Ibid.*, p. 394.
[96]  *Ibid.*, p. 401.

Heyst stumbled into the room and looked around. All the objects in there – the books, the gleam of old silver familiar to him from boyhood, the very portrait on the wall – seemed shadowy, unsubstantial, the dumb accomplices of an amazing dream-plot ending in an illusory effect of awakening and the impossibility of ever closing his eyes again.[97]

Thus his father's philosophy turns out to be not tough, realistic, an assessment of "hard facts", but more shadowy, insubstantial, and false than the romantic optimism or religious faith it was meant to supplant. "Enchanted Heyst", as he is called early in the novel, is released from his father's spell, but only to see the evil he has permitted to flourish during his dream of skepticism and aloofness. Heyst's recognition of life comes too late. His bond with his dead father has been indeed a bond with death.

In a novel the purpose of which is to affirm human bonds as a source of strength and value, Conrad has demonstrated that the uncritically accepted human tie can lead to destruction. Heyst's bond to the girl is creative; his bond to his dead father destructive. Heyst, in identifying himself with his father, has acted without adequate self-knowledge and loses his own sense of reality. With Lena the self-described "man of universal scorn and unbelief" [98] begins to feel a "greater sense of his own reality than he had ever known in his life".[99] The unexamined inheritance and an uncritically accepted filial bond carry with them death and destruction. Victory over their evil may come only as the final revelation in tragedy comes, immediately before the action that sends the hero, triumphant in self-knowledge, to his death.

I do not want to claim too much for *Victory*. As recent critics have demonstrated, its affirmative message and the means by which Conrad presents that message (the character of Lena and the relationship between Lena and Heyst) are ineffective and unconvincing. Nevertheless, inspired by some of his deepest feelings, Conrad compellingly portrayed a destructive philosophy in the lives of a father-teacher and a son-disciple.

[97]   *Ibid.*, p. 403.
[98]   *Ibid.*, p. 199.
[99]   *Ibid.*, p. 200.

In depicting in *Chance, Nostromo*, and *Victory*, a brutal poet, a
tormented merchant, and a cynical philosopher, Conrad avoided
portraying specific aspects of his own father. But the fictional
sons, a shy and chivalrous sea captain, an idealistic capitalist, and
a tender-hearted skeptic, all reflect aspects of Conrad's own character. Moreover, the forms of the heritage – an impossibly high
standard of conduct, a disaster to be redressed, a philosophy carefully taught to a lonely youth – recall in one way or another the
influence of Apollo Korzeniowski. Just as Apollo Korzeniowski,
in urging Conrad "only to be a Pole", warned him against all
courses of action, so the three fathers in *Chance, Nostromo*, and
*Victory* make impossible negative demands upon their sons:
Captain Anthony must avoid any indelicate action; Charles Gould
must renounce his inheritance; Axel Heyst must make no ties.
These points of similarity – elusive as they are – explain why
Conrad portrayed with such personal conviction the disasters inherent in the uneasy bond between the generations.

## II

## UNCLE AND NEPHEW: THE CONCEPT OF PROFESSION AND THE SPIRITUAL FATHER

After the death of Apollo Korzeniowski, Tadeusz Bobrowski became the guardian of Conrad, replacing Conrad's father. The relationship between uncle and nephew was affectionate and enduring. In later life Conrad often praised his uncle, stressing the beneficial effects of his influence.

I cannot write about Tadeusz Bobrowski, my Uncle guardian and benefactor without emotion. Even now, after ten years, I still feel his loss. He was a man of great character and unusual qualities of mind. Although he did not understand my desire to join the mercantile marine, on principle, he never objected to it. I saw him four time during the thirty [sic] years of my wanderings (from 1874-1893) but even so I attribute to his devotion, care, and influence, whatever good qualities I may possess.[1]

As Conrad indicated, Tadeusz Bobrowski exerted a steadying rational and moral influence on him, which was, as Bobrowski often suggested, diametrically opposed to the influence of Conrad's father. Because Bobrowski particularly persuaded Conrad that he should avoid his father's lack of a definite profession, Conrad was proud to show his uncle his progress in the profession of the British Merchant Service, and later tried to demonstrate to himself that writing was a similar profession. The pattern of Conrad's relationship with his uncle recurred several times in Conrad's life; in both his careers Conrad felt that he was the son or apprentice to a spiritual father who initiated him into his profession and also that he himself served as a spiritual father for younger seamen and writers. Deeply moved by these relationships, Conrad por-

[1]    Letter to Kasimir Waliszewski (Dec. 5, 1903), Najder, p. 239.

trayed similar ones in three novels, *The Shadow Line*, *Lord Jim* (where the relationship between Marlow as spiritual father and Jim as son is one of the most profound and moving relationships in his fiction), and *Nostromo*.

I

The strength and continuity which Conrad attributed to Tadeusz Bobrowski's influence may be surprising. Bobrowski did not become Conrad's guardian until the boy was eleven, after the thorough indoctrination undertaken by Korzeniowski. In addition, Bobrowski did not have the vivid, forceful personality of Conrad's father. Furthermore, Bobrowski saw his nephew infrequently. Even in Poland Conrad did not live with his uncle. Bobrowski's property was in the Ukraine in Russian Poland, and the family had agreed that Conrad was probably safer in Cracow in Austrian Poland where he had begun his formal education before his father's death.[2] Perhaps this last fact actually strengthened Bobrowski's influence. As an adolescent Conrad did not associate his dislike of school with his uncle. However, three more significant reasons account for the strength and continuity of Bobrowski's influence upon Conrad. Bobrowski tempered his strong moral outlook with understanding charity; he felt that Conrad was like a son to him; and, finally, he was probably influenced by feudal traditions concerning the relationship of a boy and his maternal uncle.

Although the chief characteristic of Bobrowski's mind was his sense of moral consequence, from which flowed the conduct of his own life and his advice to Conrad, this sense of moral consequence was modified, and indeed made more effective, by his efforts to understand the lives and minds of others. In making an unequivocal moral judgment, he did not withdraw his charitable interpretation of motives and events. His succinct judgment upon Conrad's paternal grandfather, a boastful irrational man, demonstrates both Bobrowski's sense of moral consequence and his

[2] Aubry, *Joseph Conrad, Life and Letters*, I, p. 146.

charity: "Living amongst his personal, family, and political-patriotical illusions, the brave captain spent his old age in poverty, and in 1863 saw the consequences of his convictions." [3] Conrad himself once commented on this balance of morality and charity in his uncle's character by describing Bobrowski as a "man of rigorous logic, if of infinite charity".[4]

Bobrowski's affection for Conrad also strengthened his influence. He thought of Conrad as a son. Having lost his own wife and daughter,[5] he was strongly drawn to the orphaned Conrad, especially because Conrad was the only son of his sister. Evelina Bobrowska had been the only girl among several brothers who formed, Conrad later explained, "an extraordinary Sister-Cult ... from which I profited when left an orphan".[6] Bobrowski's patience was strained when in response to an urgent telegram he had to cross Europe not only to watch his nephew recover from a wound, received in either a duel or an unsuccessful suicide attempt, but also to pay Conrad's considerable debts. But he explained to a friend: "Had he been my own son I wouldn't have done it but – I must avow – in the case of my beloved Sister's son, I had the weakness to act against the principles I had hitherto held." [7] Furthermore, Bobrowski probably felt particularly responsible for Conrad; the marriage of Evelina Bobrowska to the impractical author must have depended in part upon Bobrowski's consent; he was the head of the family after their father's death. Conrad too felt that his uncle was like a father to him. To Edward Garnett he explained, "I stand more in the relation of a son than a nephew." [8]

The relationship between Conrad and Bobrowski, generally characterized by unstrained affection and good advice, may have been strengthened and even partially determined by a common pattern of feeling and behaviour in the tradition-directed, semi-feudal society of rural Poland. Anthropologists and students of medieval literature have shown that people of widely varying cul-

---

[3]   *Memoirs*, in Morf, p. 9.
[4]   *The Mirror of the Sea*, pp. 153-54.
[5]   Aubry, *The Sea Dreamer*, p. 29.
[6]   *Garnett Letters* (Jan. 20, 1900), p. 166.
[7]   Letter (March 12/24, 1879), Najder, p. 177.
[8]   *Garnett Letters* (Jan. 20, 1900), p. 166.

tures regard the relationship between a young man and his maternal uncle as extremely important. Relatively free of the psychological difficulties inherent in a father-son relationship, the bond between nephew and uncle is warm and frank. The uncle often teaches his nephew an occupation and helps to initiate him into maturity.[9]

His influence strengthened by all these conditions, Bobrowski strove to make his nephew a useful and moral man, a man with a good deal of self-control. "I consider it my duty", he wrote to the nineteen-year-old Conrad, "by advice and reminders to keep you on the right path: that is to say on the path of reason and of duty".[10] Bobrowski advised Conrad by reminding him of those weaknesses of the Korzeniowski family which led directly to misfortunes and those strengths of the Bobrowski family which could lead to success. He insisted on this contrast because he was attempting to inculcate an idea of rational and practical duty irreconcilable with Apollo Korzeniowski's belief in the primacy of duty to the fatherland.

Bobrowski tried to teach his nephew that he was a combination of two contrasting biological inheritances. One was to be encouraged, the other discouraged. The Nałecz Korzeniowski in Conrad, according to Bobrowski, endangered him because its romantic imagination encouraged risky financial speculation and other unrealistic, grandiose plans.[11] Restlessness and carelessness were also Korzeniowski traits, and Bobrowski viewed Conrad's desire for adventure and his frequent change of plans as evidence of his paternal heritage. He pointed out that the temperamental melancholy of the Korzeniowskis resulted from the inevitable disappointments they brought upon themselves. Furthermore, their melancholy brooding deepened the sense of disappointment.

But Bobrowski, with considerable shrewdness, did not merely find fault with the Korzeniowskis. He pointed out that on the better side of their character they displayed sincerity of feelings,

[9]　George C. Homans, *The Human Group* (New York, Harcourt Brace, 1950), pp. 217-19, 252-59.
[10]　Letter (Sept. 27, 1876), Najder, p. 37.
[11]　Letter (July 18/30, 1891), *ibid.*, p. 147.

energy, and initiative. This recognition of their good traits probably reinforced for Conrad the truth of his uncle's criticism, simply because his uncle's attitude seemed so just. In addition, his uncle's admissions of the limits of his own comprehension probably strengthened the impression that his criticism made upon his nephew. One letter filled with advice concludes:

Anyhow, that's what I think! You will do as you wish, for in all aspects connected with your career I leave you absolute freedom as I am a great believer in it on principle and I realize well that I cannot express my opinion, however firmly I hold it, without knowing the circumstances in which you are situated. As a man of a clearly defined position I feel sympathetic to people of the same kind. There has never been anything of an adventurer in me, so I sigh for a regular position for you as well.[12]

About the Bobrowski influence itself, Conrad's uncle was not quite so explicit. However, he implied its principal features by the obvious point of view from which he criticized the Korzeniowskis. In contrast to Conrad's Korzeniowski-like loss in Marseilles of his Polish books and family photographs, Bobrowski notes that he himself had saved his mother's picture for over forty years.[13] When Conrad was considering some financial speculation, his uncle reminded him. "Since you are a Nałecz, beware of risky speculations based only on hope." [14] And he emphasized the supposed differences between the families by quoting a proverb: "Hope is the mother of fools and calculation the Father of the sober-minded." [15] Modesty distrust of the imagination, prudence, ever-vigilant regard for consequences, and duty, all these are extolled in Bobrowski's letters.

Generally, in his uncle's view, the saving traits Conrad inherited from his mother ought to control or negate the dangerous traits of his paternal heritage. At his most generous, however, Bobrowski hopes – with the kind of hope that is actually advice and encouragement – that the two strains might unite to produce a truly superior man.

[12] Letter (May 18/30, 1880), *ibid.*, p. 63.
[13] Letter (Sept. 27, 1876), *ibid.*, p. 38.
[14] Letter (Aug. 3/15, 1881), *ibid.*, p. 73.
[15] *Ibid.*

I see with pleasure that the Nałecz in you has been modified under the influence of the Bobroszczaki, as your incomparable Mother used to call her own family after she flew away to the Nałecz nest. This time I rejoice over the influence of my family, although I don't in the least deny that the Nałeczes have a spirit of initiative and enterprise greater than that which is in my blood. From the blending of these two excellent families in your worthy person there should spring a race which by its endurance and wise enterprise will astound the whole world! Pray God that may happen. Amen![16]

Naturally, Bobrowski wrote this way only when he approved of Conrad's behaviour and wanted to see more like it. But although necessary, joining endurance and initiative – staying and spurting, as Conrad was to say in *Lord Jim* – was extremely difficult.

Elsewhere, Bobrowski used as a symbol of the romantic temperament the image of the bird – flying to seek new scenes and adventures, perched precariously and momentarily on a branch, or suddenly leaving a comfortable branch for no discernible reason.

When the telegram summoned him to care for Conrad in Marseilles, he complained: "Naturally I could not fly to him straight away like a bird." [17] In 1880 Bobrowski urged naturalization saying: "It is impossible to be a 'Vogel frey' all your life." [18] The image and its meaning having been impressed upon him, Conrad used it in his autobiographical novel, *The Shadow Line*, to describe his unaccountable and irrational abandoning a position of second mate on a steamer: "I left it in that, to us, inconsequential manner in which a bird flies away from a comfortable branch." [19]

While it is possible that the two halves of the temperament might be integrated through vigilant discipline, no amount of adjustment and modification could bring about permanent agreement between the concept of duty held by Apollo Korzeniowski and that held by Tadeusz Bobrowski. Apollo Korzeniowski, of course, saw duty as the unwavering devotion to the Polish cause despite disappointment, circumstances, or the claims of his per-

---

[16] Letter (June 28, 1880), *ibid.*, p. 66. Baines explains *Bobroszczaki* as "a facetious form of the surname, meaning 'the Bobrowski family' " (p. 66).
[17] Letter to Stefan Buszczynski (March 12/24, 1879), Najder, p. 176.
[18] Letter (May 18/30, 1880), *ibid.*, p. 63.
[19] *The Shadow Line*, p. 5.

sonal life. Bobrowski's conception was quite different, and significantly, he saw it as part of a philosophy which specifically rejected Polish Messianism and insurrection.

In rejecting Messianism, insurrection, and the primacy of patriotic duty, Bobrowski agreed with the new realistic movement in Polish culture which re-thought the problems of history and politics. Criticizing the romantic idealization of Poland's past, the realists studied Polish history with less patriotic fervor. They analyzed the weaknesses of the old royal republic, which for Korzeniowski and the romantics had been an ideal. In 1869, the year of Korzeniowski's death, the men who formed the new government of Austrian Poland formulated and published a new political doctrine. Oscar Halecki summarizes its intent: "Condemning the revolutionary policy of the insurrections, its authors recommended the Poles to work within the sphere of legality, and put them on their guard against all dangerous illusions." [20] At the same time they did not deny by these prudent ideas the patriotic hope of eventual national independence and urged Poles not to forget their nationality merely because they were not committed to insurrection.

Bobrowski directly reflected these new ideas expressing the temper of the era of "organic work". Noting the danger of the new era, the growth of indifference toward politics and Poland, he rejoices that his nephew takes an interest in the Polish problem; but he warns him that Panlavism is a false hope for Poland, pointing out that it is only a disguise for Russification. His analysis of the situation and his program for individual and national behaviour demonstrate how a sensitive and intelligent man responded to the dilemmas of his time.

I am certain that eventually out of this chaos some form of federation will emerge, but by that time I shall be long dead and possibly you too. In the meantime, since like pariahs we are deprived of our own political and national rights, we more than the others, have to preserve our individuality and our own standpoint, till the time comes when Nemesis, as a result of our own efforts, spins out some

[20]   Halecki, p. 262.

situation which will give use the right to have a real national existence – and possibly something more.[21]

Bobrowski too believed in the importance of nationality, and he
shared Korzeniowski's opinion of Russia as an international
criminal. In contrast, however, he had no faith in the transcendent
importance of the nation and accepted, with reluctance, the lack
of opportunities for action. In another letter he made his criticism
of Polish Messianism clear when he contrasted the romantic view
of Poland and its Messianic destiny with his own more sober view
of nations and individuals.

Our nation unfortunately, As Słowacki so truly remarked – although
he himself was not immune from the accusation – is a "peacock
among nations", which in simple prose means that we are a collection
of proclaimed and generally unrecognized celebrities – whom no one
knows, no one acknowledges and no one ever will! So that if both
Individuals and Nations were to make "duty" their aim, instead of
the ideal of greatness, the world would certainly be a better place
than it is! [22]

Thus Bobrowski attempted to guide Conrad away from his father's
attitude toward duty to his own, from "dreaming of being the
chosen Apostle of the people", as he says further in this letter, to
toiling "as a modest tiny ant", a "part of the team". Similarly in
Lord Jim, Conrad was to contrast following the "dream" with
fighting "in the ranks". Bobrowski explained that his idea of duty
was firmly based on the circumstances of his life, that it was not
made up of easy platitudes.

Perhaps you will tell me that what I have said is but the words of a
man who has always been comfortable in the world, "qui a eu tou-
jours chaud"; but this is not so – you know this well. I have gone

---

[21]  Letter (Sept. 11/23, 1881), Najder, p. 80. Conrad's apparent interest in
Pan-Slavism is puzzling. During the rest of his life, he insisted on Poland's
affinity with the West and grew angry when readers found Slavic qualities
in his writing. Mrs. Hay notices this disparity (pp. 298-300) but goes too
far, I believe, in suggesting that Conrad was being influenced by the Pan-
Slavism in the Dostoevsky novels he was reading. It seems more reasonable to imagine that the young Conrad had suggested to his uncle the possibility of Poland's achieving political autonomy through the Pan-Slavic
Movement.
[22]  Letter (Oct. 28/Nov. 9, 1891), Najder, p. 154.

through a lot, I have suffered over my own fate and the fate of my
family and my Nation, and perhaps just because of these sufferings
and disappointments I have developed in myself this calm outlook
on the problem of life, whose motto, I venture to say, was, is, and
will be "usque ad finem". The devotion to duty interpreted more
widely or narrowly, according to circumstances and time – this con-
stitutes my practical creed which – supported as it is by the experience of sixty years – may be of some use to you? [23]

Duty, then, for Tadeusz Bobrowski, was not primarily patriotic
but practical. It was not fulfilled by attempts to realize an ideal
despite the improbability of success, but rather by attempts to
bring more modest goals to pass. It was not the transcendent
religio-political duty of "only to be a Pole" but rather the "duty
according to circumstances and time". No less strong and compelling than romantic duty, its motto, *usque ad finem*, was meant
seriously.

Devoted as Conrad was to his uncle and plausible as were some
of his uncle's arguments, Conrad could hardly have accepted
Bobrowski's insistence on the contrast existing between all the
Bobrowskis and all the Korzeniowskis. He must have realized that
his uncle had oversimplified the distinction between the two families in order to conduct his moral education. When Bobrowski
criticized the romantic, revolutionist, and unrealistic pride of the
Korzeniowskis in his letters to Conrad, he knew that his own
family was not free from the same taint. Even in his posthumous-
ly published memoirs Bobrowski made only the most restrained
references to the Korzeniowski-like danger in his own family. Yet
the excesses and demands of revolutionary patriotism brought
about the early deaths of his brother Stefan and his sister Evelina,
Conrad's mother. Both of them, although Tadeusz Bobrowski did
not like to say so, had willingly engaged in activities of which he
disapproved and which belied the family habit of realistically
facing facts. It seems almost ironic that Bobrowski advised his
nephew to follow the reasonable traits of his mother. The Korzeniowski inheritance may have meant only danger for Conrad,
but the Bobrowskis had their own share of unreason.

Stefan Bobrowski, like his brother-in-law Apollo Korzeniowski,

[23]   *Ibid.*, p. 155.

belonged to the "Reds" or extremist wing, the party of action among Polish patriots.[24] One of the first and most active promoters of the revolutionary movement, he helped organize the Central National Committee which planned and directed the revolution. When the revolution broke out on January 22, 1863, representatives of the Whites (the conservatives, who had been reluctant to revolt) also joined the committee. But the course of the insurrection wavered because the Whites and the Reds on the committee could not agree on a chief to direct the revolt. Finally, they concurred on Marian Langiewicz and sent Count Adam Grabowski, a moderate who had proposed Langiewicz for the post, to offer him the position. Unfortunately, after only nine days as dictator Langiewicz fled the country. Not only did Stefan Bobrowski sign the proclamation in which the Central National Committee announced that it was taking back the power delegated to Langiewicz, but he also blamed Count Grabowski for the choice of Langiewicz. Bobrowski's accusation was fantastic. Count Grabowski, he said, did not represent the revolution and the true Polish cause at all, but acted for the cautious landlords, who feared the unsettling social results of a revolution which had already proclaimed to the peasants free title to their lands. Stefan Bobrowski went on to say that the reactionaries had plotted to have Langiewicz appointed in order that he might fail and the revolution be defeated. It was an elaborate rationalization of disappointed hopes. Although Stefan Bobrowski was not alone in making this accusation, he was the most vociferous in seeking a scapegoat. The charge could not remain unanswered, and Count Grabowski sought quasi-legal means of settling their differences for which a court of honor was assembled. After it cleared Grabowski of the charge of treachery, Grabowski asked Bobrowski to withdraw what he had said and to assent to the judgment of the court. No formal apology other than the admission of mistake was demanded. Grabowski even offered his hand to his accuser, but Bobrow-

---

[24] The story of Stefan Bobrowski's political career and his duel comes from H. Sutherland Edwards' *The Private History of a Polish Insurrection* (London, 1865), I, pp. 199-202. The book is based on Edward's experiences as a reporter for the *Times* in Poland during the uprising.

ski, unwilling to accept the judgment of the court of honor, refused. Evidently he renewed his charges. The two men quarreled, and although there were many attempts to reconcile them, a duel became inevitable. It took place in Silesia and Bobrowski was mortally wounded.

His conduct contradicts the traits claimed for the family by his brother. Stefan Bobrowski took an active part in politics; he joined the radical wing of the party of revolution. Finally, his intensely emotional involvement in Polish nationalism became indistinguishable for him from his aggressive sense of personal honor. In his memoirs Tadeusz Bobrowski mentioned Stefan's death briefly in this manner, according to Morf: "The tragic fate of his brother Stefan, for instance, is related soberly, unemotionally, in a few lines written in a mood which could be expressed thus: I always thought this would happen." [25]

Although Tadeusz Bobrowski often advised his nephew to imitate his mother rather than his father, Evelina Korzeniowska does not reveal in the few details we have of her life and character the sort of rational prudence with a regard for consequences that characterized Bobrowski himself and which he constantly encouraged in his letters. Bobrowski described her in his memoirs [26] with a good deal of restraint; yet a close look at the text and a consideration of information omitted by Bobrowski reveals that she was less perfect by a good deal than she appeared in his letters to her son. Her early life was marked by tension and unrest. Bobrowski contrasts Evelina with her younger sister Teofila who, before her early death, seemed to embody all the feminine traits he approved of. Teofila appealed with "her good sense, the admirable sweetness of her nature, her exceptional facility and ease

[25] Morf, pp. 6-7. According to Najder, Tadeusz Bobrowski's *Memoirs* make out Stefan Bobrowski to be a member of an "anti-Jacobin" group (p. 18). Tadeusz Bobrowski does not even mention another unstable family connection. His own maternal uncle was one of the most erratic and untrustworthy Polish exiles in Mickiewicz's circle in Paris in the 1840's. See Hay, pp. 34-36.

[26] Conrad himself translated this passage in order to include it in *A Personal Record* as an example of his uncle's conversation with him during a visit to Poland. *Joseph Conrad, Life and Letters*, I, p. 7.

in daily relations".[27] Conrad's mother did not excel in these domestic virtues. She had genuine gifts, but they made her personality intense and unstable.

Your mother – of far greater beauty, exceptionally distinguished in person, manner, and intellect – had a less easy disposition. Being more brilliantly gifted, she also expected more from life. At that trying time, especially, we were greatly concerned about her state. Suffering in her health from the shock of her father's death (she was alone in the house with him when he died suddenly) she was torn by the inward struggle between her love for the man whom she was to marry in the end and her knowledge of her dead father's declared objection to that match. Unable to bring herself to disregard that cherished memory and that judgment she had always respected and trusted, and on the other hand, feeling the impossibility to resist a sentiment so deep and so true, she could not have been expected to preserve her mental and moral balance. At war with herself, she could not give to others that feeling of peace which was not her own.[28]

Behind the balanced style and the dignified abstractions expressing the conflict of love and duty, one can sense the tension of the Bobrowski household alternating between silent conflict and passionate argument and recrimination. Although the Bobrowski objections to Apollo Korzeniowski are explicitly clear elsewhere in his memoirs, Tadeusz avoids alluding to them in the passage dealing with his sister. His account of her extraordinary fidelity to her father's wishes for six years after his death [29] suggests that the rest of the family continued the father's objections to the match.

According to her brother, the inner tension of her life was resolved by her marriage, and his account of her life concludes with her filling an ideal role beyond both criticism and close examination.

It was only later, when united at last with the man of her choice, that she developed those uncommon gifts of mind and heart which compelled the respect and admiration of our foes. Meeting with calm fortitude the cruel trials of a life reflecting all the national and social misfortunes of the community, she realized the highest conceptions

---

[27]  *A Personal Record*, p. 28.
[28]  *Ibid.*, pp. 28-29.
[29]  Aubry, *The Sea Dreamer*, p. 20.

of duty as a wife, a mother and a patriot sharing the exile of her husband and representing nobly the ideal of Polish womanhood.[30]

She probably deserves the high praise, but in presenting and analyzing her character as a type of ideal duty, Bobrowski purposely distances himself and, as he had done in the case of Stefan, forgoes any critical particulars. He says nothing of her temperamental affinity with her husband and her part in his revolutionary activities. And he successfully concealed for a century the fact that she was arrested, tried, and convicted with her husband by proclaiming the patriotic fiction that she chose to join him in exile.[31] One suspects that Evelina's temperament did not easily accommodate itself to approved social roles. Energy that in more conventional circumstances might have been consumed in frustration found an adequate outlet in her marriage to a rebel and a poet.

Only once in his letters to Conrad does Bobrowski hint that his nephew's temperamental ills may originate in his mother as well as his father. Discussing Conrad's "pessimistic disposition", he writes: "Both in you as an individual and in what you inherited from your parents I detect the dreamer – in spite of your very practical profession – or perhaps because of it." [32] But this is merely one slight exception to Bobrowski's method in a program of moral education. At other times he repeatedly urged Conrad to control his paternal heritage of unreason, melancholy, pride, and romantic idealism by fostering his maternal heritage of good sense, modesty, and devotion to duty defined by circumstances.

II

Tadeusz Bobrowski did more than simply exhort his nephew in general terms to follow reason and do his duty. He sought to make his idea of duty workable by counselling the boy to choose a profession and remain faithful to it. Persuaded by these arguments,

---

[30]  *A Personal Record*, p. 29.
[31]  Najder, p. 6.
[32]  Letter (Oct. 28/Nov. 9, 1891), *ibid.*, p. 153.

which he further developed in his writing, Conrad attempted to live up to his uncle's ideal of profession in both his sea and literary careers.

Profession was based, Bobrowski explained, on education, and by developing a profession Conrad might avoid his father's failings to which an incomplete education and the lack of a definite profession had materially contributed. Thus in Conrad's mind the idea of professional duty formed an antithesis to his father's concept of patriotic duty. Bobrowski emphasized the importance of education and profession in the first letter he wrote him after his father's death.

Without a thorough education you will be worth nothing in this world, you will never be self-sufficient, and a thorough education is gained only by thoroughly mastering the beginnings of every subject which is necessary for every cultivated man – which we hope you wish to become and we hope to see you become; therefore, my dear boy, apply yourself to mastering thoroughly their first principles. ... Therefore, not that which is easy and attractive must be the object of your studies but that which is useful, although sometimes difficult, for a man who knows nothing fundamentally, who has no strength of character and no endurance, who does not know how to work on his own and guide himself, ceases to be a man and becomes a useless puppet. Try therefore, my child, not to be or become such a puppet, but to be useful, hard-working, capable and therefore a worthy human being – and thereby reward us for the cares and worries devoted to your upbringing.[33]

With his idea of profession, Bobrowski also criticized the Korzeniowskis' attempts at business and politics. After Conrad left Poland, Bobrowski constantly urged him to settle in a single profession. He discouraged Conrad's desire to leave the sea and become the secretary of a Canadian railroad magnate. His reasons are significant, and his attitudes form the base of some of Conrad's ideas about profession. Bobrowski does not mention the possibility of financial failure as a reason for his dissuasion, but emphasizes rather his disapproval of changing from one profession to another, which makes "people become 'déclassé', who never having warmed a place for themselves nor having built anything

33   Letter (Sept. 8/20, 1869), *ibid.*, p. 153.

for themselves".[34] In addition to these dangers coming from constant change of occupations are dangers attendant on the absence of a profession and its ethics as the center of Conrad's working life.

You must see it for yourself – does it agree with personal dignity and reason to tie oneself to the fate of another man – however great he might seem – and in this particular case to some American business-man or politician? It is much more dignified and sensible to devote your life and tie your future to a certain profession, putting into it your work and determination. You chose for yourself the profession of seaman, – you can expand on it further by trading – well and good – pursue this as far as you can and you will get somewhere. By changing from one career fortuitously to another you may encounter on your way nothing but deception and pain! [35]

An important part of Bobrowski's definition of profession and his nephew's development of that concept is just this distrust of businessmen and politicians and these reservations about basing a career on serving one man. Almost borrowing his uncle's words for *The Duel*, Conrad has his rational hero, an officer under Napoleon, reflect "upon the uncertainty of all personal hopes, when bound up entirely with the prestigious fortune of one incomparably great it is true, yet still remaining but a man in his greatness".[36]

Bobrowski had specifically objected to trusting businessmen and politicians. His refusal to grant professional status to the businessman appears strange on the surface because he himself might be regarded as a businessman. But his career of estate management and ownership composed a traditional occupation complete with rights and duties. As a member of the Polish country gentry, he disparaged the less stable career of the industrial entrepreneur, who must seize the main chance, or of the politician, who depends upon the fickle electorate and questionable intrigue. Bobrowski's distrust of business and politics involved more than a desire for security. Unlike professions, these occupations – as Conrad, following his uncle's advice, came to see them – lack inherent codes

[34]  Letter (May 18/30, 1880), *ibid.*, p. 63.
[35]  *Ibid.*
[36]  *A Set of Six*, p. 216.

of values and standards of behavior by which a man can conduct his life. A code of ethics or sense of responsibility has to be imposed externally on business and political activity. Such imposition is likely to be ineffectual or deluding. In "Heart of Darkness" notions of a mission of benevolent civilizing hide ruthless colonial exploitation. More subtly, in *Nostromo*, some of the characters delude themselves into discovering a satisfying philosophy in business expansion. Lacking codes of ethics and essentially responsible relations between people, both business and politics encourage excessive and anarchic individualism, or its corollary, uncritical discipleship. Conrad's rejection of the nineteenth-century cult of individualism and hero-worship had its first statement in the admonitions of his uncle. As a Korzeniowski Conrad felt the fascination of business and politics. As a Bobrowski he perceived their dangers and tragic possibilities.

What positively defined profession, as Conrad and his uncle saw it? Economic security is the least aspect of profession. Neither is the value of a profession a matter of class or even the reward of an elaborate formal education. Viewed significantly, a profession or craft has a long and honorable history with clearly marked traditions which, if they do not actually prescribe behavior for all aspects of life, have a restraining moral effect upon the character. The absence of profession usually proves disastrous in Conrad's view of life. One of the significant things Marlow learns about Kurtz is his lack of definite profession. Profession provides, for Conrad, the most satisfactory substitute, in an age without dogma, for more general codes of behavior that in earlier eras, with or even without supernatural sanction, had created genuine moral strength. Conrad's ideal was that a man's profession, his true work, should also be a vocation, a calling, and some of the old religious meanings cling to the world.

One must not give the impression that Conrad's concept of the true profession, any more than his concept of duty, is purely rational. The true profession is a conscious ordering and directing of an unconscious prompting, a vocation which declares itself in its own time. In *A Personal Record* Conrad compares his tutor's final acceptance of his "mysterious vocation" of the sea with

Pulman's own later vocation to medicine. The account of Adam Pulman's career as a charitable physician in a small Galician town is punctuated with references to Conrad's own successfully advancing career at sea.[37] Both vocations declared themselves, he states, and both took discipline; both, he implies were honorable professions.

Conrad could see that he was following his uncle's principles in his life as a sailor. He moved steadily upward in a clearly marked path of advancement, taking examinations for certificates, filling positions of ever increasing responsibility, receiving testimonials of good service from captains and owners, and, not the least of satisfactions, receiving the approval of his uncle for his professional advancement and performance of duty. The whole conduct of life – facing dangers in oneself, among one's shipmates, and in the elements – seemed prescribed if not insured by the seaman's code of duty and responsibility.

When he left the sea and took up the career of an author, he carried with him the ideas of profession that he had originally learned from his uncle. As a novelist, however, he had some difficulty in seeing in his career the outward marks of profession. We can speak of the *craft* of fiction, of *professional* novelists, of periods of *apprenticeship*, and even of *masterpieces* in discussing literature, but these terms are merely useful metaphors imported from the recognized crafts and professions. Conrad knew that there was an essential difference between his two careers. He knew that the creative artist works alone no matter what help he might have from interested friends, perceptive critics, or a literary tradition, no matter what support he might feel from the accepted standards of his age or even from popular success. He knew that the loneliness of a ship's captain responsible for the welfare of his crew was not comparable to the loneliness of the novelist writing at his desk. He knew that continuous work during the orderly routine of sea duty completed the sailor's job, but that eight hours of strain at his desk might produce nothing at all. He knew that the institutions that make up literary life and that judge its members and work were not nearly so well defined or accurate as the

[37]   *A Personal Record*, pp. 44-45.

British Merchant Service. He knew all this by experience and apparently accepted it as the conditions under which a creative writer works. Yet he retained the need to think of it as a profession.

Because Conrad was aware that writing differed from the other professions and that his uncle would probably not approve of his becoming a writer like his father, he did not become commited to writing until after his uncle's death. For almost five years he struggled with *Almayer's Folly*, inhibited by the possibility of his uncle's disapproval. Conrad unintentionally revealed this fear in his account of the adventures of the manuscript of *Almayer's Folly* in *A Personal Record*. There is a significant difference between what Conrad says of the perils of his manuscript as it accompanied him throughout the world and what he says of it in Poland. He emphasizes its near loss in the waters of the Congo and in a Berlin railroad station. But the danger it undergoes in Poland seems to be exposure to critical eyes. In his Warsaw hotel room, he says, it lay in an open suitcase while he chatted with an old acquaintance.[38] At Bobrowski's estate, Conrad goes out of his way to say, "the manuscript was deposited unostentatiously on the writing-table placed between two windows. It didn't occur to me to put it away in the drawer".[39] By risking its discovery Conrad seems to have satisfied the demands of his conscience that he allow his uncle a chance to pass judgment on this new activity, which, Conrad probably feared, his uncle would see as unhappy proof of his Korzeniowski inheritance. The period of greatest struggle with this first novel falls between his return from Poland in the fall of 1893 to Bobrowski's death in February 1894.[40] But when, as Albert Guerard points out,[41] the news of his uncle's death came to Conrad, he suddenly was able to finish the novel easily.

Although the death of his uncle permitted him to devote his life to writing, he did find it necessary to regard himself in this new occupation as a craftsman, a member of a profession associated in

[38]   *Ibid.*, p. 19.
[39]   *Ibid.*, p. 27.
[40]   Aubry, *The Sea Dreamer*, p. 194.
[41]   Guerard, p. 11.

a deep intimacy with other writers. This need and this belief in profession, originating in Tadeusz Bobrowski's advice, had important consequences in his writing and his personal relations.

Conrad had to see himself in the role of author, but his uncle's opinion of his father discouraged some of the obvious aspects of his role. Bobrowski's reiterated criticism of Apollo Korzeniowski as a mere dilettante impressed Conrad so that he disliked many of the customary urban literary activities of the man of letters. They recalled his father's career. Conrad disliked attending the theater as well as social gatherings of the literary world; he sometimes refused to lend his name and pen to worthy causes; he found helping Ford to edit the *English Review* both tedious and nerve-wracking. He avoided London as much as possible, writing in the country or on the continent. Furthermore, those parts of his output which most belong to the professional literary milieu, the essays, the author's notes on life and letters, often undertaken simply for the money, gave him very little satisfaction and are for the most part the weakest and least characteristic of his writing.

He often expressed dislike of his essays, referring to them as "silly".[42] This dislike for his essays was well-founded. Whenever Conrad addressed the public in his writings as an essayist or man of letters on the subject of his own works, a situation of general literary concern, or the problems of authorship, his prose became embarrassed, artificial, and derivative. His essay attacking the dramatic censor, for example, is clumsy and ludicrous; its metaphors are over-elaborated, and its attempt to make short repetitious sentences devastating is ineffective.[43] On less serious subjects he often adopted the mask of the elegant trifler.[44] But the insincerity in his attempts at clever irony and of his expressions of sophisticated ennui and superiority as well as his pretense of a languid disdain for work only reveal how ineptly Conrad played the uncongenial role of the man of letters. Although uncomforta-

---

[42] *Garnett Letters* (Feb. 2, 1898), p. 130; (July 20, 1905), p. 193; *Joseph Conrad, Life and Letters* (Feb. 3, 1898), I, pp. 227-28.
[43] "The Censor of Plays", *Notes on Life and Letters*, pp. 76-80.
[44] See Author's Note, *The Mirror of the Sea*, p. vii; "The Ascending Effort", *Notes on Life and Letters*, p. 71; Author's Note, *Notes on Life and Letters*, pp. v-viii.

ble at taking part in its more social and public activities, Conrad nevertheless felt that he had some status in the world of literature or the "Republic of Letters", as he called it.[45] Ford Madox Ford recounts, probably with some humorous exaggeration, Conrad's desire to make an official, formal announcement of their decision to collaborate. In the manner of candidates for membership in the French Academy paying an official call on an Academician, they drove to see H. G. Wells, who was selected as the local representative of the Republic of Letters. Ford said he felt "like a brown paper parcel on a seat beside a functionary in a green uniform, decorated with golden palm leaves and a feathered cocked hat".[46]

Far more serious than this incident were Conrad's friendships with fellow writers. Of course he had some practical and unexceptional reasons for developing these friendships. These men provided intellectual stimulation, the opportunity to discuss problems of technique, valuable advice, a chance to learn more of English life and language, as well as that hard core of truly literate readers on which a reputation is based. In addition to greater and lesser intrinsic reasons for acquiring literary friends, Conrad wanted to fill the role of the professional novelist. This role involved visits, criticism of one another's manuscripts, the exchange of new books, and dedications. The simple existence of these literary acquaintanceships was valuable to Conrad, because he felt they marked the life of the professional writer. This role was not a pose designed to impress others or bolster the ego of a man unsure of his talents. Conrad's genuine anguish over his abilities was unconnected with his conception of his role as author. He simply had to prove to himself, that although, Korzeniowski-like, he had changed occupations and left a career in a clearly marked profession or craft, he still followed his uncle's ideal, the value and necessity of which had become a part of him.

In Conrad's correspondence with other authors he expressed his belief in the profession of letters and the natural bond between

---

[45] *Notes on Life and Letters*, p. 80.
[46] Ford, *Joseph Conrad: A Personal Remembrance* (Boston, Little, Brown, 1924), p. 44.

all members. Thanking Arnold Bennett for a gift of *Anna of the Five Towns* and praising the book, Conrad wrote:

It is indeed a thing *done*: good to see and friendly to live with for a space. This is the final impression – the whole feeling freed from that quarrelsomeness of one craftsman appreciating another – if you do me the honour to take me for a fellow craftsman.[47]

The modesty concerning his own achievement expresses not merely politeness but also his need to be accepted as a fellow craftsman by Bennett. The seaman's bond of fellowship and mutual security achieved through work Conrad attempted to perceive in his career as a writer.

He also sought in the writer's life some substitute for the approval he had received as an inherent part of his life as a seaman. He was troubled because the writer's life seemed to lack such an authority. Public popularity could not be trusted. Fisher Unwin's attempt to interest him in cheap fiction showed him decisively that the institutions of publishing could not be trusted to evaluate the writer's work. While acceptance by *Blackwood's Magazine* and admission into the circle of "Maga's" contributors gave him satisfaction, *Blackwood's* rejection of *Romance*,[48] a group of Edward Garnett's critical essays,[49] and his own story "The Brute"[50] disappointed his trust in their judgment. His extensive experience with critics who misunderstood his work showed him that the men professionally engaged in evaluating literature were often inadequate. In *A Personal Record* he developed at length the parallels between sea and literary life, but he indicated firmly that there were very few similarities between "sea criticisms" of work ill done and bad notices of a new book on the one hand, and, on the other, between sea appreciations (certificates of competence from ship captains) and literary appreciations praising his writing.

Everything can be found at sea, according to the spirit of your quest – strife, peace, romance, naturalism of the most pronounced kind, ideals, boredom, disgust, inspiration – and every conceivable oppor-

[47]   Letter (Nov. 6, 1902), *Joseph Conrad, Life and Letters*, I, p. 306.
[48]   *Blackwood Letters*, p. 132.
[49]   *Ibid.*, pp. 134-35.
[50]   *Ibid.*, pp. 188-89.

tunity to make a fool of yourself – exactly as in the pursuit of literature. But the quarter-deck criticism is somewhat different from
literary criticism. This much they have in common, that before the
one and the other the answering back, as a general rule, does not
pay.[51]

But Conrad did find satisfaction in signs of approval – or what
he interpreted as signs of approval from fellow authors. In a letter
to Cunninghame Graham, he draws the most explicit parallels between the satisfactions of literary recognition by a fellow author
and the satisfactions from approval of conduct at sea. Conrad felt
that the parallels between signs of approval in the two careers
were more than a useful metaphor. They represented a deep, psychologically necessary similarity. To Cunninghame Graham, who
had just dedicated a book to him, he wrote:

This moment I receive *Progress*; or rather the moment (last night)
occured favourably to let me read before I sat down to write.
    Nothing in my writing life (for in the sea life what could approach
the pride of one's first testimonial as a "sober and trustworthy officer"!) has given me greater pleasure, a deeper satisfaction of innocent vanity, a more distinct sense of my work being tangible to
others than myself – than the dedication of the book so full of
admirable things, from the wonderful preface to the slightest of the
sketches within the covers.
    ... And with every masterly turn of phrase, masterly in pictur-
esque vision and in matchless wording, my pride grows till it equals
– nay – almost surpasses, – the pride of that long ago moment, in
another existence, when another sort of master of quite a different
craft vouched with his obscure name for my "sobriety and trustworthiness" before his fellows, well able to judge and amongst whom
I believed my life was destined to run to the end.[52]

Conrad rather elaborately interpreted this friendly dedication as
a kind of official approval for himself as a novelist. The fact that
his work was "tangible to others than myself" was important to
Conrad, who often feared its unreality. To reach a fellow author
was proof that he was a member of the brotherhood of writers and
that his work was judged worthy. Since Conrad had six years earlier expressed distrust of Cunninghame Graham's literary judg-

[51]    *A Personal Record*, p. 109.
[52]    Letter (Feb. 2, 1905), *Joseph Conrad, Life and Letters*, II, p. 10.

ment,[53] his appreciation of the dedication arose from psychological necessity rather than from a desire for useful criticism.

When Arnold Bennett praised *'Twixt Land and Sea* in a letter, Conrad responded: "It is indeed a rare happiness for a craftsman to evoke such a response in a creative temperament so richly gifted and of a sincerity so absolutely above suspicion as all your work proclaims you to be."[54] *Craftsman* and *work*, these reveal the nature of Conrad's rare happiness.


## III


Conrad did not limit the significance of profession to the sustaining relations of men who loved the fine art of their craft. The contrast in Conrad's mind between his intensely disturbing childhood experiences with his father, who taught him to be a good Pole, and the long, steady influence of his uncle, who sought to make him a useful and moral man, created for him a type for one of the most significant human relationships. Conrad saw as an ideal and projected into some of his own relationships the figure of the spiritual father who teaches his son the profession which the son has already chosen or accepted for himself and initiates the son into the mature bond of fellow craftsmen. Because, as Conrad saw early, his own father had neither a profession nor a set of rational workable ideals, the role of the spiritual father must be filled by a man with a profession and workable ideals and without the automatic claim of blood father.

The men whom Conrad perceived to be his spiritual fathers did not simply replace the inadequate and even misdirected Apollo Korzeniowski nor merely substitute for Bobrowski. In initiating Conrad into his two professions, they of course supplemented Bobrowski, who had urged Conrad to adopt a profession although he could not pass on his own to him. But they were not merely practical extensions of Bobrowski, like Adam Pulman, Conrad's tutor. Rather, these men whom Conrad viewed as his spiritual

---

[53]  *Garnett Letters* (Sept. 16, 1899), p. 154.
[54]  Letter (Nov. 25, 1912), *Joseph Conrad, Life and Letters*, II, p. 142.

fathers represented a justification of himself to his uncle, who had disapproved of Conrad's going to sea and who very likely would have had grave doubts about his nephew's becoming an author.

Of course, a man taking up two unusual and demanding occupations far from home might well develop close relations with more experienced practitioners. If we possessed merely the external details of Conrad's years at sea and a brief summary of Edward Garnett's aid to Conrad in his first years as a writer in Britain, then discussing Conrad's elders at sea as well as Garnett as his spiritual fathers would be interpreting far too elaborately the familiar pattern of the old hand showing the apprentice the ropes. But in addition to the general facts about the part played by these men in Conrad's career, we have more particular details about the quality of the relationships and – of most importance – we have Conrad's own account of the relationships in language unmistakeably indicating his attitude. In both cases the metaphor of father and son, rather, that is, of *spiritual* father and son, governs Conrad's view of the relationships.

Conrad expressed his life at sea in terms such as "filial piety to the sea and ships", "professional ancestors", "initiation", "brotherhood"; he even used "nursery" and "cradle" as epithets for the Mediterranean and its ships on which he first served. Before he met Dominic Cervoni, who captained their smuggling vessel the *Tremolino*, he had been allowed by the Marseilles Pilots Association to accompany them in their boats which waited at the harbor mouth to provide incoming ships with pilots. Conrad's description in *A Personal Record* of this band of professional men and their activities shows them to be his first experience of the professional brotherhood of the sea that could provide acceptable routine, sanction, and security. These men, with their monk-like hooded cloaks [55] and their pre-dawn stop at a harbor islet to "break a crust and take a pull at the wine bottle",[56] a suggestive sacrament of good fellowship, watched over his "sea-infancy".[57]

---

[55]  *A Personal Record*, p. 123.
[56]  *Ibid.*, p. 134.
[57]  *Ibid.*, p. 124.

But the true initiation into the craft of sea life came two years (and several voyages) later through the mediation of Dominic Cervoni. Jean-Aubry describes the Corsican, scornful of upper class beliefs and restrictive institutions, yet faithful to his friends and commitments.

Dominic Cervoni was Conrad's real initiator into the art of the sea. His long experience, the sureness of his eye, the controlled strength of his character, awoke in this young man not only a strong liking but an admiration and affection which were never to be effaced from his heart. Cervoni for his part took an interest in this young foreigner, so enthusiastic and eager to learn. Cervoni's knowledge was not limited to the sea; he passed on to his avid disciple his views about the world of men and things – views which were both humane and yet completely free of illusions. Dominic made himself the Mentor of this seagoing Telemachus: an unusual Mentor in his contempt for law, his warm scepticism, and his cold-blooded taste for dangerous adventures so compatible with the hot-blooded one in the heart of his impatient disciple. In Dominic Cervoni Conrad found a man older than himself capable of completely understanding youthful follies, who would try to make them at least appear reasonable. What more could this young Pole want or ask just then?[58]

In *The Mirror of the Sea* Conrad himself depicts Dominic filling the role of spiritual father. Conrad symbolizes Dominic's membership in the craft by a description:

On board the *Tremolino,* wrapped up in a black *Caban,* the picturesque cloak of Mediterranean seamen, with those massive moustaches and his remorseless eyes set off by the shadow of the deep hood, he looked piratical and monkish and darkly initiated into the most awful mysteries of the sea.[59]

His cloak especially seems symbolic of his membership in a monastic-like order into which he was initiating Conrad. Conrad returned to this detail in his Author's Note to *Nostromo* where he speaks of Dominic's "monkish hood".[60]

Dominic was not an isolated influence on the young seaman. Other men repeated and reinforced Dominic's lessons. One of these spiritual fathers was the captain of Conrad's ship discussed

[58] Aubry, *The Sea Dreamer,* pp. 64-65.
[59] *The Mirror of the Sea,* p. 164.
[60] *Nostromo,* Author's Note, p. xxii.

in the section of *The Mirror of the Sea* called "Initiation". The youthful Conrad, setting out eagerly to rescue the crew of a sinking derelict, felt that his captain's warning against taking chances with his own boat crew was mere "cold blooded caution" worthy only of scorn.[61] But when Conrad saws the derelict's crew exhausted by the cruel strength of the sea, his "romantic love to what men's imagination had proclaimed the most august aspect of Nature" [62] perished, and he realized that his captain's skepticism and caution were more realistic and mature attitudes.

In a letter to his publisher, William Blackwood, Conrad paid tribute to the many seamen who had served as his spiritual fathers and who had instilled in him the simple, strong values of the sea.

A wrestle with wind and weather has a moral value like the primitive acts of faith on which may be built a doctrine of salvation and a rule of life. At any rate men engaged in such contests have been my spiritual fathers too long for me to change my convictions – if I have pulled off my sea-boots, hung the sou'wester on a peg and made a tasteful trophy of my pet marline spikes.[63]

In his literary life Conrad had only one spiritual father, Edward Garnett. Although Garnett was eleven years Conrad's junior, his greater experience in the literary world and the obvious absence of the marks of profession in a writer's life intensified Conrad's need to feel that Garnett was his spiritual father. Conrad referred frequently to him as such and depended upon him for advice and support. Unfortunately, Conrad's attitude made it very difficult for him to become independent when he no longer needed a literary mentor.

Like Dominic Cervoni, Garnett did not meet and influence Conrad until he already had some experience in his new craft. A publisher's reader, Garnett advised accepting Conrad's first novel. As soon as he met Conrad, Garnett convinced him to continue writing. The death of Bobrowski and the acceptance of *Almayer's Folly* had not led Conrad to commit himself definitely to writing.

---

[61] *The Mirror of the Sea*, p. 139.
[62] *Ibid.*, p. 141.
[63] Letter to William Blackwood (Aug. 26, 1901), *Blackwood Letters*, p. 133.

In the Author's Note to *An Outcast of the Islands*, Conrad recalled his mental condition when he had completed *Almayer's Folly*.

Neither in my mind nor in my heart had I then given up the sea. In truth I was clinging to it desperately, all the more desperately because, against my will, I could not help feeling that there was something changed in my relation to it. *"Almayer's Folly"*, had been finished and done with. The mood itself was gone. But it had left the memory of an experience that, both in thought and emotion was unconnected with the sea, and I supposed that part of my moral being which is rooted in consistency was badly shaken. I was a victim of contrary stresses which produced a state of immobility. I gave myself up to indolence. Since it was impossible for me to face both ways I had elected to face nothing. The discovery of new values in life is a very chaotic experience; there is a tremendous amount of jostling and confusion and a momentary feeling of darkness. I let my spirit float supine over that chaos.[64]

Garnett helped him out of this impasse. Garnett's encouragement to write merely "another" appealed to Conrad because it seemed less binding on his ultimate professional plans than a decision to "go on writing".[65] Garnett made this congenial suggestion at their first meeting, and thus began one of the most significant friendships of Conrad's life. Conrad insisted in letter after letter, and undoubtedly also in conversation, that Garnett was his literary father from whom he learned his craft, who gave him advice on his relationships with other writers, and who judged his work as worthy and unworthy.

The relationship between the two men was very close (especially from 1894 to 1898 when Conrad submitted his manuscripts to Garnett for approval and revision). Conrad became absolutely dependent upon Garnett artistically. A letter of Conrad's concerning Garnett's opinion of "Karain" illustrates how the relationship functioned for Conrad as he viewed it in one of his less anxious moments:

Thanks for all you say about the story. If it is tolerable it is only because you have recalled me to a tolerable mood. I will not now try to explain what chaotic impulses guided me in writing – but as

---

[64]  *An Outcast of the Islands*, Author's Note, p. vii.
[65]  *Ibid.*, p. vii.

I wrote I tried to remember what you said. My dear fellow you keep me straight in my work and when it is done you still direct its destinies! And it seems to me that if you ceased to do either life itself would cease. For me you are the reality outside, the expressed thought, the living voice! And without you I would think myself alone in an empty universe.[66]

Circumstances help account for this sensation. Aside from the inexperienced Galsworthy and Edward Noble, to whom Conrad gave critical advice, Conrad had almost no literary friends during his first few years as an author except Garnett. The intensity of the sensation, however, arises from facts other than the mere conditions of his early writing life. Plagued all of his life by the sense of his own unreality and of the unreality and unintelligibility of his stories, he came to regard Garnett in these early years as the only reality, the force which persuaded Conrad that he existed. By "reality" Conrad meant the individual's sense of his continuing conscious existence which has meaning and value for other people. Possibly, Conrad's sense of himself as an isolated man making his sole contact and communication with a father-figure whose interest proves his existence and worth grew out of his childhood years of isolation in Russia with his own father, or the years at sea where, despite the meaningful bond of the sea, his correspondence with his uncle was his only point of contact with his Polish reality and the chief source of love and value.

In his letters to Garnett he recurred frequently to the father-son metaphor as the most meaningful definition of their relationship. Explaining the unfortunate results in "An Outpost of Progress" of overly conscious planning, he wrote,

... when I consciously try to write or construct then my ignorance has full play and the quality of my miserable benighted intelligence is disclosed to the scandalized glance of my literary father. This is as it should be.[67]

When Garnett sent Conrad three chapters of a book on London, he was writing, Conrad was grateful, but aware that Garnett was trying to reverse their roles. Conrad asserted that although he had wanted to see the manuscript,

---

[66] *Garnett Letters* (April 20, 1897), p. 97.
[67] *Ibid.* (Aug. 14, 1896), p. 66.

I did not care to ask. I didn't know whether you cared to let anybody read your work in fragments, and besides, it is a monstrous thing for the children to call their fathers to account – to literary account which is more terrible than a trial for a crime.[68]

Conrad did not criticize the manuscript in anything other than a warmly appreciative way, although years later when Conrad no longer depended upon Garnett for approval and advice, he ana- lyzed at length the weaknesses of Garnett's plays. Such a gesture as Garnett's asking Conrad's advice made the inevitable break a less difficult passage to independent maturity. It was Conrad, however, rather than Garnett who brought about the change.

Probably the frustrating struggle to write *The Rescue*, which – despite interruptions to write much other fiction – Conrad felt compelled to complete, as well as Garnett's disturbingly adverse criticism of "The Return" made Conrad wish to become indepen- dent. He saw that Garnett's aid was beginning to damage his writ- ing. With Garnett's help he had recently completed two excellent pieces, *The Nigger of the "Narcissus"* and "Karain". But the subsequent work done for Garnett's approval, chapters for *The Rescue* and "The Return", had been both difficult to compose and poor in quality. Furthermore, the work done independently, "Youth", "Heart of Darkness", and *Lord Jim*, often with Ford's non-paternal advice, was of high merit. Consciously or uncon- sciously Conrad must have felt that he had to free himself from Garnett's blighting hand.[69] The spiritual father was in danger of becoming the real father, with a claim on his son irrespective of its good or ill effects. The task of dissociation from his advisor was made difficult, of course, simply because Conrad had intensi- fied their relationship by viewing it as paternal and filial. It had developed under these terms and would have to be altered under the same terms.

Conrad finally expressed his independence from Garnett by announcing his decision to move where he could collaborate with

---

68   *Ibid.* (Jan. 19, 1897), pp. 83-84.
69   Richard Herndon in his dissertation, *The Collaboration of Joseph Conrad with Ford Madox Ford* (Stanford, 1957), has suggested that in part Conrad began working with Ford in order to free himself from Garnett.

Ford. In November 1898, he announced completion of the move to Pent Farm (which Garnett disliked): "I reckon you disapprove. 'I rebel! I said I would rebel' (d'you know the quotation)." [70] Garnett recognized it as a line from Turgeniev's *Fathers and Sons*.

Although Conrad stopped sending Garnett his manuscripts in late 1898, he was still appreciative of Garnett's approval when in 1899 he sent him parts (typescript and magazine proofs) of the already accepted *Lord Jim*. The fact that he allowed the novel to begin appearing serially before he had completed it shows his new confidence; yet his independence from Garnett disturbed him. In his letters of 1899 and 1900 he excused himself with a variety of reasons for not sending Garnett his manuscripts. Characteristically, he apologized for the change in their relationship in terms of the prodigal son.

I feel to you like a son who has gone wrong and what with shame and recklessness remains silent – and yet nourishes the hope of rehabilitation and keeps his eyes fixed steadily on some distant day of pardon and embraces.

It will come, it will come and whether the prodigal comes to you or you come to the prodigal some poor innocent calf is sure to suffer. I've written. Are you any the wiser? Are you disposed to forgive?[71]

A year later the break came. In a letter, Garnett praised the completed *Lord Jim* but undiplomatically claimed that the book fell awkwardly into two parts. Conrad began his answer by apparently accepting the accuracy of this criticism, but in the rest of the letter Conrad covered *Lord Jim*, his literary aspirations, and all his other works with blame and humiliation. This abasement is amazing because *Lord Jim* had been favorably reviewed and Henry James, whose literary status and judgment were beyond question, had just written Conrad to praise the book.[72] In fact Conrad sent James's letter along to Garnett, perhaps as proof that Garnett was wrong. Garnett was clearly disturbed by Conrad's extreme disparagement of his work and upon receiving Conrad's letter wrote to Galsworthy: "I have attacked Conrad critically, *re* the last two-fifths

---

[70]   *Garnett Letters* (Nov. 7, 1898), p. 148.
[71]   *Ibid.* (Sept. 16, 1900), pp. 154-55.
[72]   *Ibid.* (Nov. 12, 1900), pp. 171-73.

and the end of *Lord Jim*. He more than accepts what I have said: He goes too far in acceptance." [73] Perhaps Conrad's excessive humility in accepting Garnett's criticism here came partly from a sense of guilt over having disobeyed or deserted his spiritual father. But mainly, he was probably angry at Garnett for not recognizing that *Lord Jim* was the finest thing he had written. The correspondence between the two stopped completely for seven months, resuming at last in the summer of 1901 with a group of letters in which Conrad politely advised Garnett about writing a critical article and then tried to place it for him in *Blackwood's*.[74] Then after almost a year of silence Conrad refused what must have been Garnett's request that they renew their old relationship: "I am simply afraid to show you my work; and as to writing about it, this I can't do." [75] Conrad followed this statement with his usual deprecating remarks about his ability, but it seems clear that by this time the relationship of spiritual father and son was finished, that Conrad neither wanted nor needed Garnett's advice, and that although he valued his friendship, he felt neither dependent upon Garnett nor guilty that he had offended or disappointed him by not submitting his work.

Circumstances had made terminating the actual relationships with the previous spiritual fathers a good deal easier. Tadeusz Bobrowski had been in Poland and had insisted on Conrad's free choice; Dominic Cervoni had disappeared after the *Tremolino* sank; and the various captains and officers had been his superiors for what was usually only a ninety day passage. Yet the relationship with Garnett did at last develop into a settled friendship, and long after Conrad had become independent, he referred to the old relation affectionately as an important stage in his development. Sending a copy of *The Duel* to Garnett's sixteen year old son David in 1908, he insisted charmingly on their kinship as brothers.

But still I send you the little volume as I want you to have something of mine, from myself, in memory of the days when we both were considerably younger – and less wise.

[73] Letter (Nov. 15, 1900), *Letters from John Galsworthy*, ed. Edward Garnett (London, Scribners, 1934), p. 24.
[74] *Garnett Letters*, pp. 174-79.
[75] *Ibid.* (June 10, 1902), p. 180.

... You were a child then, and I but an infant – a literary infant – whose first steps were – like your own – watched over by your mother and father, though I don't mean to say with the same anxious interest. That's a bond between us surely.[76]

Conrad often appealed to Garnett in later years on the basis of their earlier friendship:

Don't put off your promised visit too long. Yes, it is a far cry from 1894 when this literary child was born to you. For you know you can't get out of it however you may regret it. You are responsible for my existence.[77]

Why don't you come and pat me on the head or hit me or assert your paternity in some way. You'll find me most dutiful.[78]

Not only did Conrad act as a spiritual son in both his sea and literary careers, but he also performed the functions of spiritual father for young seamen and writers. At sea he took special care in training young men, new to the merchant service. Galsworthy, who was on the return voyage of the *Torrens* from Australia, noticed his gentleness with the apprentices, especially with a youth fearful of going aloft.[79] According to Jean-Aubry, Conrad received all his life grateful letters from men who had had their sea training under him. When Conrad's publisher sent on to him some letters of inquiry from one of his former apprentices on the *Highland Forest*, Conrad commented: "He was one of the score or so of boys that passed through my hands when I was chief officer of various ships. It's pleasant to see that the pains I took to make good seamen of them are not forgotten by those grizzled men." [80] In 1923 another of his former pupils wrote him:

From the reading of the chapter "Poland Revisited" I gather that you have a son: if this is so, may I say something in this letter to him. I dislike flattery in any form, but I would like him to realize what a marvellous personality you have. I have loved you more than any

[76]   *Ibid.* (Dec. 22, 1908), p. 217.
[77]   *Ibid.* (Jan. 12, 1911), p. 222.
[78]   *Ibid.* (Nov. 5, 1912), p. 243.
[79]   John Galsworthy, "Reminiscences of Conrad", *Castles in Spain* (New York, Scribners, 1927), p. 102.
[80]   Letter to Hugh R. Dent (April 3, 1917), *Joseph Conrad, Life and Letters*, I, pp. 187-88.

man I ever knew except my own father and I revere the memory that
was made upon the most irresponsible of human beings, the schoolboy, because I had only just left school when I had the honour of
being your boy. I remember so distinctly the trouble you took in the
silent watches of a tropical night to teach me the different ropes.
This was thirty years or more ago.[81]

In his literary life too, Conrad acted many times as spiritual father. He read and criticized the writings of Ford Madox Ford,
Edward Garnett, Edward Noble, Hugh Clifford, John Galsworthy,
and Norman Douglas, and took an interest in introducing the
young Polish author Bruno Winawer to the English public by
translating one of his plays.[82] Jean-Aubry, who consulted Conrad
at length about his translations of several of Conrad's books into
French, insisted on Conrad's paternal attitude toward him.[83]
Richard Curle, whose devoted friendship Conrad prized during
his last years, recalled that Conrad had offered him help at a bad
time in his life, saying: "I am an old man and you might be my
son. Why not see if I can do anything?" [84] And in a letter accom-
panying a gift for Curle, Conrad wrote: "When I reflect that if I
had made an early marriage I could have been (easily) a father of
a man your age, this way seems permissible between you and
me." [85] "One could, indeed", Curle commented, "have talked to
him as to a Father Confessor".[86] John Galsworthy too paid tribute
to Conrad for his help: "He was indefatiguably good to me while
my own puppy's eyes were opening to literature, and I was still in
the early stages of that struggle with his craft which a writer worth
his salt never quite abandons." [87]

As a literary father to Galsworthy, Conrad seems to have taken
special care that their relationship did not undergo the strains that
had come about in his own relationship with Garnett. Writing to

[81]   *Ibid.*, I, p. 156.
[82]   *Ibid.*, II, pp. 260-63.
[83]   Jean-Aubry, "Introduction", *Lettres Françaises* (Paris, Gallimard, 1929),
p. 10.
[84]   Richard Curle, *The Last Twelve Years of Joseph Conrad* (London,
Sampson, Low, Marston and Co., 1928), p. 9.
[85]   *Ibid.*, p. 10.
[86]   *Ibid.*, p. 15.
[87]   Galsworthy, "Reminiscences of Conrad", p. 112.

Galsworthy just a year after Garnett's unfortunate criticism of *Lord Jim*, Conrad concluded a letter, filled with advice and criticism, in a manner reminiscent of his uncle:

That the man who has written once the *Four Winds* has written now the M[an] of D[evon] volume is a source of infinite gratification to me. It vindicates my insight, my opinion, my judgment, and it satisfied my affection for you, – in whom I believed and am believing. Because this *is* the point: I *am* believing. You've gone now beyond the point where I could be of any use to you, otherwise than just by my belief. It is if anything firmer than ever before, whether my remarks above find their way to your conviction or not. You may disagree with what I said here but in my main convictions we are at one.[88]

This letter, however, did not mark the end of Conrad's advising and encouraging Galsworthy. Galsworthy recalled that it continued in force to 1905, and even after that the two remained close. Galsworthy read the manuscript of *The Secret Agent* in 1906,[89] and Conrad criticized at great length the manuscript of *Fraternity* in 1908.[90]

Of all the relationships in his life Conrad found these associations between spiritual father and son, between master and apprentice, the most profound and satisfying. Other relationships either broke under stress or remained incomplete, often superficial. His relationship to his father, of course, was intensely disturbing. Toward fellow sea captains he was often haughty and aloof.[91] Before his marriage he suffered a series of rejections by women which developed his misogyny. His marriage was successful largely because his wife patiently assumed the roles of mother and nurse; she was unable to be an intellectual companion.[92] He was an extremely erratic father to his two sons.[93] Even with his

[88]  Letter (Nov. 11, 1901), *Joseph Conrad, Life and Letters*, I, p. 302.
[89]  *Joseph Conrad: Life and Letters*, II, p. 37.
[90]  *Ibid.*, pp. 76-82, 85-86.
[91]  Aubry, *The Sea Dreamer*, p. 140.
[92]  These conclusions emerge from reading Mrs. Conrad's *Joseph Conrad and His Circle*.
[93]  Conrad was not altogether an adequate father to his own sons. Some of the tensions and misunderstandings as well as the reasons for them between the worried, restless, temperamental author and his sons are revealed in these sources: Conrad's letters to Gide, *Letters Françaises*, pp.

collaborator Ford Madox Ford, he maintained fairly formal relations, avoiding real intimacy.[94] He of course enjoyed knowing fellow professionals like Bennett, Wells, and Walpole, but except for his intimacy and frankness with Cunninghame Graham and Stephen Crane, his truly profound relationships with other writers, with Garnett, Galsworthy, Jean-Aubry, and Curle, took the form of the association between spiritual father and son. These relationships as well as those with his uncle, Dominic Cervoni, and other seamen, both younger and older than Conrad, proved to be his most enduring, profound, and meaningful. It should not be surprising then, when we turn to his fiction, to discover that he portrayed this relationship with a good deal of emotion and significance.

## IV

In three novels, *The Shadow Line*, *Lord Jim*, and *Nostromo*, Conrad treats the relationship between a young seaman and an older man serving as his spiritual father. In the first two of these Conrad also briefly treats by way of contrast the young protagonist's real father (or a man taking the place of his real father) whose influence or heritage the hero must overcome. The value of the spiritual father's influence varies in these three novels. In *The Shadow Line* Conrad presents his most optimistic view of the effect of the relationship on the young man. In *Lord Jim* he shows that the spiritual father is not always able to help the young man. Finally in *Nostromo* he shows that a spiritual father can be a destructive influence. What makes for these differences is the presence or absence of profession in the lives of the characters. In *The Shadow Line* both spiritual father and son are seamen, and

---

119, 186; Richard Curle, *The Last Twelve Years of Joseph Conrad*, pp. 147-48; Jessie Conrad, *Joseph Conrad and his Circle*, pp. 255-61; and Borys Conrad, "A Famous Father and His Son", *New York Times Book Review*, LXII (Dec. 1, 1957), pp. 7, 74.
[94] In *Joseph Conrad: A Personal Remembrance*, Ford suggested this lack of intimacy several times; see pp. 24-25, 70, 74, 127-28, 129.

the father leads the son to professional maturity. In *Lord Jim* the spiritual father is a seaman, but the son can no longer follow the sea because of a serious dereliction of duty. In *Nostromo* both father and son have left the sea, and the ideals of romantic liberalism have replaced the seaman's code of professional duty.

I shall discuss *The Shadow Line* first because it is closely related to those experiences of Conrad which I have just analyzed, and because it somewhat simplifies and idealizes Conrad's view of the spiritual father. Although this simplification reduces its value as fiction, relating it slightly to the pompous and sentimental essays about the sea which Conrad wrote in his later years, its schematic quality makes the book informative and clarifies the complexities of the much greater novels, *Lord Jim* and *Nostromo*. The process of literary decline (to be discussed at length in the next two chapters) had not gone so far as to falsify Conrad's account of sea-life.

The history of its composition suggests why *The Shadow Line* surpasses most of the prose of the later years. When Conrad wrote it, he was deeply concerned with the relation of the autobiographical material to two important contemporary aspects of his own life. One was filial, the other paternal. The 1914 visit to Poland, Albert Guerard has speculated,[95] reminded Conrad how severely Tadeusz Bobrowski had criticized first his desire to go to sea and later his erratic conduct. The novel answers both these criticisms by telling Conrad's own success story. Conrad himself described the other concern in explaining the composition of *The Shadow Line*. In The Author's Note, Conrad emphasizes the anxieties brought on by the First World War. With considerable modesty he asserts that he had experienced a strong "feeling of identity" between the exceptionally clear memories of his first command and the contemporary trials of an entire generation.[96] He dedicated the book "to Borys and all others who like himself have crossed in early youth the shadow-line of their generation". Thus when he was writing the novel, he was concerned with the justification of his own life to an older generation – his uncle and the men he

---

[95] Guerard, p. 20.
[96] Author's Note, *The Shadow Line*, pp. vi-vii.

regarded as his professional forefathers – and with the coming maturity of his own son and his generation.

In *The Shadow Line* Conrad presents the positive aspects of the relationship between a young man and his spiritual father. Although the young captain in the novel seems largely responsible for his own success in meeting all his difficulties (of a deadly calm, a fever-ridden crew, useless mates, as well as his own temptation to collapse superstitiously in defeat), it is an older seaman, Captain Giles, who helps him obtain the command and later sets his approval on the young captain's painfully learned wisdom of maturity. In Conrad's world Captain Giles stands for all the virtues of profession. His character is based on Captain Patterson, probably the last of the men whom Conrad saw as his initiators into the craft.[97] But Conrad portrays him so that he also suggests other men who had served as his spiritual fathers. The Ulyssean traits of Captain Giles (his skill in navigation, his reputation for wonderful adventures, and a mysterious tragedy in his life) link him, according to Paul Wiley, to Dominic Cervoni, Conrad's first professional father whom in *The Mirror of the Sea* he had described in Ulyssean terms.[98] More significantly he recalls Tadeusz Bobrowski, that man "of rigorous logic if of infinite charity". During his first interview with the narrator, Giles disapproves of the young man's irresponsibility "in a benevolent heavy-uncle manner".[99] In their final interview, he praises the young man's newly developed maturity, radiating "benevolence ... with a 'kind uncle' smile".[100] Thus for Conrad, Captain Giles seems to represent his uncle: a source of continuing affectionate interest and moral authority, to which has been added professional wisdom.

Unlike Marlow in *Lord Jim*, Giles unerringly discriminates between seamen who *can* be trusted to mature and those who will become lazy and unreliable. It is easy, Giles points out, for a white seaman to become demoralized in the East with native owners and

---

[97]  *Joseph Conrad, Life and Letters*, I, p. 102.
[98]  Paul Wiley, *Conrad's Measure of Man* (Madison, University of Wisconsin Press, 1954), p. 201.
[99]  *The Shadow Line*, p. 14.
[100]  *Ibid.*, p. 131.

native crews. Of the drugged, insensible officer of a rajah's yacht, he says: "I remember him first coming ashore here some years ago ... He was a nice boy. Oh! these nice boys ... Some of them do go soft mighty quick out here."[101] The seaman who has gone soft in the undemanding service in the East has become what could have been predicted for Jim.[102] Giles is quick to perceive that the narrator is at a crucial point in his life, that the glamour of seamanship has worn off, and that he needs to develop the perfect love of the craft to replace his immature desire for constantly varying stimulation.

In a sense Giles replaces Captain Kent, the young man's former commander, in the carefully hierarchical profession of the sea. Captain Kent had also perceived that something was wrong with his first mate.

> As I was going out of the chart-room he added suddenly in a peculiar wistful tone, that he hoped I would find what I was so anxious to go and look for. A soft cryptic utterance which seemed to reach deeper than any diamond-hard tool could have done. I do believe he understood my case.[103]

Just as Marlow had brought Jim's case to Stein, so Captain Kent discusses the young seaman's case with Giles, who indeed had already taken an interest in him. Kent tells Giles that he is sorry to lose an excellent officer but also points out the young man's irrationality.[104] Conrad's four brief allusions to this consultation indicate its importance and that from it stemmed Giles's active interest.

The shrewdness of his two spiritual fathers annoys the young man because he perceives that they are right. Captain Kent sees his difficulties as psychological. Captain Giles sees them as moral also and knows that his present state of mind is dangerous. The young man resents Giles's paternal intrusion into his affairs, preferring to drift with circumstance and his own irresponsible impulses. But ultimately he has to recognize Giles's wisdom and

---

[101]   *Ibid.*, p. 14.
[102]   *Lord Jim*, p. 13.
[103]   *The Shadow Line*, pp. 5-6.
[104]   *Ibid.*, p. 15.

authority. In their first conversation Giles demands to know why he has left his position so inconsequentially. Realizing that he cannot answer the question and that Giles is suggesting a similarity between him and the white seaman who had gone soft, he becomes angry and disturbed: "I said to myself that I ought to shut up that moralist; and to him aloud I said with challenging politeness: "Why...? Do you disapprove." [105] Giles retreats from this open hostility saying that he does disapprove "in a general way", but he does not end his interest in the young man. When the young seaman rationalizes that he had given up his job because he wanted to return home, Giles comments skeptically, "I have heard that sort of thing so often before." [106]

The young man is very sensitive and attempts to protect himself against sober examination of his irrationality by aggression and by defense mechanisms. In a parody of rationality he decides that Captain Giles is insane and that he must protect his own sober self-possession, one of the prime seamanlike virtues for Conrad, by breaking off a conversation in which "the sense of the absurdity was beginning to exercise its well-known fascination".[107] He projects his own defensive feelings into what he observes in a casual acquaintance. With great exaggeration, he describes the aimiable official at the Harbor Office, who immediately becomes sober when he hears that the young man has signed off his ship for good in order to go home.

He did not look at me again till he handed me my papers with a sorrowful expression, as if they had been my passports for Hades....

I didn't know him outside the official building, but he leaned forward over the desk to shake hands with me, compassionately, as one would do with some poor devil going out to be hanged; and I am afraid I performed my part ungraciously, in the hardened manner of an impenitent criminal.[108]

The narrator reveals here not so much the attitudes of the official as his own guilty defiance at criticism. At one point he admits that

[105] *Ibid.*, p. 14.
[106] *Ibid.*, p. 15.
[107] *Ibid.*, p. 24.
[108] *Ibid.*, pp. 7-8.

his anger at anyone's questioning his leaving the ship is "childish irritation".[109] At the same time, however, he assumes all the privileges and attitudes of a seaman – staying at the Officers' Seamen's Home and feeling a sense of superiority to all shore people and their petty affairs.

Even after Giles has obtained a command for him, he feels he must justify himself. When Giles tells him that Kent had thought him a little mad for leaving the ship, the young man replies, "Oh, leaving his ship". Then, as though he were doing the older man a favor, he defends his action by saying, "What I really wanted was to get a fresh grip. I felt it was time. Is that so mad?"[110] Giles makes no reply to this *post facto* explanation. At this point the young captain is grateful to Giles for his command, but he is not yet prepared to acknowledge the older man's worth until he has gone through the sobering tests of getting his ship through the becalmed gulf.

Although *The Shadow Line* lacks the symbolic and psychological richness of "Heart of Darkness", the young captain's terrible journey out of the gulf is comparable to Marlow's trip up the African river. It illustrates the second half of the Vergilian maxim that the descent into Avernus is easy but the return is difficult. Just as the link between Marlow and Kurtz is once asserted to be paternal, so the young captain's horror at the evil and madness of his recently deceased predecessor arises from a similar sense of kinship. Both Kurtz and the dead captain have betrayed the trust of a position of command. Both Marlow and the young captain begin their journeys by an irrational action and discover at the furthest point of navigation the evil that a man similar to themselves can do. Before he hears of his predecessor, the young captain thinks of his ship: "She was there waiting for me, spellbound, unable to move, to live, to get out into the world (till I came), like an enchanted princess."[111] Marlow looks forward to meeting the famous Kurtz. "The approach to this Kurtz ... was beset by as many dangers as though he had been an enchanted princess sleeping in

[109]   *Ibid.*, p. 18.
[110]   *Ibid.*, p. 42.
[111]   *Ibid.*, p. 40.

a fabulous castle." [112] And Marlow's own predecessor, the dead captain of the Congo steamboat, was killed when he lost all restraint and began to beat a Negro who he imagined was cheating him. Both Marlow and the young captain save themselves by hard work and the strict performance of duty.

Conrad frames the story of the insane destructive predecessor (told to the young captain by the first mate) between two related meditations on command. The young captain enters his cabin for the first time. He sits in the captain's chair and begins to meditate on the succession of men who had sat there and on what their "composite soul, the soul of command" might tell him.

"You, too!" it seemed to say, "you, too, shall taste of that peace and that unrest in a searching intimacy with your own self – obscure as we were and as supreme in the face of all the winds and all the seas, an immensity that receives no impress, preserves no memories, and keeps no reckoning of lives." [113]

Except for the faintest hint of self-indulgent introspection, this seems like sober wisdom, an acceptance of isolation and insignificance. But as the young captain continues to meditate, he turns confidently to the line of succession, forgetting what he has learned about failure both from experience and from Captain Giles.

Deep within the tarnished ormolu frame [of the mirror], in the hot half-light sifted through the awning, I saw my own face propped between my hands. And I stared back at myself with the perfect detachment of distance, rather with curiosity than with any other feeling, except of some sympathy for this latest representative of what for all intents and purposes was a dynasty; continuous not in blood, indeed, but in its experience, in its training, in its conception of duty, and in the blessed simplicity of its traditional point of view on life.

It struck me that this quietly staring man whom I was watching, both as if he were myself and somebody else, was not exactly a lonely figure. He had his place in a line of men whom he did not know, of whose souls in relation to their humble life's works had no secrets for him. [114]

This is a beautiful expression of Conrad's ideal of profession, but

[112] "Heart of Darkness", *Youth*, p. 106.
[113] *The Shadow Line*, p. 53.
[114] *Ibid.*

the young captain in his confidence and exhilaration mistakes it for an achieved reality.

He is unexpectedly interrupted in this self-satisfying meditation by the mate, who reluctantly informs him about the former captain's madness. The story forces the young captain to revise his conceptions of the dynasty of command and the "blessed simplicity of its traditional point of view on life".

I was already the man in command. My sensations could not be like those of any other man on board. In that community I stood, like a king in his country, in a class all by myself. I mean an hereditary king, not a mere elected head of a state.[115] I was brought there to rule by an agency as remote from the people and as inscrutable almost to them as the Grace of God.

And like a member of a dynasty, feeling a semi-mystical bond with the dead, I was profoundly shocked by my immediate predecessor.

That man had been in all essentials but his age just such another man as myself. Yet the end of his life was a complete act of treason, the betrayal of a tradition which seemed to me as imperative as any guide on earth could be. It appeared that even at sea a man could become the victim of evil spirits. I felt on my face the breath of unknown powers that shape our destinies.[116]

Not only in this scene does his predecessor disturb the captain, but during the entire tortured progress through the becalmed gulf, the captain must struggle against his fevered mate's conviction that the malevolent ghost of the dead captain wants to destroy the ship and is hindering their advance. Conrad's account of the ultimate victory over the dead captain weakens this aspect of the story; the mate's recovery and the young captain's mental association test by which he makes sure that his mate is no longer superstitious are a little flat. Nevertheless, the captain's struggle against belief in the evil power of the dead suggest the terrific menace of failure and collapse, reminding us that these also are part of man's heritage.

[115] Conrad's insistent distinction between "an hereditary king" and "a mere elected head of state" is probably a Polish reference. The Polish throne had been elective. Conrad is taking care that the image describing the young captain's position indicates the close bond with his predecessor.
[116] *The Shadow Line*, p. 62.

The dead captain stands, of course, in direct contrast with Captain Giles, who is sanity and duty personified. In a very general way this contrast represents the differences between Apollo Korzeniowski and Tadeusz Bobrowski. The real father passes on to his son madness and destruction from which he can save himself only by carefully following the example and advice of the spiritual father.

When the captain finally gets his ship back to port, he discusses his new-found wisdom with Captain Giles. It consists of two closely related ideas. Giles says, "One must not make too much of anything in life, good or bad." The young man replies that it is difficult to "live at half-speed".[117] In this interchange they are criticizing his earlier mental state which shifted from apathetic disillusionment to naive exhilaration. The second piece of advice develops the idea of controlling this wide and violent swing of emotions. "A man should stand up to his bad luck, to his mistakes, to his conscience, and all that sort of thing." [118] We should not dismiss this as a careless equation of bad luck and guilt. Despite the conversational vagueness of the final phrase, Conrad has arranged his other three terms in order. The necessity of standing up to bad luck is an obvious piece of advice as is the wisdom of facing one's mistakes so as to take responsibility for them and to learn from them. But standing up to one's conscience is a more subtle idea. It means that a man must not allow his guilt over moral errors so to interfere with the performance of his duty as to immobilize him. And it means an acceptance of evil and irrationality in himself without minimizing their importance. Giles concludes by emphasizing his approval of hard work and by insisting that "a man has got to learn everything – and that's what so many of those youngsters don't understand".[119] As a spiritual father Captain Giles has shrewdly perceived the young man's difficulties, rescued him from his chaotic impulses, given him a chance to prove himself, provided him a model of steadfast professional duty, and finally phrased for him the meaning of his experience.

[117]   *Ibid.*, p. 131.
[118]   *Ibid.*, pp. 131-32.
[119]   *Ibid.*, p. 132.

Despite Giles's importance, the story suffers from lack of depth
in its portrayal of him. Except for a few suggestive details he has
no character outside of his role of spiritual father. The mysterious
tragedy in his life is never explained, and nothing is made of the
contrast between his fairly sedentary life in the present and his
former wonderful adventures. (Conrad had emphasized the pathos of a similar contrast in Captain Whalley in "The End of the
Tether".) Giles's motives for helping a capable young man reach
maturity are never made clear. When the young seaman asks
Giles why he has gone to the trouble to get him a command, Giles
does not answer and begins speaking about something else. His
farewell to the young captain on the way to his ship is brief and
unemotional. Both scenes hint at a paternal feeling in Giles, but
the hints are too insubstantial for any discernible effect. The
young captain takes a personal interest in Giles at the end of their
acquaintance, but the passage is so brief as to reveal nothing about
Giles nor about the possibilities of their relationship. Giles comments on the young man's outburst that there will be little rest for
him on this voyage:

"Yes, that's what it amounts to," he said in a musing tone. It was
as if a ponderous curtain had rolled up disclosing an unexpected
Captain Giles. But it was only for a moment, merely the time to let
him add: "Precious little rest in life for anybody. Better not think
of it."
  We ... parted ... just as he began to interest me for the first
time. . . .[120]

Sometimes the simplified idealization of the spiritual father harms
the characterization of Giles. The narrator insists heavily and
repetitiously on the "benevolence" of the older seaman. He describes him as so flawless and self-confident a character as to
make him partially unconvincing. Conrad intends the reader to
see that the narrator's frequent annoyance at Captain Giles's
complacency is mistaken; the total portrayal of Giles, however,
unwittingly suggests dense complacency. Perhaps earlier in his
career, Conrad would have questioned the motives of a benevolent
old meddler. He has given Giles some of his uncle's traits, but

[120]   *Ibid.*, p. 133.

could not give him his uncle's motives and did not attempt to give him Marlow's complex motives.

In *Lord Jim* Conrad portrays a similar relationship, but does it with considerably more psychological and moral complexity. Dramatizing in full the profound relationship between a young man and an older man who tries to serve as his spiritual father, Conrad employed all he had learned about the relationship from his own experiences in both roles. He put aspects of himself in both Jim and Marlow. In one sense the novel is a prolonged development of the fantasy that comes to every adult who finds himself deeply involved with the rearing and educating of those younger than himself and wonders what it would have been like if he had had an older friend like himself.

The relationship between Jim and Marlow differs significantly from Conrad's own experiences as either spiritual father or son and from the relationship portrayed in *The Shadow Line*. It lacks the bond of profession. Yet Conrad judges Jim, Marlow, and their friendship by standards of behaving, feeling, and communicating derived from profession. The fact that they conform outwardly to the ideal of the professional father and son only makes the inward lack more poignant and Conrad's judgment more severe. We can see this most simply in one of Marlow's first reactions to Jim. The disparity between Jim's seamanlike, trustworthy appearance and the reality of his jump disturbs Marlow deeply because it calls into question both the effectiveness of the seaman's code of duty and Marlow's own role in passing on this code to young seamen. Jim's failure to stay at his post aboard the endangered ship threatens Marlow's whole complex of satisfying and justifying memories. He begins to doubt the stability of an important part of his life. In his first long meditation about Jim he recalls the many boys whom he had trained. He thinks of the satisfaction he feels years later whenever he meets one of them who has become an officer. If he were to return home, he says confidently, within two days he would be overtaken by a young chief mate who would recall his first coming aboard. Repeated details make this a ceremony in Marlow's mind. Quickly passing over the possibility of the boy's being accompanied by a mother and older sister, he expands in detail a typical incident in which a boy is brought aboard by his father, who must relinquish his claim on his son so that he may learn a profession and gain maturity. The father in this composite memory is a "decent middle-aged" man who stays aboard too long and has to be hastened ashore from the departing ship. There is nothing embarrassing or awkward in this memory. It follows a traditional form satisfying to the emotions. The father, though hastened, is treated with respect. "All very proper. He has offered his bit of sacrifice to the sea, and now he may go home pretending he thinks nothing of it..." [121] This accepted ritual of transfer from the real father to the profession leads in Marlow's experience to the satisfying meeting years later at the dock-gates with the young officer.

By-and-by, when he (the young sailor) has learned all the little mysteries and the one great secret of the craft, he shall be fit to live or die as the sea may decree; and the man who had taken a hand in this fool game, in which the sea wins every toss, will be pleased to have his back slapped by a heavy young hand, and to hear a cheery sea-puppy voice: "Do you remember me, sir? The little So-and-so." [122]

But the memory of Jim intrudes into Marlow's justifiable pride in himself as a teacher of seamen and a judge of men.

I tell you this is good; it tells you that once in your life at least you had gone the right way to work. I have been thus slapped, and I have winced, for that slap was heavy, and I have glowed all day by the virtue of that heavy thump. Don't I remember the little So-and-so's! I tell you I ought to know the right kinds of looks. I would have trusted the deck to that youngster on the strength of a single glance, and gone to sleep with both eyes – and, by Jove! it wouldn't have been safe. There are depths of horror in that thought.[123]

The depths of horror for Marlow are not simply the fear that he is inadequate as a judge of seamen; no commander, however perceptive and responsible, could see the danger of employing Jim. The entire profession with its safeguards of training and tradition, its "fixed standard of conduct",[124] becomes insecure.

[121]  *Lord Jim*, p. 45.
[122]  *Ibid.*
[123]  *Ibid.*
[124]  *Ibid.*, p. 50.

Because Marlow still feels that his relationship to Jim is analogous to his relationships with successful young seamen, his sense that he cannot help Jim is painful. Not only as an older professional does he feel inadequate, but, as he becomes more involved with Jim, he feels inadequate as a spiritual father. Jim turns to Marlow as to an older and wiser seaman. In one scene he thanks Marlow for listening to him: " 'You are an awful good sort to listen like this', he said. 'It does me good. You don't know what it is to me. You don't' ... words seemed to fail him." [125] This appeal makes Marlow again aware of Jim as a young seaman. But the relationship has grown so since he first met Jim that Marlow now feels a closer identification with him. Characteristically, Marlow eases into this intensely meaningful confession by stages of apparent casualness and off-hand jocularity.

He was a youngster of the sort you like to see about you; of the sort you like to imagine yourself to have been; of the sort whose appearance claims the fellowship of these illusions you had thought gone out, extinct, cold, and which as if rekindled at the approach of another flame, give a flutter deep, deep down somewhere, give a flutter of light ... of heat! [126]

Jim, at last finding the words he was searching for, continues his thanks and appeal.

"You don't know what it is for a fellow in my position to be believed – make a clean breast of it to an elder man. It is so difficult – so awfully unfair – so hard to understand." [127]

This statement makes Jim obscure to Marlow. But here as elsewhere Marlow's assertion of Jim's mysteriousness, of mists obscuring him, represents not so much genuine bewilderment as Marlow's withdrawal from a disturbing identification or from one of Jim's appeals. Marlow's apparent withdrawal reveals how deeply and unexpectedly Jim has touched him. Jim's appeal to him as an "elder man" has reminded Marlow not of their differences but their similarities. He meditates on the bond of the sea which is

---

[125] *Ibid.*, p. 128.
[126] *Ibid.*
[127] *Ibid.*

strengthened by the swift and thorough disillusionment common to the experience of all seamen.

Hadn't we all commenced with the same desire, ended with the same knowledge, carried the memory of the same cherished glamour through the sordid days of imprecation? What wonder that when some heavy prod gets home the bond is found to be close; that besides the fellowship of the craft there is felt the strength of a wider feeling – the feeling that binds a man to a child.[128]

Marlow's statement must be examined closely, for it does not exactly fit Jim's case. Marlow's affection for Jim and his desire to serve as a spiritual father have momentarily obscured Jim's failure. The literal sense of this statement is actually related to an idea found in other Conrad narratives. The kind of disillusionment which Marlow talks about here is simply a seaman's disappointment when he realizes the sea's cruel strength. In *Youth*, for example, a middle-aged Marlow mourns the loss of his youthful resilience and illusions. At the beginning of *The Shadow Line* the young seaman feels the loss of his illusions. But the chain of ill effects that threatened to follow his disillusionment were avoided by a command and the development of a sense of professional duty. Jim's case is different, because his illusions and unwarranted desires have gotten him far deeper into trouble than the shortcomings of young Marlow or the young captain. Although Jim appears to Marlow as though he were at the shadow line or the point of initiation, he is actually retreating from professional maturity. Jim looks like a good young man in the kind of youthful trouble that "greybeards wag at solemnly while they hide a smile",[129] but, as Marlow well knows when Jim's appeal to him as a spiritual father is less compelling, his trouble is far more serious and irremediable. Indeed, Marlow has such an insight earlier in this long conversation. There, when he describes his role as a father confessor to Jim, he makes it clear that his metaphor expresses a desire or and ideal rather than a reality.

Didn't I tell you he confessed himself before me as though I had the power to bind and to loose? He burrowed deep, deep, in the hope of

---

[128]    *Ibid.*, p. 129.
[129]    *Ibid.*

my absolution, which would have been of no good to him. This was one of those cases which no solemn deception can palliate, which no man can help; where his very Maker seems to abandon a sinner to his own devices.[130]

Jim wants to confess his troubles to Marlow, not his sins. He wants to receive simple approval for his excuses, not the absolution that a priest might give the repentant sinner. Jim is abusing the relationship. If the role of the spiritual father is filled for the son's genuine benefit, the son must accept judgment and follow advice.

The relationship between Marlow and Jim is the central father-son relationship in the book. Other ones throw light upon it by contrast and similarity. Early in the novel, the actions of Captain Brierly establish that Conrad's portrayal of sea life assumes a father-son relationship between a captain and his officers. Before Brierly commits suicide, he writes two letters that he hopes will give his chief mate Jones the command of the vessel. Jones says: "He wrote like a father would to a favorite son, Captain Marlow, and I was five-and-twenty years his senior..." [131] Brierly's suicide makes ludicrous all the seamanlike care with which he carried it out. His act of paternal responsibility toward his chief mate proves specious, for Jones does not get the command. Brierly's paternal role and his suicide prefigure Jim's role as savior in Patusan and his selfish suicide. Jones and Marlow are also linked. Jones writes to Brierly's father of his son's suicide, but he receives no answer – "neither Thank you, nor Go to the devil! – nothing! Perhaps they did not want to know." [132] This foreshadows Marlow's perception that no one at home would inquire about Jim [133] and explains why he does not write to Jim's father, whose simple moral views and narrow experiences would not permit him to comprehend Jim's failure and motives. In each case the man with a filial or paternal relation remains alone with the unhappy memory which he cannot share with the real father.

In more specific fashion the relationship between Jim and

---

[130]  *Ibid.*, p. 97.
[131]  *Ibid.*, p. 62.
[132]  *Ibid.*, p. 64.
[133]  *Ibid.*, p. 223.

Marlow is paralleled by similar relationships which Jim forms with two other men. Marlow first arranges for the disgraced seaman to work for Mr. Denver, an eccentric elderly bachelor, owner of a rice mill somewhere in the East.[134] Denver becomes fond of the young man and has him live in his house. When Jim courteously crosses the room to open the door for his employer, Denver feels "more in touch with mankind than I had been for years". Jim senses Denver's feelings. He recalls to Marlow that Denver had slipped his hand under his arm.[135] Just as Jim's future seems secure, the former second engineer of the *Patna* come to work at the mill, and Jim feels that he can no longer stay where someone knows of his disgrace. Ironically, the engineer, who has no intention of informing on Jim, acknowledges Jim's new position. He addresses him as "Mr. James". To Marlow, Jim explains, "I was called Mr. James there as if I had been the son." Jim cannot bear the thought of confessing to Denver, who has rapidly become "more like a father", and he ruins this chance by leaving without explanation. This brief and clear episode foreshadows Jim's complex relationship with Stein.

Marlow takes Jim's case to Stein, a wealthy German trader in the East. Stein too has paternal motives for wishing to help Jim. Because an old Scotsman had once adopted Stein as his son and heir, Stein will himself be a father to Jim. As a young man in the East without fortune or prospects, Stein had been befriended by an old Scots trader who had become a power in a native state. Stein recounts to Marlow the ceremony with which M'Neil had announced his adoption of the young German. "Look, queen, and you rajahs, this is my son ... I have traded with your fathers, and when I die he shall trade with you and your sons." [136] Even before meeting Jim, Stein decides to give him his Patusan property.

---

[134]   *Ibid.*, p. 187-91.

[135]   This is a particularly Conradian gesture of paternal affection. Jean-Aubry recalls a paternal pressure on his arm during discussions of the French translations of Conrad's work (Introduction, *Lettres Françaises*, p. x) and Rudolph Megroz, who had just discussed with Conrad the sensation of turning thirty (the shadow line), felt Conrad's hand under his arm as they crossed a hotel lobby: *A Talk with Joseph Conrad and A Criticism of his Mind and Method* (London, Elkin Matthews, 1926), p. 35.

[136]   *Lord Jim*, p. 206.

Stein's paternal response to Jim has a less altruistic side than this generous desire to repay a debt to a man from the British Isles. Stein desires not only to give Jim a second chance, but to see Jim make up for some particular failures of his own. Apart from saying "Stein characteristically enough had a sentimental motive" for aiding Jim,[137] Marlow does not comment on these motives. Yet sufficient details are given to suggest them to the reader. The trading post left to Stein by the Scotsman was in Celebes. After considerable success there – holding out against sieges in a dynastic war, marrying a native princess, surviving an ambush, capturing a rare butterfly – suddenly Stein's world collapses. The native ruler, his friend, is assassinated. Stein's wife and daughter die.

According to Marlow, grief rather than danger causes Stein to leave,[138] but according to the version Jim reports after talking directly to Stein, he "had to make a dash for dear life out of the country".[139] With Stein came Doramin and his people. Doramin and the Bugis finally settle in Patusan, perhaps accompanied to their new home by Stein himself, for Marlow once guesses that Stein had been to Patusan "either in his butterfly-hunting days or later ... when he tried in his incorrigible way to season with a pinch of romance the fattening dishes of his commercial kitchen".[140] The position of the men of Celebes in Patusan is, however, fairly precarious, for they are menaced by a roving robber band and by the tyrannical sultan. Moreover, Stein's trading post, intended to make the Bugis prosperous, has failed. Stein still feels some obligation to Doramin and his people especially because he and Doramin had been "war-comrades"[141] and before parting had promised eternal friendship, exchanging tokens. Doramin gave Stein a silver ring,[142] and Stein gave Doramin a pair of pistols he had received from M'Neil.[143] The gift of pistols symbolized

137 Ibid., p. 229.
138 Ibid., p. 207.
139 Ibid., p. 233.
140 Ibid., p. 219.
141 Ibid., p. 233.
142 Ibid.
143 Ibid., p. 264.

Stein's desire to share with Doramin his paternal heritage and to restore Doramin to the position and prosperity he had known in Celebes.

After hearing Jim's story from Marlow, Stein identifies his own defeat in Celebes with Jim's disgrace. Although Marlow thinks of Stein as a romantic success, one who has followed the dream "with unfaltering footsteps",[144] Stein corrects him, "And do you know how many opportunities I let escape; how many dreams I had lost that had come in my way. ... It seems to me that some would have been very fine – if I had made them come true." Stein then sends Jim to Patusan to restore Doramin and his people to prosperity. For Stein, Jim will be a son, just as Stein had been a son to M'Neil to take up an inheritance, a responsibility, and carry it forward.

And Jim, a generation later, begins to re-enact Stein's jungle adventure. Within two years he establishes peace and order; he increases the power and wealth of Doramin and the Celebes people; his success encourages Doramin to think of establishing his son Dain Waris on the throne. And Jim becomes a "war-comrade" to Dain Waris. Conrad's employment of the symbolic ring and pistols makes this parallel clear. Stein gives the ring to Jim, who uses it to introduce himself to Doramin. And as Jim and Dain Waris prepare to attack the robber band, Doramin watches approvingly, M'Neil's pistols on his knees.[145]

Stein is greatly satisfied with Jim, and he sends Marlow to tell Jim that he is giving him his trading post, goods, and house in Patusan.[146] But finally Jim's sonship to Stein ends disastrously. After a loss of reputation resulting from a second failure to protect people in his charge, Jim virtually commits suicide. Just as Jim had been unable to stay with Denver once his shameful past threatened to be known, so he cannot continue to live in Patusan once the natives' belief in him has collapsed. Feeling his honor sullied again, he must clear it by offering himself as a sacrifice. The

144   *Ibid.*, p. 217.
145   *Ibid.*, p. 264.
146   *Ibid.*, p. 247.

"call of his exalted egoism" [147] leads him to renounce an inheritance almost within his grasp. Again the symbolic ring and pistols take a part. Jim had given Stein's ring to Dain Waris, from whose body his father has taken it. As Doramin rises to shoot Jim with M'Neil's pistol, the ring falls at Jim's feet. Jim dies, perhaps satisfied by his expiation, but all of Stein's paternal hopes for him are destroyed.

The biographical origin of the relationship between Stein as spiritual father and Jim as son is evident in the fact that Conrad gives to Stein his uncle's motto, *usque ad finem*. But the motto expresses not only that duty which reason perceives to be defined by circumstances, as Tadeusz Bobrowski had once explained it, but also the duty to the inner necessities of the romantic personality, an idea of duty reminiscent both of Conrad's own inexplicable desire to go to sea and his father's personality. The character of Stein itself combines elements of both Conrad's father and uncle. Marlow insists that he is "romantic" but respects his judgment. A refugee from the liberal revolution of 1848, Stein is also a man of practical intelligence. He argues that man must immerse himself in the "destructive element", that is, he must "follow the dream – and so – *ewig – usque ad finem*".[148] But Bobrowski-like, Stein also argues that man must accept failure and disappointment and that to follow the dream demands exertions which, like the swimmer's efforts in his metaphor, keep the man balanced and safe from the drowning that comes from passivity or the wrong kind of activity.

Incapable of taking such subtle advice, Jim follows his own dream to the very end only as self-fulfillment. In so doing Jim has profoundly disappointed the three men whom he led to look upon him as a son. Jim's betrayal of the seaman's code of professional duty had marred his relationship with Marlow; his desertion of Denver and his self-sacrificing death had destroyed the beginnings of two other filial relationships. And, of course, his failure with Denver and Stein's trust also betrayed Marlow, who had recommended him to them. Both Denver and Stein had seen in Jim a

[147] *Ibid.*, p. 416.
[148] *Ibid.*, p. 215.

son, a new self, who with his youth and energy would fulfill their hopes. Marlow too had seen in Jim a younger, more idealistic self. Jim's failure leaves Denver and Stein lonely and unhappy. Denver writes bitterly to Marlow:

Allow me to say, lest you should have some more mysterious young men in reserve, that I have shut up shop definitely and forever. This is the last eccentricity I shall be guilty of. De not imagine for a moment that I care a hang. . . .[149]

Stein, whose shock and grief at Jim's death Marlow describes in detail, is left to care for Jim's widow, another victim of his desertion. "Stein has aged greatly of late. He feels it himself and says often that he is 'preparing to leave' . . . while he waves his hand sadly at his butterflies." [150] And Marlow remains troubled and unhappy as he thinks of Jim.

Denver and Stein have perhaps demanded more of Jim than they had a right to. Marlow had after all asked Denver merely to employ Jim and Stein simply to help him. But in both cases Jim had responded to paternal overtures in a way that made the men assume that they could count on him. Marlow's own disillusionment is not so great. He sees Jim's tremendous egoism very early in their acquaintance, and his delight in Jim's success in Patusan is continually restrained by his doubts about its meaning. Nevertheless, the relationship between Marlow and Jim has been a failure. Self-knowledge, profession, and duty are the objects to the relationship. But these objects were prevented by the non-professional circumstances of the friendship, by Jim's pride, by his refusal to accept his own weakness and guilt, and, finally by Marlow's reluctance to accept fully the role of spiritual father. To have done so he would have thoroughly admitted Jim's weaknesses, not simply his failure. Captain Brierly had done so and, seeing the weaknesses as his own, had committed suicide. The very thing that draws Marlow to Jim – the disturbing sense of identification – makes Marlow unable to be a full and saving spiritual father. Too much like a real father, and one similar to his son, Marlow lacks

---

[149]   *Ibid.*, p. 189.
[150]   *Ibid.*, p. 417.

the detachment that Conrad demanded of the spiritual father.

In *Lord Jim*, Conrad pessimistically examines a bulwark against evil, failure, and irrationality. He comes to the conclusion that under severe tests the relationship between a young man and his spiritual father can fail.

In his next novel, *Nostromo*, Conrad shows further shortcomings possible in the relation of a spiritual father to the younger man who looks to him for guidance and truth. The personal sources of this relationship differ from Conrad's sources for Jim and his three father surrogates. In a startling juxtaposition of two contrary influences upon his own life, Conrad places a character based on the independent and skeptical Dominic Cervoni under the influence of a figure suggestive of his own father. (From both portrayals he excluded the sophistication of the originals, embodying this trait and its dangers in still another character, Decoud.) In Giorgio Viola, the self-exiled Garibaldino, Conrad portrays aspects of Apollo Korzeniowski by emphasizing in the Italian's character, patriotism, personal selflessness, and a disappointment so deep that it "had instilled into him a gloomy doubt of ever being able to understand the ways of Divine justice".[151] Even Viola's full white beard recalls the older Korzeniowski. Like many Poles in the nineteenth century, this Italian had fought in other revolutions while awaiting the opportunity to liberate and unite his homeland. When the cause of united Italy passes from the idealistic Garibaldi to the cynical politician Cavour and when despite revolutions the kings and emperors seem still firmly established, Viola retires defeated and disappointed to keeping an inn in South America. Disappointment, however, has not robbed him of his ideals, for he still believes passionately and unquestioningly in a romantic nationalism, clearly irrelevant to a semi-barbarous nation divided between rural feudalism and sham democracy and about to be precipitated into modern industrial capitalism and imperialism. Conrad characterizes his political idealism:

His austere old-world Republicanism had a severe, soldier-like standard of duty, as if the world were a battlefield where men had to fight

[151] *Nostromo*, p. 29.

for the sake of universal love and brotherhood, instead of a more or less large share of booty.[152]

Although often made ridiculous by the difference between his vast ideals and the reality of his humble inn, Viola is a figure of great dignity and pathos.

While Viola is a static character undergoing no essential change in the novel, Nostromo is a dynamic character in whose life the effects of romantic idealism work themselves out. Nostromo is Dominic Cervoni gone ashore, deprived, like Jim, of the bond of the sea, and also, as Conrad points out in the Author's Note, lacking Dominic's pride of ancestry and clan loyalty.[153]

The relationship of Viola and Nostromo recalls Stein's befriending Jim, for it too is a sympathetically portrayed friendship between an exile from the "old humanitarian revolutions" and an attractive egoistic young man. Like Stein sending Jim to Patusan where he may re-live Stein's romantic tropical adventure, old Viola persuades Nostromo, a sailor, to desert his ship just as he himself had done years earlier. And just as Stein had the welfare of an unprotected girl in mind when he gave Jim his second chance, so Viola thinks of Nostromo as a husband for one of his daughters. Viola's interest in Nostromo is more subtly selfish than this wish to provide for a daughter. Like Stein, Marlow, and Denver, Viola sees the splendid young man as a son, a substitute for his own dead boy. Although Nostromo chafes uneasily under Viola's appeals to him as "all his son would have been",[154] he accepts a filial role which is strengthened by his never having known his own parents.

Viola passes on to Nostromo his two dominant attitudes: distrust of the upper classes and a disdain for money and personal advantage. Viola's philosophy, however, adversely affects Nostromo: "He has encouraged much of the Capataz's confounded nonsense", one character comments.[155] Unlike old Viola Nostromo does not live in a dream of past republicanism, for "his prestige

---

[152]    *Ibid.*, p. 313.
[153]    *Nostromo*, Author's Note, p. xxii.
[154]    *Nostromo*, p. 468.
[155]    *Ibid.*, p. 320.

is his fortune".[156] Like Jim in Patusan, he is the prisoner of the admiration he receives. The *Cargadores*, of which Nostromo is the *Capataz*, counterfeit the professional fellowship of seamen. Not a sober professional group like the Marseilles Pilots' Association, the *Cargadores* are more noted for their colorful costume and aggressive solidarity. Although they do load and unload ships efficiently, they exist primarily for the vanity of Nostromo and the members. Conrad points out their motives for defending the Custom House against the insurgent mob bent on stealing the load of silver.

The Company's lightermen, too, natives of the Republic, behaved very well under their Capataz. An outcast lot of very mixed blood, mainly negroes, everlastingly at feud with the other customers of low grog shops in the town, they embraced with delight this opportunity to settle their personal scores under such favourable auspices.[157]

After Viola, aided by his shrewd peasant wife, has persuaded Nostromo that the praise of the rich, as well as the adulation of the selfish mob, is worthless, Nostromo loses his motive for utter trustworthiness. His dislike of the wealthy, now erected into a principle, becomes reason enough to keep the load of silver ingots which has fallen into his hands. Romantic idealism has proven a false guide. The cult of the hero, Viola's worship of Garibaldi, has encouraged egoism; and distrust of the rich and powerful has justified theft. Despite the complications of the foolish love story bringing about the final catastrophe and seriously marring the last chapters, it is appropriate that Viola unwittingly kill Nostromo, who has both carried out and betrayed his naive ideals. With the best intentions the spiritual father may prove as ill an influence as the real father.

Indeed, Conrad has constructed this relationship as a parallel to the relation between Charles Gould and his father. Both sons mingle loyalty with disloyalty and confuse ideals with vanity. As a sanction for the principles behind each relationship stands a political idealist, easily mistaken for an adventurer, who dies defeated. Viola frequently invokes Garibaldi, like himself a sailor

[156] *Ibid.*
[157] *Ibid.*, p. 14.

turned revolutionist, as a precedent, and Charles Gould recalls his uncle, a businessman turned politician who vainly attempted to bring "social order" and "rational liberty" [158] to Costaguana, as a moral model for his own re-opening of the silver mine. Garibaldi was at last wounded and imprisoned and Harry Gould was arrested and shot by the insurgent regime which overthrew his own. These failures link together and prefigure the more subtle failures of Gould and Nostromo, wealthy but isolated, both victims of a misunderstood inheritance.

*Nostromo,* apparently the least autobiographical of Conrad's novels, thus brings together concerns stemming from the contrary influences of Apollo Korzeniowski, romantic patriotism and the strong tie of blood, and of Tadeusz Bobrowski, profession and the bond between spiritual father and son.

---

[158] *Ibid.,* p. 46.

## THE FATHERLAND: "PRINCE ROMAN", THE
## POLISH ESSAYS, AND *LORD JIM*

During the last twelve or thirteen years of his life, Joseph Conrad solved the problems originating in the opposing Bobrowski and Korzeniowski strains in his character. Exhausted by continued poverty and illness, Conrad made peace between the warring halves of his personality through a series of illogical maneuvers which relaxed the tension from which his best work had proceeded. He lost that earlier, productive mental state which had combined an uneasy symphaty for Apollo Korzeniowski and the obligations of Messianic patriotism with a clear sense that the practical moral and professional viewpoint of Tadeusz Bobrowski was necessary for life. Because in his later years he developed an almost uncritical approval for his father and Poland, Conrad no longer felt the force of his uncle's analysis of his father's weaknesses.

Signs of inner reconciliation began to appear after a severe illness in 1910, and they were first manifested in "Prince Roman", a short story in which Conrad for the first time whole-heartedly accepted romantic nationalism. Soon after this time Conrad became less reticent about his father; he discussed him with some frankness four years later in "Poland Revisited", revealing much more, however, about his own conflicting feelings as a child than about his father. His reconciliation with his father's nationalism went still farther during the First World War and shortly after when he espoused the tenets of romantic nationalism in essays defending Poland's right to independence and to all of her former territories. These essays throw light on a passage in *Lord Jim* in which he had used some of the same ideas with great artistic subtlety to project Marlow's relationship with Jim. Finally, in 1919 Conrad openly defended his father in the Author's Note to *A Personal Record*, where, after insisting that his father was a "patriot" rather than a "revolutionist", he suggests similarities between his father and his uncle and attempts to prove that his uncle had been mistaken in his criticism of his father.

I

This enforced reconciliation between the two sides of Conrad's personality, and the subsequent literary decline, follow a period of ill health preceded by considerable financial and personal anxieties. In the latter half of 1909 after fourteen barely saleable volumes in as many years of writing life, he felt that his financial problems would never be solved. He had just quarreled irrevocably with Ford Madox Ford over the form of *Some Reminiscences* appearing in Ford's *English Review*. Ford had disturbed Conrad with his accusation that their form was "ragged",[1] and, as if to substantiate Ford's criticism, Conrad was having trouble in finding an American journal to publish them.[2] Even the Conrads' faithful maid, Nellie Lyons, who had joined them in France three years earlier when the children were desperately ill, was herself critically ill, and Conrad's aristocratic conscience led him to provide for her stay in the hospital and convalescent home.[3] Deeply in debt, he feared that he would be unable to pay for Borys' schooling.[4] Then in January 1910 Conrad's perennial gout and a pulmonary illness attacked him with great violence. It was his most serious illness since his return from Africa twenty years earlier.[5] Confusion over doctors and a wrong diagnosis aggravated Conrad's illness, and during its course he became delirious and began to hold impassioned conversations with the characters of

[1]  Letter to Ford Madox Ford (July 31, 1909), *Joseph Conrad, Life and Letters*, II, p. 101.
[2]  Letter to John Galsworthy (July 13, 1909), *ibid.*
[3]  Letter to John Galsworthy (Monday night, 1909), *ibid.*, II, p. 106.
[4]  Letter to J. B. Pinker (Monday, Oct., 1909), *ibid.*, II, pp. 102-03.
[5]  Jessie Conrad, *Joseph Conrad and his Circle*, pp. 142-46.

*Under Western Eyes*, which he had completed a short time before.[6] Mrs. Conrad, who tended him, thought it the worst of his
illness that she had seen, and Conrad himself felt that even the
painful attack he was suffering in the last year of his life did not
seem so severe.

I confess that the periods of pain have been extremely severe, and
only to be compared with a bad illness I had after finishing *Western
Eyes* and before I wrote *Chance*. But at that time I was really in danger on account of high temperatures lasting for days.[7]

Conrad was fifty-three when he recovered, and he had become an
old man. His convalescent habits seem to have been prolonged for
several years. Jean-Aubry recalled that between 1910 and 1914
Conrad did very little travelling and received only a few visitors
in the country.[8] It was almost inevitable, therefore, that Conrad
would not be so intensely involved with his own work.

In 1911, the year after his long illness, Conrad demonstrated in
a short story his unqualified acceptance of romantic nationalism
and his reconciliation of the conflicting Bobrowski and Korzeniowski forces in his mind. In "Prince Roman", as Gustav Morf
points out, Conrad defends his father's impractical patriotism
against the worldly wisdom of his uncle.[9] Thus he insisted on the
close connections and even similarities between the hero, a historical figure in the revolution of 1830, and both Apollo Korzeniowski and Tadeusz Bobrowski; further he shows that Bobrowski, from whose memoirs Conrad took the story, praised the
prince; in addition, he thoroughly answers or dismisses all criticism of the insurrection of 1830; finally, he makes clear that the
chief critic, a character whom he models on Bobrowski, is converted from rational disapproval to sympathy for the "patriotic
impulses of the heart". Conrad pays particular tribute to Polish
romanticism by giving his hero traits drawn from Polish Messian-

[6]   Jessie Conrad, letter to D. S. Meldrum (Feb. 6, 1910), *Blackwood Letters*, p. 192.
[7]   Letter to Mr. and Mrs. F. N. Doubleday (Jan. 7, 1924), *Joseph Conrad,
Life and Letters*, II, p. 332.
[8]   Aubry, *The Sea Dreamer*, p. 257.
[9]   Morf, pp. 198-99.

ism, and, more significantly, by borrowing ideas, setting, a character, and a peculiarity of Polish speech from the masterpiece of Polish romanticism, Adam Mickiewicz's *Pan Tadeusz*. Not surprisingly, Conrad's reconciliation of the influences of father and uncle and his acceptance of romantic nationalism result in a story generally inferior to his best work. Nevertheless, he narrates the climax, a moment of critical moral choice for the romantic hero, with great effectiveness, employing the methods of his best writing.

Conrad was especially anxious that "Prince Roman" be read as history. He disliked the idea that "Prince Roman" might be printed in a collection of purely fictional short stories and at one time hoped that he could publish it with *The Shadow Line* and include a preface that would distinctly explain their autobiographical origins.[10] Later, he planned to use "Prince Roman" as a part of a second volume of reminiscences.[11]

In characterizing the hero and commenting on his life, Conrad joins the best qualities of both his father and his uncle. Conrad makes quite specific the connections between the prince and the Korzeniowskis. The prince, speaking to Tadeusz Bobrowski in 1868, recalls that he had been a comapnion in arms of Teodor Korzeniowski, the paternal grandfather of the eleven year old Conrad who is present listening to their conversation. The prince goes on to praise Teodor Korzeniowski, saying, somewhat mysteriously, "He was one of those who knew." [12] Thus in the presence of Tadeusz Bobrowski Prince Roman sets his approval on a man whose career Bobrowski had criticized for its weaknesses. Conrad insists, moreover, on the aristocratic associations and status of the Korzeniowskis: "My grandfather was a neighbour of the S– family in the country but he did not know Prince Roman, who however knew his name perfectly well." [13] Becoming acquainted at the last stand of the revolution, the two patriots

---

[10]    Letter to J. B. Pinker (early 1917), *Joseph Conrad, Life and Letters*, II, p. 181.
[11]    Jessie Conrad, *Joseph Conrad as I Knew Him* (Garden City, N. Y., Doubleday Page, 1926), p. 159.
[12]    *Tales of Hearsay*, p. 35.
[13]    *Ibid.*, p. 48.

promise to inform one another's families in case of death or capture. This incident is immaterial to the plot; its purpose is to reinforce the association of the patriotic prince and the Korzeniowskis. Conrad also makes a point of saying that 1828 was the year of the prince's marriage and his own father's birth.[14] The second detail is inaccurate. Apollo Korzeniowski was born in 1820. Whether Conrad, often confused about exact dates, purposely altered the facts or not is unimportant. He merely wished to assert another connection. Prince Roman's personal affinities with Apollo Korzeniowski are less overt. The prince's grief over the death of his beautiful young wife recalls Korzeniowski's despair after his wife's death and the generalized description of the princess' attractions – "her beauty, her charm, and the serious qualities of her mind and heart" [15] – might have been one of Tadeusz Bobrowski's tributes to his sister. The most significant link between Prince Roman and Conrad's father is their concept of patriotic duty, beyond reason, beyond question, beyond all other obligations.

Prince Roman, however, is not merely an idealized Korzeniowski; he is also shown to have affinities with the Bobrowskis. The Bobrowskis approve highly of the prince. Tadeusz Bobrowski introduces the child to the prince who shakes the hand of the grandchild of his old companion in arms and pats him on the head. The gesture, though a commonplace one, suggests approval and blessing, a patriotic laying-on of hands. Far from disapproving of this gesture of an old revolutionist toward the child, the son and grandson of revolutionists, Bobrowski interprets the scene for the boy: "My uncle addressed me weightily: 'You have shaken hands with Prince Roman S–. It's something for you to remember when you grow up.' " [16] One detail of the story joins the prince's character and activities with Tadeusz Bobrowski. After his many years of exile in Russia, the prince returns to Poland, not to die like Apollo Korzeniowski, but to become a public benefactor, helping with his advice, influence, and wealth, the unfortunate of his

---

[14]   *Ibid.*, p. 30.
[15]   *Ibid.*, p. 31.
[16]   *Ibid.*, p. 25.

neighborhood. He especially aids other returned exiles. This, of course, also describes Bobrowski's benevolence. A widower like the prince, he was the guardian of many orphans and often saved properties which were in danger of confiscation because of the revolutionary activities of relatives. The story concludes with a conversation between Bobrowski and the prince about obtaining an official position for a deserving man. The two gentlemen are thus seen engaged in the same worthy cause.

The brief final paragraph of the story represents a total reconciliation of the two halves of Conrad's personality. Bobrowski has expressed surprise that his recommendation should also be necessary to obtain the position for such a deserving young man. Conrad emphasizes the prince's answer.

> "And to this day [the narrator concludes] I remember the very words: 'I ask you because, you see, my daughter and my son-in-law don't believe me to be a good judge of men. They think that I let myself be guided too much by mere sentiment.' " [17]

This answer shows that the prince performs his good deed, similar to the good deeds of Bobrowski, out of motives more like those of Apollo Korzeniowski, and it also indicates that these motives are criticized largely by people indifferent to the fate of Poland, people of whom both Bobrowski and Korzeniowski would disapprove. The prince's daughter, as Conrad has already established, represents the generation after the insurrections which was not so much critical as indifferent to them. "His daughter married splendidly to a Polish Austrian *grand seigneur* and, moving in the cosmopolitan sphere of the highest European aristocracy, lived mostly abroad in Nice and Vienna." [18] The prince's request for Bobrowski's recommendation unites the two men in disparaging the compromising generation, especially the aristocrats who are now useless because they have forgotten their country. The daughter and her husband's criticism that the prince is "guided too much by mere sentiment" may have been, as Morf suggests, a typical Bobrowski criticism of Apollo Korzeniowski, but the scene indicates

---

[17]   *Ibid.*, p. 55.
[18]   *Ibid.*, pp. 53-54.

that Bobrowski listens to the prince with perfect sympathy, understanding that the daughter and her husband do not realize that
true sentiment is the basis of sound judgment. In Conrad's experience his uncle had criticized the fanatical patriotism which began
hopeless revolutions that left Poland in a worse condition after
they were crushed than the nation had been in when they were
undertaken. In the short story this criticism is specifically detached from Tadeusz Bobrowski and put elsewhere.[19]

Not only does "Prince Roman" show Tadeusz Bobrowski's
admiration for a Polish revolutionist, but it refutes or discredits
any criticism that he or others might make of Polish nationalism.
Conrad does this through direct author's comment and through a
short debate between Prince Roman and his father Prince John.
In the introduction to the story Conrad rejects all criticism of
patriotism.

It requires a certain greatness of soul to interpret patriotism worthily
– or else a sincerity of feeling denied to the vulgar refinement of
modern thought which cannot understand the august simplicity of a
sentiment proceeding from the very nature of things and men.[20]

Commenting on the story Conrad pretends to take up criticism of
the prince's determination to fight to the very end of a revolution
already defeated. But by the end of this short discussion he has
thoroughly discredited any person who might hold these views.

This looks like mere fanaticism. But fanaticism is human. Man has
adored ferocious divinities. There is ferocity in every passion, even
in love itself. The religion of undying hope resembles the mad cult
of despair, of death, of annihilation. The difference lies in the moral
motive springing from the secret needs and unexpressed aspirations
of the believers. It is only to vain men that all is vanity; and all is
deception only to those who have never been sincere with themselves.[21]

---

[19]  In order to show Tadeusz Bobrowski as an admirer of national risings
Conrad had to omit any reference to the revolution of 1863 of which both
Bobrowski and the historical Prince Roman Sanguzko disappeared. See
Ludwik Krzyzanowski, "Joseph Conrad's 'Prince Roman': Fact and Fic-
tion", *Joseph Conrad Centennial Essays*, ed. Ludwik Krzyzanowski (New
York, The Polish Institute of Arts and Sciences in America, 1960), p. 58.
[20]  *Tales of Hearsay*, p. 35.
[21]  *Ibid.*, p. 48.

Stein in *Lord Jim* had made a similar defense of Jim's secret needs and unexpressed aspiration that drove him to seek a place where his reputation, his view of himself, and his deeds all harmonized. But Stein is only one of the commentators on Jim, and Marlow remains disturbed and skeptical about what he hears. This paragraph in "Prince Roman", however, expresses Conrad's own views, and comes perilously close to saying that good intentions excuse anything.

More specific criticism of the revolt of 1831 is put into the mouth of Prince Roman's father, to whom Conrad gives some of the traits and opinions of his uncle. But as with the charge of fanaticism, Prince John's criticisms are soon met, and the Bobrowski point of view is reconciled with revolution. The conflict between the two men is short and insignificant. The old prince merely expresses his views – more applicable to 1863 than 1830 – and then acquiesces in his son's patriotic decision.

Old Prince John, moved and uneasy, speaking from a purely aristocratic point of view, mistrusted the popular origins of the movement, regretted its democratic tendencies, and did not believe in the possibility of success. He was sad, inwardly agitated.

"I am judging all this calmly. There are secular principles of legitimity and order which have been violated in this reckless enterprise for the sake of more subversive illusions. Though of course the patriotic impulses of the heart. . . ." [22]

Conrad has attributed to the old prince the prime quality of his uncle, the sense of moral consequence. Prince John further meditates on "this unhappy struggle which was wrong in principle and therefore destined to fail".[23] The terms in which Prince John expresses his critical opposition are significant. The violated "principles of legitimity and order" are "secular". *Secular*, as Albert Guerard points out, had been one of the favorite words of the early Conrad.[24] We may recall the "secular trees" of "Heart of Darkness". But in the phrase, "secular principles" in "Prince Roman", the word has lost its unique Conradian overtones of the

---

[22]    *Ibid.*, p. 40.
[23]    *Ibid.*
[24]    Guerard, *Conrad the Novelist*, p. 262.

brute endurance of a godless universe and has taken on its customary meaning antonymous to *religious* or *sacred*. Although the word *sacred* is not used in this story, it is implied here. *Sacred* became for the older Conrad a word of vague emotional uplift and approval. In *Victory* he applies "sacred" to the Christ-like Lena, a Magdalen and soiled dove who sacrifices herself that the hero may know the truth and live. The "secular principles" in "Prince Roman" are opposed to that other Christ figure, Poland with its "sacred traditions of freedom", as Conrad was to put it eight years later. The "unhappy struggle" is wrong then, but only according to secular principles. Higher principles, perceived by the "patriotic impulses of the heart", prove it right.

Not only does "Prince Roman" defend the politics of Apollo Korzeniowski to Tadeusz Bobrowski and other critics, but it also pays tribute to Polish romanticism by insisting on the emotional basis of patriotism, by depicting in the hero qualities reminiscent of Polish Messianism, and, most significantly, by borrowings from Mickiewicz's *Pan Tadeusz*. Conrad makes it clear that the basis of patriotism is feeling. Chastened by personal sorrow, the prince intuitively responds to his country and her sorrows. The death of the prince's wife

had opened his heart to a greater sorrow, his mind to a vaster thought, his eyes to all the past and to the existence of another love fraught with pain but as mysteriously imperative as that lost one to which he had entrusted his happiness.[25]

And later the narrator also comments on the irresistible appeal of Poland for her people.

Conrad reveals his indebtedness to Polish romanticism more specifically by making Prince Roman express his patriotism in the terms of Polish Messianism. Messianism's quasi-religious emphasis on humility and sacrifice are inherent in the hero's explanation of his desire to fight as an enlisted man under an assumed name.

There is no question here of leadership and glory. I mean to go alone and to fight obscurely in the ranks. I am going to offer my country

[25]   *Tales of Hearsay*, p. 41.

what is mine to offer, that is my life, as simply as the saddler from Grodek who went through yesterday with his apprentices.[26]

One might imagine that the prince's name, experience, and ability would serve his country better than pseudonymous humble service. The author of *Lord Jim* would have searchingly analyzed this romantic desire to "fight obscurely in the ranks" and to offer oneself as a sacrifice. Here Conrad simply approves of a plan which earlier he would have seen as a subtle ministering to the ego. An author's comment also indicates the Messianic qualities of Prince Roman's character: "Thus humbly and in accord with the simplicity of the vision of duty he saw when death had removed the brilliant bandage of happiness from his eyes, did Prince Roman bring his offering to his country." [27] Because the terms *offering* and *vision*, and the ideas of humility and sacrifice are usually found in a religious context we can see how closely Conrad is approaching the language and assumptions of Polish Messianism.

Conrad pays tribute to the romantic nationalism of Poland most significantly in his borrowings from the literary work considered the Polish national epic, Adam Mickiewicz's *Pan Tadeusz*. Learning about the poem in his childhood, Conrad valued it highly all of his life because it symbolized his Polish heritage. Both his father and his uncle admired the poem and encouraged Conrad to read and appreciate it. Apollo Korzeniowski had taught his son to read it aloud during exile; it was doubtless one of the means by which he taught him the duty of "only to be a Pole". Tadeusz Bobrowski had given Conrad a copy when the youth left Poland for France and the sea. When Conrad lost his copy, along with his other Polish books and an album of family photographs, Bobrowski wrote him that he could replace it at a Polish bookstore in Paris where he also might meet Ladislas Mickiewicz, the son and biographer of the poet.[28] Over thirty-five years later Conrad showed his Polish friend Joseph Retinger two volumes bound in black linen, one an album of photographs and the other a copy of *Pan*

---

[26]   *Ibid.*, p. 43. The historical Prince Roman served as a captain, not an enlisted man, and assumed another name to protect his family and their property. See Ludwik Krzyzanowski, p. 39.

[27]   *Tales of Hearsay*, p. 44.

[28]   Letter (Sept. 27, 1876 old style), Najder, p. 38.

*Tadeusz.* "Nothing else have I saved ... from my inheritance", he told Retinger, "but these faded daguerreotypes and this book, which I never tired of reading on my unending journeys." [29]

Both "Prince Roman" and *Pan Tadeusz* are, of course, expressions of Polish patriotism. "Prince Roman" particularly resembles *Pan Tadeusz* in its social and political conservatism, its setting, and the character of its hero. Relying directly on Mickiewicz's text, Conrad has unmistakeably borrowed one minor character, Yankel, the patriotic Jewish innkeeper, from Mickiewicz. Also like Mickiewicz, Conrad portrays a character who employs Latin phrases in order to elevate his praise of the hero's patriotism. All these borrowings indicate Conrad's accord with the romantic nationalism of his father.

Both *Pan Tadeusz* and "Prince Roman" are socially and politically conservative. Expressing values similar to those in Conrad's story, the old judge in the epic contrasts half-digested notions of equality imported from pre-Napoleonic France, along with foppish fashions, with the leading traits of the traditional society of rural Poland based on a studied and sincere courtesy in all social relationships and situations. [30] Conrad's story briefly invokes the rich social harmony of the old Polish country estate, one of the principal themes of the epic.

Mickiewicz also provided Conrad with the geography of the story. Both their works take place in Lithuania, a section of northeastern Poland where Conrad had never been, but which is usually the setting for the local color writing of Polish romantics. Conrad seems to have shifted his story to the more conventionally romantic province, for when the historical prince joined the revolt, he left from his father's estate in Volhynia, a province to the south of Lithuania, not far from the homes of the Bobrowskis and Korzeniowskis. [31] Mickiewicz was born in the Lithuanian town of

[29]  Retinger, p. 29.
[30]  Mickiewicz, *Pan Tadeusz*, trans. George Rapall Noyes (London, Everyman's Library, 1930), pp. 12-17. Many of these parallels between *Pan Tadeusz* and "Prince Roman" are also pointed out by Ludwik Krzyzanowski, who further suggests that the theme of patriotic conversion recalls several of Mickiewicz's works (pp. 54-57).
[31]  Bobrowski, *Memoirs*, in Morf, p. 195.

Nowogrodek which he names in the epic's invocation of the Virgin,[32] as well as in the second stanza of "Grazyna", a narrative poem loved by Conrad as a child. In "Prince Roman" Conrad refers to Grodek, "a tiny market town nearby", the ancestral estate of the hero.[33] Just off-stage in both epic and short story is the brilliant social world of St. Petersburg where one can forget one's duty to be Polish.

Conrad may have had *Pan Tadeusz* in mind when he portrayed the hero of his story, although the factual account in Bobrowski's memoirs supplied the particular details that recall Mickiewicz's hero. Both literary works present the figure of the man who, proud of his family name, sinks personal grief in patriotic service under an assumed name. Curiously, Mickiewicz's poem has a more Conradian hero than Conrad's own story. Jacek Soplica, filled with remorse for having killed the father of the woman he loved because the father had prevented their marriage, expiates his crime by a life-time of working for the Polish cause disguised as a monk. Prince Roman's grief, however, is largely that of loss, not of guilt. Yet Conrad suggests that the prince's happiness in his marriage had blinded him temporarily to his imperative duties toward his suffering fatherland. Jacek's murder is considered unpatriotic because he committed it during a Russian attack on the castle of his fiancé's father and because the Russian governors henceforth looked on him as an accomplice. Just as Jacek Soplica must leave his country, where he has the chance for considerable power, in order to redeem himself personally and patriotically, so Prince Roman must abandon a promising career in the Imperial Guards to serve Poland.

The most striking link between the two works is the fact that they share a character, Jankiel, the patriotic Jewish innkeeper. Both works, of course, reflect a simple fact of Polish rural life, and a few similarities do not necessarily prove Conrad's borrowing. Innkeepers in Poland were often Jews; Jankiel (Yankel in Conrad's anglicized spelling) is a common name among Polish Jews; Jankel's long coat, one presumes, was a typical Jewish gar-

---

[32] Mickiewicz, *Pan Tadeusz*, p. 1.
[33] *Tales of Hearsay*, p. 39.

ment; and eastern European Jewish men all wore beards. But only Conrad's borrowing can account for close resemblances in the descriptions of the characters and for their common patriotism. An important descriptive sentence in "Prince Roman" probably echoes a similar sentence in the epic. Mickiewicz wrote:

In the centre of the room stood the host, Jankiel, in a long gown that reached to the floor, and was fastened with silver clasps; one hand he had tucked into his black silk girdle, with the other he stroked in dignified fashion his gray beard.[34]

In "Prince Roman" Conrad writes:

The innkeeper, a portly dignified Jew, clad in a black satin coat reaching down to his heels and girt with a red sash, stood at the door stroking his long silvery beard.[35]

And the Jew's inn is described with a similar metaphor in both works. Concluding an elaborate description of the traditional Jewish design of the inn, Mickiewicz says:

In a word, from a distance the tottering crooked tavern was like a Jew, when he nods his head in prayer; the roof is his cap, the disordered thatch his beard, the smoky, dirty wall his black frock, and in front the carving juts out like the cyces [the phylactery] on his brow.[36]

Conrad's brief description runs:

The roadside inn with its stable, byre, and barn under one enormous thatched roof resembled a deformed, hunch-backed giant, sprawling among the small huts of the peasants.[37]

Although the Jewish innkeeper and his inn were common facts in Polish rural life and a convention in Polish literary culture, the patriotism of Jankiel and Yankel is unusual; Jews were supposed to be indifferent to the fate of the land where they lived. Despite considerable prejudice in Poland, Polish nationalism, however, unlike Russian and German nationalism, was not anti-Semitic.

---

[34] Mickiewicz, *Pan Tadeusz*, p. 42.
[35] *Tales of Hearsay*, p. 39.
[36] Mickiewicz, *Pan Tadeusz*, p. 44.
[37] *Tales of Hearsay*, pp. 38-39.

Mickiewicz's Jankiel attempts to reconcile the quarrelling parties of Poles, thus helping to unite them against the common enemy, the Russians. He ultimately becomes a provisions officer in the liberating army of Napoleon. Conrad's Yankel supplies the prince with information about the patriotic revolt in the south and provides his grandson as a guide for the prince to the nearest party of insurgents.[38] A sentence in Conrad's story links it openly to the national epic. Yankel says:

I was already a married man when the French and all the other nations passed this way with Napoleon. Tse! Tse! That was a great harvest for death, no! Perhaps this time God will help.[39]

Conrad also shares Mickiewicz's affectionate amusement at the old-fashioned habit of educated Poles to lard their speech with Latin words and phrases, especially in highly rhetorical expressions of patriotism. In *Pan Tadeusz* the Chamberlain uses Latin words and phrases drawn from the life of the ancient Romans and from law. His greatest outburst of Latin comes as he announces that Jacek Soplica's years of heroic service to the fatherland have cleared his name forever. In "Prince Roman" Master Francis, one of the minor nobility attached for generations to the prince's family, breaks into a mixture of Latin and the vernacular when he rhetorically praises the prince's decision to join the rebellion.

The old man understood. His extended hands trembled exceedingly. But as soon as he found his voice he thanked God aloud for letting him live long enough to see the descendant of the illustrious family in its youngest generation give an example *coram Gentibus* of the love of his country and of valor in the field. He doubted not of his

---

[38]   Conrad is not the only author of prose fiction to borrow Mickiewicz's Jankiel. Joseph Kraszewski's *The Jew* (trans. Linda Da Kowalewska, New York, Dodd Mead, 1890), a novel published in 1866 about the Insurrection of 1863, also portrays a patriotic Jewish innkeeper named Jankiel who lives in a small town which, however, is located in ethnic Poland. Kraszewski admits his indebtedness to Mickiewicz. As though he were Conrad's Yankel grown old, Kraszewski's Jankiel says, "I have been through all this before, in 1809, 1812, and 1831. What the result will be now, God only knows; but I fear the worst" (p. 41). It is possible that Conrad read *The Jew* as a schoolboy in Cracow. Kraszewski was a prolific popular novelist whose work reflected directly the problems of the day.

[39]   *Tales of Hearsay*, p. 39.

dear Prince attaining a place in council and in was worthy of his
high birth; he saw already that *in fulgore* of family glory *affulget
patriae serenitas.*[40]
This speech has a patriotic significance even beyond its links with
*Pan Tadeusz.* It suggests the Messianic heroes of other Polish
romantic literature. Master Francis's joyful thanksgiving seems to
be modelled on the passage in Saint Luke in which Simeon rejoices at seeing the infant Christ.[41]
These echoes of *Pan Tadeusz* in "Prince Roman" are significant. The poem itself was a symbol of Polish nationalism. For
Conrad to employ it as a source of setting, characters, and themes
signified that Polish material no longer disturbed him as it once
had. He had made peace with his father. The uneasy balance between the two sides of his character had come to rest with the
weight apparently on the side of his father. *Pan Tadeusz* is a highly appropriate instrument for this reconciliation. Its intrinsic
merits as well as its symbolic value were appreciated by both Korzeniowski and Bobrowski. It expresses Polish patriotism without
any coloring of Messianism or even any great hatred of the Russians. Love of one's fatherland is a prime virtue, but Mickiewicz
assumes in this poem that it is a universal quality, not the private
mystique of the Poles. Such a view harmonizes very well with the
life and thought of Conrad which encompassed cosmopolitanism
and the patriotism of several lands. The movement in the epic toward union with Poland by reconciliation of discordant elements
– two feuding families, the minor gentry and great lords, quarrelling friends, Poland and Lithuania – provides a model for the
psychological process within Conrad which was expressed by
"Prince Roman". It is highly probable that Conrad could see in
the characters resemblances to himself and his own family. The
character named in the title, young Tadeusz Soplica, is the son of
Jacek Soplica whose romantic, amorous and patriotic career has
points in common with Apollo Korzeniowski's. After Jacek's dis-

[40]   *Ibid.*, p. 42. Ludwik Krzyzanowski restores Conrad's correct Latin:
*patriae*, not *patride*, by comparing the magazine text of 1911 with the post-
humously published *Tales of Hearsay* (p. 69).
[41]   Luke 2 : 29-32. Conrad's Latin, however, does not come from the
Vulgate.

appearance into a religious order and secret political activities, young Tadeusz becomes the ward of his uncle the Judge, a dignified, prosperous, and generous country gentleman who represents all the solid conservative virtues of the class to which the Bobrowskis clearly belonged. Young Tadeusz himself, after the private feud turns suddenly into an insurrection against the Russian troops sent to quell it, must leave the country. As a simple, happy, patriotic young aristocrat whose character unites the romantic charm of his father without his bent toward crime and atonement with his uncle's social position and property without his gravity, Pan Tadeusz may well have appealed to the aging Conrad, anxious for peace and reconciliation, anxious to settle his own Polish problem.

That the achievement of a personal peace is in some ways detrimental to Conrad's fiction is evident in the complicated and ineffective technique of the story. The framework for the narrative seems unnecessarily intricate and at times rather dull. About 1910 an English writer recalls that during a conversation of ten years earlier a Pole told a story. Obviously no more than an expository device for abstract discussion of patriotism and aristocracy in a world that fails to appreciate them, this conversation lacks the dramatic interchange between Marlow and his audience in *Lord Jim*, "Youth", and "Heart of Darkness", and between Conrad and his imaginary audience in *A Personal Record* and *The Mirror of the Sea*. The Pole then introduces his story with an anecdote, but unlike the manner in which the story of Nicholas Bobrowski's canine meal was introduced in *A Personal Record*, the childhood anecdote is not related to the theme of the story. The Pole tells that as a child he had escaped from the schoolroom to "hear about a particularly wolfish wolf" only to meet a "man who was preëminently a man amongst men". This man is a prince, but unfortunately for the child's fairy-tale conceptions of princes, he is very old, bald, and deaf. This anecdote is interesting and charming, but it bears no relationship to the story of the sterling patriot who never betrayed his country or his integrity. In *A Personal Record* Conrad had made clear that there was a significant connection between Nicholas Bobrowski's meal of Lithuanian dog

eaten during his selfless military service for Poland and his own
"fantastic meals of salt junk and hard tack upon the wide seas",[42]
symbolic of his self-indulgent love of adventure. But the contrast
between a "wolfish wolf" and a "man who was preëminently a
man amongst men" is purely mechanical and verbal. The child's
horrified fascination with the meal of dog, his certainty that he
would not have eaten the dog, and his grandmother's remark –
"Perhaps you don't know what it is to be hungry"[43] – these form
a more telling childhood relation to the story of the patriot than
the accidental encounter of a truant schoolboy with a patriot
prince in the billiard room. The significance of the prince's life to
the adult narrator is merely that of an example for an argument.
Once the story itself has begun, the carefully introduced, authenti-
cated, and even partially characterized Polish narrator largely
disappears. Although he refers to "my grandfather" and "my
uncle", he is merely in fact the old-fashioned totally omniscient
author moving freely and without warning into the minds of all
his characters, and pausing occasionally for expository comment
essentially detached from the characters' thoughts and from any
personal meaning the story may have for himself.

Conrad's anxiety that the story might be judged as a piece of
fiction was quite proper. It is most significantly read as autobiographical revelation. While the relationship between the mature
Conrad and his background forms one of the chief interests of *A
Personal Record* similar concerns in "Prince Roman" are perceptible only after considerable biographical study. As a work of
pure literature its value is limited.

Nevertheless, the story has an appeal independent of biographical interest. What gives the story its impact is the presentation of
the climax. The prince's moment of superb integrity comes directly from Bobrowski's memoirs and even there has striking effect.
But at this point in the story, almost for the first time, Conrad
brings his full fictional gifts into play. The Polish narrator loses
some of his assured and unconvincing omniscience and begins to
speak with emotion, as involved with Prince Roman and his moral

[42]  *A Personal Record*, p. 35.
[43]  *Ibid.*, p. 34.

choice as Marlow had been with Jim. The narrator's description of the prince at the climax is not simply an announcement of what the prince is thinking at the moment. Rather, the narrator guesses, speculates, interprets gestures and tone of voice, and expands the situation into terms of a universal moral problem – i.e., he employs the modes of character portrayal and analysis that we associate with Conrad's best writing which shows meaning not as conclusions but as a search ever nearing conclusions.

Conrad's narrator approaches the mental state of the prince by indirection. He first asks questions about the prince standing before the military court.

Within those four sinister walls shutting out from him all the sights and sounds of liberty, all hopes of the future, all consoling illusions – alone in the face of his enemies erected for judges, who can tell how much love of life there was in Prince Roman? [44]

This question suggests a kind of total surrender, a despair and longing for peace. The next two questions suggest a loss of patriotic love and duty: "How much remained in that sense of duty revealed to him in sorrow? How much of his awakened love for his native country?" The narrator himself now truly enters the story as he comments on Polish patriotism, not merely as a motivating sentiment in the personages of 1831, into whose story he is intruding to make an explanation, but as a profound concern of his own.

That country which demands to be loved as no other country has ever been loved, with the mournful affection one bears to the unforgotten dead and with the unextinguishable fire of a hopeless passion which only a living breathing, warm ideal can kindle in our breasts for our pride, for our weariness, for our exultation, for our undoing.[45]

We have authentic Conrad in this passage, not second-hand Mickiewicz or Walter Scott. The narrator realizes the call of duty, the irresistible appeal of the fatherland, but he also perceives the drawbacks to this love of the sacred lost cause of the homeland. The narrator is very much concerned about a man who has a chance to save his life and gain his liberty if he will betray his

[44]    *Tales of Hearsay*, p. 51.
[45]    *Ibid.*

country. *Betray* is perhaps too strong a term, for the prince is merely asked to agree with his previously bribed judges that, overcome by grief, he joined the revolt unaware of the significance of his actions. For the presiding judge's phrasing of this excuse Conrad employs the rhetorical structure of the official proclamation: elaborate introductory participial modifiers, indicating in vague terms overwhelming emotions, then followed by the grammatical subject.

Distracted by excessive grief after his young wife's death, rendered irresponsible for his conduct by his despair, in a moment of blind recklessness, without realizing the highly reprehensible nature of the act, nor yet its danger and its dishonour, he went off to join the nearest rebels on a sudden impulse. And that now penitently....[46]

We are again at a moment of marginal crime, of ambiguous action. Up to this point in the passage the narrator has suggested that the prince has concealed his apathy from his judges lest they think him discouraged or crushed. The reader's closest and most authentic glimpse into the prince's mind has been this consideration of what the judges may be thinking about his conduct. At the moment of choice even this evasive view is withdrawn and a purely external view of men and their actions is made to carry the full weight of the scene.

But Prince Roman was silent. The military judges looked at him hopefully. In silence he reached for a pen and wrote on a sheet of paper he found under his hand: "I joined the national rising from conviction."

He pushed the paper across the table. The president took it up, showed it in turn to his two colleagues sitting to the right and left, then looking fixedly at Prince Roman let it fall from his hand. And the silence remained unbroken until he spoke to the gendarmes ordering them to remove the prisoner.[47]

We are at one of those supreme moments of the romantic ego which fascinated Conrad. Conrad does not indicate the full moral import of the scene, but its power is nonetheless present through the employment of Conrad's best and most characteristic narra-

---

[46]  *Ibid.*, pp. 52-53.
[47]  *Ibid.*, p. 53.

tive manner. At least once then in this story, Conrad has broken through the surface compromise between his warring elements to give genuine merit to an important scene.

II

"Prince Roman" shows that Conrad, having completed the basic task of inner reconciliation, was ready to speak more openly of his father, a readiness quite different from his earlier shame and reticence about him. Conrad was also willing for the first time to reveal his alienation from his father that began at the time of Korzeniowski's death and to associate his own guilt over deserting Poland with his father. But not long after he expressed these sentiments in the autobiographical essay, "Poland Revisited" (1915), he dissipated that patriotic guilt by writing two essays in which he defended, by a series of dubious arguments based largely on the premises of romantic nationalism, Poland's right to independence and to the whole of her former territories in the East.

During most of his life Conrad had avoided speaking of his father. In private he let friends like Garnett and Ford know that he was embarrassed by his father's career. When Conrad provided information about himself for publication, he emphasized the influence of the Bobrowskis, often insisting on their patriotism, and presented only a few facts about his father. In a letter to Garnett in 1900 he makes a point of the patriotism of all the Bobrowskis – concealing, of course, the death of Stefan Bobrowski in a duel under the phrase, "died assassinated" – but says very little about his father.[48] In his letter to Kasimir Waliszewski in 1903,[49] Conrad carefully selects those facts about his father which will produce a favorable impression. First he mentions that his father was the son of a captain in the Polish army and had managed an estate. Conrad is, of course, emphasizing his father's connections with agriculture and military life, the two traditional and honorable occupations for a Polish gentleman. Of Apollo Korzeniowski's

---

[48]   *Garnett Letters* (Jan. 20, 1900), p. 166.
[49]   Letter (Dec. 5, 1903), Najder, p. 239.

literary career Conrad only mentions Buszczynski's biography, *A Forgotten Poet*. And of Apollo Korzeniowski's political carreer Conrad merely cites the facts of the move to Warsaw, his father's imprisonment, and their exile. Presumably a fellow Pole like Waliszewski would be able to supply a good deal of circumstantial information on the basis of these few facts, but except for saying that Korzeniowski's funeral was the occasion for a demonstration of university students, Conrad avoids discussing his father's politics. In this letter he is almost as evasive about his father as he is about his uncle Stefan, whom he refers to simply as "a well-known personality in 1863", but he speaks at length of Tadeusz Bobrowski. Similarly, in his early autobiographical writing, Conrad mentions his father briefly but not in connection with Polish patriotism. In *A Personal Record* he emphasizes the patriotic sacrifices of his mother and his maternal great uncle Nicholas Bobrowski, but describes his father only as introducing the child to literature. In these early statements, both public and private, Conrad also avoids saying anything which would reveal the differences between his father's family and his mother's family which his uncle had repeatedly pointed out to him.

After composing "Prince Roman", in which he made peace with his father's ideas, Conrad wrote much more freely about his father. Ultimately he was to form a highly idealized and uncritical image of him. Before that time, however, he wrote an essay which contains his first extended portrait of his father and admits to his own uneasy feelings about Poland. "Poland Revisited" (1915) holds a half-way position between his earlier embarrassment and reticence about his father and his later pride and defense of him. In this essay Conrad for the first time openly refers to his father's patriotism, which, of course, he presents favorably. Korzeniowski appears in his old age in Cracow, a dying man of great spiritual stature, almost a saint of patriotism. But for all his readiness to describe his father, Conrad avoids specific discussion of Korzeniowski's disastrous political career and of the degeneration of his religious faith into "mysticism touched with despair", the phrase with which in 1900 he had characterized for Garnett his father's religion after the death of his wife Evelina.

Despite the idealizing which is usually a sign of diminished literary power in Conrad, the essay also expresses Conrad's own uneasy guilt over his leaving of Poland. Thus his reaction to his father resembles his reaction to his patriotic great uncle Nicholas Bobrowski, recorded earlier in *A Personal Record*. What makes "Poland Revisited" significant is that in it for the first time Conrad associates his feelings for Poland with his father.

The essay suggests conflicts in Conrad's attitude toward his father and Poland at the time of Korzeniowski's death in 1869 and of Conrad's revisit to Poland in 1914. Conrad's text, in a very moving passage of about two pages,[50] concentrates on the eleven year old boy's fear that his lack of tears is interpreted by onlookers as a lack of grief. But he describes also his loss of religious faith and the strange refrain, "It's done", which rang in his head during his father's funeral procession. Thus Conrad suggests a grief and despair far deeper than the tears which might be expected from an orphan whose loss is being assuaged by the love and sympathy of relatives and friends and who is being assured by an entire city that his father had died nobly in a great cause which still unites the boy with all of his countrymen. The passage indicates that Conrad lost not only his father, but also, his religious faith and his trust in his country. When Korzeniowski died, Conrad says, "I don't think I found a single tear to shed. I have a suspicion that the Canon's housekeeper looked on me as the most callous little wretch on earth." Conrad may have associated the housekeeper's possible disapproval of him with the fact that a nun, one of his father's nurses, had thought the books he was reading unsuitable for a child. The long sickness and approaching death of his father had shaken the boy's religious faith. "I had also moments of revolt which stripped off me some of my simple trust in the government of the universe." Conrad's alienation from his father was not confined to the loss of faith and the fear that he appeared unfeeling to the Canon's housekeeper. He also felt alienated from the entire population of the town, in which Korzeniowski's funeral procession was a public event. The citizens of Cracow

---

[50] *Notes on Life and Letters*, pp. 168-69.

honored Korzeniowski's fidelity to the Polish cause. Conrad walked dry-eyed behind the hearse.

The day of the funeral came in due course and all the generous "Youth of the Schools", the grave Senate of the University, the delegations of the Trade-Guilds, might have obtained (if they cared) *de visu* evidence of the callousness of the little wretch.

Here he seems to fear that his lack of feeling was evident to the citizens, divided by class and occupation but united in loyalty to a patriotic creed "which the simplest heart in that crowd could feel and understand". The phrase "*de visu* evidence" suggests condemnation by a court of law, and the parenthetical modifier "if they cared" suggests further alienation. One sentence in this account of his father's funeral procession indicates that the death of the Messianic patriot may have been complexly associated in his son's mind with the Christian faith: "There was nothing in my aching head but a few words, some such stupid sentences as 'It's done', or, 'It's accomplished' (in Polish it is much shorter), or something of the sort, repeating itself endlessly." One suspects that the child was repeating the last words from the cross, It is finished, or, in Latin *Consummatus est*. Poland, father, and faith had become unreal to the child for whom they had made up an intensely demanding universe. The high literary quality of this passage comes from Conrad's presentation of the difference between the lonely child aware of his individuality, and the child's environment, made up of patriotism, "piety, resignation, and silence".[51]

There were limits, however, to how far Conrad could go in recalling and considering these memories with their heavy claims upon him. He emphasizes that the return to Cracow and his father's memory was a perilous journey:

I felt more and more plainly that what I had started on was a journey in time, into the past; a fearful enough prospect for the most consistent, but to him who had not known how to preserve against his impulses the order and continuity of his life – so that at times it presented itself to his conscience as a series of betrayals – still more dreadful.[52]

[51] *Ibid.*, p. 158.
[52] *Ibid.*, p. 149.

Note that in this passage Conrad moves protectively from the first to the third person (from "I" to "him") when he is about to take up one of the basic anxieties of his life. The idea of a journey into the past recalls the perilous journey in "Heart of Darkness", but the journey into time in this essay is incomplete. Conrad's return to his Polish past was interrupted by the outbreak of the First World War, and the need for action in the present cut short the private psychological exploration. The theme of the essay, that the demands of the present and fears for the future deny the claims of memory, accurately expresses what happened to Conrad. Undoubtedly Conrad invokes the dark journey into the past with such thoroughness because he was aware that it had not been completed. In "Poland Revisited" then, Conrad was willing to discuss his father to some extent, but in terms largely laudatory; with greater frankness he was willing to discuss his own conflicting feelings of alienation from his father and of guilt for having deserted Poland.

This guilt, which Conrad expiated by his service to Poland during World War I and its aftermath, was of long standing. His father had thoroughly indoctrinated him with the duty of "only to be a Pole". Although he left Poland, he knew that Poles wherever they find themselves must work for the good of the fatherland. The romantic poets he had read with his father as a child made it clear that the Pole in exile may, and indeed must, still serve his country. In *Anhelli*, Slowacki contrasted types of loyal and disloyal Polish exiles. Mickiewicz wrote *The Books of the Polish Nation* as a guide in faith and morals for the exiles. In *Pan Tadeusz* he had written:

The Pole, though famous among the nations because he loves his native land more than life, is nevertheless always prepared to abandon it, and to travel to the ends of the earth, to live long years in poverty and contempt, struggling with men and with fate – so long as amid the storm there shines upon him this hope, that he is serving the Fatherland.[53]

Not only was Conrad familiar with the duty of the exile to serve his fatherland from the works of the Polish romantics, but he heard the question of the exile's loyalty directly applied to him-

[53]   Mickiewicz, *Pan Tadeusz*, p. 256.

self. Even Tadeusz Bobrowski, who had little sympathy for the intensities of Messianic patriotism, when suggesting that his sailor nephew compose travel sketches for a Warsaw paper said: "It would be an exercise in your native tongue – that thread which binds you to your country and countrymen, and finally a tribute to the memory of your father who always wanted to and did serve his country by his pen." [54] On his honeymoon in 1896 Conrad had received a letter from his cousin Charles Zagorski which delicately opened the subject of the exile's loyalty.

We heard of your literary debut from Marguerite [Poradowska]. As I held your book in my hand, I felt so to speak, a double sadness: first, I was sorry not to be able to get to know the work of your mind, and then I regretted that as a result of the exceptional conditions of life your talent should be lost to our literature and become the fortune and heritage of foreigners, although they are not foreigners to you, since you have found among them the wife who loves you.[55]

Conrad accepted the reproach, for, when Zagorski died two years later, Conrad regretted that he would never be able "to confess to him my entire life and to be understood by him." [56] In 1899 the question of Conrad's service to Poland was publicly discussed. Three Polish literati debated in a Polish newspaper whether Joseph Conrad was serving the cause of Poland although established far from it, or whether, by leaving, he had betrayed the fatherland. The controversy disturbed Conrad deeply, and, it is speculated, resulted in part in the composition of *Lord Jim*.[57] Conrad's

---

[54]   Letter (June 10/28, 1881), Najder, pp. 71-72.
[55]   Letter (March 21, 1896), quoted by Aubry, *The Sea Dreamer*, p. 216.
[56]   Letter to Mrs. Aniela Zagorska (Feb. 6, 1898), Najder, p. 224. Translation mine from French.
[57]   Aubry, *The Sea Dreamer*, pp. 236-40. The first person to suggest that *Lord Jim* reflects Conrad's remorse over leaving Poland at a time of her misfortunes was the Polish novelist Maria Dabrowska in 1926 (*The Sea Dreamer*, p. 240). In 1930 Gustav Morf expanded the idea as a basis for his discussion of all of Conrad's work. Roman Dyboski repeated the idea of Conrad's patriotic remorse in his brief biography of Conrad included in *Great Men and Women of Poland*, ed. Stephen Mizwa (New York, Macmillan, 1942). In 1947 Jean-Aubry accepted it in his biography of Conrad. With Albert Guerard's discussion in 1958, the idea can be said to have received general acceptance among Conrad scholars and critics, most notably Jocelyn Baines in his biography. Leo Gurko, however, in his *Joseph*

disturbance at these charges is obviously reflected in a letter of 1901 to Joseph Korzeniowski, a Polish writer whose last name he shared.

And please let me add, dear Sir (for you may still be hearing this and that said of me), that I have in no way disavowed either my nationality or the name we share for the sake of success. It is widely known that I am a Pole and that Jozef Konrad are my two Christian names, the latter being used by me as a surname so that foreign mouths should not distort my real surname – a distortion which I cannot stand. It does not seem to me that I have been unfaithful to my country by having proved to the English that a gentleman from the Ukraine can be as good a sailor as they, and has something to tell them in their own language. I consider such recognition as I have won from this particular point of view, and offer it in silent homage where it is due.[58]

Conrad's defense of himself in *A Personal Record* against the charge of desertion and infidelity reflects most immediately the attack of 1899. When a Polish journalist interviewed Conrad early in 1914, Conrad again suggested that his success in two careers served the fatherland: "There are two personal things that fill me with pride – that I, as a Pole, am a captain in the British merchant marine and that I write English not too badly." [59] The force of the attack on his loyalty and his need to answer it lie in the fact that it was couched in terms of a national sentiment which had first been implanted in Conrad by his father, who had demonstrated his own fidelity.

Until the first World War, however, Conrad was unable to do anything directly in the service of his country. He had paid literary tribute in "Prince Roman", but the dominant mood of the story looks back from a hopeless present to a heroic time in which action was possible. He had met a young Pole, Joseph Retinger, one

*Conrad: Giant in Exile* (New York, Macmillan, 1962), asserts that the theory of guilt has validity in an imaginative sense only (pp. 15-18). But his superficial treatment of purely biographical material ignores the evidence that Conrad's guilt was personal as well.

[58]   Letter (Feb. 14, 1901), Najder, p. 234.

[59]   Maria Dabrowska, "A Polish Press Interview with Joseph Conrad", *Poland*, American edition (June, 1960), p. 27. (A complete translation of the text of an interview published in the *Tygodnik Ilustrowany*, 1914, No. 16.)

of the Poles in western Europe who was attempting to keep alive the Polish question, but before the war, which promised radical changes in Poland's status, Conrad pointed out to Retinger that he should not be so indignantly surprised at western Europe's lack of interest in the plight of Poland. Too many selfish national and international interests, Conrad insisted pessimistically, would be upset by a revival of the Polish question, and practical politicians refused to take the risk.[60]

At last, however, Conrad realized vividly that something effective might well be done for Poland, that he might discharge his old patriotic debt to his country. Persuaded by Retinger to visit Poland in the summer of 1914, Conrad saw at first hand the outbreak of the war and the terrible predicament of the Poles. They were caught in a war between the partitioning powers, and any military action – whether revolt or support of one of the powers against the others – would be to the advantage of one of their masters. In September, Conrad joined with Polish friends in Cracow to draft a "Political Memorandum".[61] Envisioning an early peace conference, Conrad pledges himself to encourage England to support Austria's liberal Polish policy. More important than the illogic of hoping England would support her enemy, Austria, rather than her ally, Russia, is the fervent tone of Conrad's promises to aid his fatherland. In less than two pages he repeats such expression as "my intentions are ... it would be my concern ... I am convinced ... basing myself on these two facts, I intend to point out...". Conrad, at last like all the faithful exiles since the partitions was trying to keep alive the Polish question.

As the war continued, the Allies began to discuss handing over to Russia all of Poland as spoils of war. Three facts supported their position: the coming defeat of Germany and Austria, the Polish revolt under Jozef Pilsudski against Russia, and Russia's position among the allies. But patriotic Poles in western Europe (like Paderewski in America) opposed this possibility. Influenced by Retinger and other members of the Polish committee in Lon-

[60] "The Crime of Partition", *Notes on Life and Letters*, p. 137.
[61] Najder, pp. 303-04.

don, Conrad composed in 1916 "A Note on the Polish Problem" for private circulation in the Foreign Office. The plans for Polish independence through an Anglo-Franco-Russian alliance were probably worked out by others, and the Note's obvious lack of an introduction suggests that it was accompanied by letters from the committee explaining the situation and plan in detail.

The text of Conrad's note reveals that in order to defend Poland's right to independence he had embraced the confusing mixture of ideas and feelings that constituted Polish nationalism. The Messianists' millenium is to be brought about by morally questionable methods; a realistic fear of Russia is coupled with an illogical hope that Russia would yield easily to Polish desires if supported by the sympathy of western Europe. As arguments supporting the plan, Conrad cites Poland's right to an independent existence and the value of a pro-Allied, pro-Western nation between "organized Germanism" and the "great might of Slavionism".[62] The exact role of Poland is not made clear, but its real function will affect "the stability of European peace".[63] Conrad's conviction that the resurrection of Poland would insure an era of international peace recalls the millenial prophecies of Polish Messianism. With a more personal conviction he expresses his strong doubts that Russia would ever respect any treaty committing her to guarantee Polish rights, once Poland was turned over to her. Illogically, he then argues that Russia could be persuaded to agree to Polish independence.

In reality Russia has ceased to care much for her Polish possessions. Public recognition of a mistake in political morality and a voluntary surrender of territory in the cause of European concord, cannot damage the prestige of a powerful State. The new spheres of expansion in regions more easily assimilable, will more than compensate Russia for the loss of territory on the Western frontier of the Empire.[64]

One may well question the political morality which suggests exchanging one area of imperial expansion for another in order to expiate a political crime.

[62] "A Note on the Polish Problem", *Notes on Life and Letters*, p. 137.
[63] *Ibid.*
[64] *Ibid.*, p. 139.

Although events quickly made this illogical note a mere historical curiosity and Conrad had presented some of its ideas more forcefully in "The Crime of Partition", Conrad was proud to publish it in *Notes on Life and Letters* (1921). In a single unapologetic paragraph, contrasting with the rest of the mediocre introduction, Conrad explains that he wrote the note out of sympathy with the hopes of his Polish friends and on the remote chance that an optimistic presentation of the plan might receive a respectful reading. His frank explanation is convincing. For reasons almost wholly extrinsic to its merit, Conrad was proud of this note. It was proof of his contribution to the Polish cause. In it he began to discharge his patriotic debt to Poland. He started to show that without any question a Pole may serve the fatherland wherever he has established himself.

Conrad reveals no embarrassment at taking part in political life. He has abandoned the principle behind his uncle's advice to find a profession rather than enter politics. Bobrowski had explained that not only was politics an unfortunate way of life, but that success as a creative writer prevented success in practical politics.[65] Conrad, early in his writing career, accepted this as accurate analysis of the shortcomings of the Korzeniowskis and as a valuable warning to himself. When Roger Casement, whom he had met in Africa, urged the author of "Heart of Darkness" to lend his support to an anti-imperialistic movement in 1903, Conrad refused. He wrote to Cunninghame Graham: "I would help him, but it is not in me. I am only a wretched novelist inventing wretched stories and not even up to that miserable game." [66] But by 1916 Conrad was happy to visit the foreign office to discuss the note on Poland. When he was leaving, the official said to him, "Well, I never thought I would have this sort of conversation with the author of *The Nigger of the 'Narcissus'*." [67] Conrad was pleased by the man's "sense of contrasts". Earlier he might have been disturbed. When Conrad's inner tension between father and uncle relaxed, he felt with much less force the applicability of his uncle's

[65]   Bobrowski, *Memoirs*, in Morf, p. 27.
[66]   Letter (Dec. 26, 1903), *Joseph Conrad, Life and Letters*, I, p. 325.
[67]   Letter to Christopher Sandeman (Aug. 20, 1916), *ibid.*, II, p. 174.

criticism of the Korzeniowski weaknesses; and these inner events coincided with the pressing opportunity to discharge his Polish debt and prove fidelity. Conrad spoke more frequently on political and patriotic matters. In 1919 the opportunity came again, and Conrad again defended his fatherland with arguments drawn from romantic Polish nationalism. Conrad feared that the Versailles conference, apparently about to invite "the mangy Russian dog" to participate, would force Poland into an inferior international position or would permanently limit its boundaries, especially in the East. A letter to Sir Hugh Clifford expresses his feelings with extreme fear and loathing.[68] The violence of his feelings caused him to make illogical statements. Bitterly complaining that British initiative was responsible for the inclusion of Russia at the peace table, he wrote: "The whole paltry transaction of conciliating mere crime for fear of obscure political consequences makes one sick." The sentences immediately following apparently are supposed to express Conrad's conviction that immoral practical compromise must be resisted. The language, however, suggests something else.

In a class contest there is no room for conciliation. The attacked class cannot save itself by throwing honesty, dignity and convictions overboard. The issue is simply life and death, and if anything can save the situation it is only ruthless courage.

It is difficult to say exactly what Conrad meant by a "class contest" although his dislike of communism could be behind this view of Russia at Versailles. The "honesty, dignity and convictions" to be preserved are evidently inherent in the attacked class, which is then free to defend itself by "ruthless courage" regardless of means. Conrad's published political writings differ only in degree from the violence of feeling and inconsistency in this letter.

Conrad's fears were excessive. Despite the efforts of Lloyd George and Woodrow Wilson, Russia had no official representatives at Versailles,[69] and the later Russo-Polish War rather than the Versailles deliberations decided the eastern boundary of Po-

---

[68]  Letter (Jan. 25, 1919), *ibid.*, II, pp. 216-18.
[69]  W. P. and Zelda Coates, *Six Centuries of Russo-Polish Relations* (London, Lawrence and Wishart, 1948), p. 94.

land. Nevertheless, January 1919 was a crucial moment for the reborn Poland. Hoping to influence British opinion, Conrad published on May 1, 1919 an essay, "The Crime of Partition", in which he vigorously defends the new Poland and her right to include all the territories of the old Royal Republic.

The text of the essay reveals how far Conrad had gone in accepting the theories of romantic nationalism. Discussing current problems in the terms of the mid-nineteenth century, he ignores or rejects all evidence not consistent with the tenets of Polish nationalism. By asserting the organic unity of all Poland, he denies the existence of non-Polish nationalism among minority groups. By idealizing the national past, he attributes anachronistic motives to the fourteenth-century union of Poland and Lithuania. By insisting on the central doctrine of Polish Messianism (that Poland died for the cause of universal liberty), he misinterprets eighteenth-century European history. Foreign as these ideas are to much of Conrad's earlier thinking, he has not in this essay wholly broken with some of his earlier ideas. He manages to harmonize this new commitment to romantic nationalism with his old disbelief in progress, and, by means of verbal hedging, he avoids literal commitment to the untenable belief in the permanence of the nation and its national spirit, an idea which, paradoxically, he had earlier expressed very enthusiastically.

The union of Poland proper with Lithuania and the Ruthenian provinces, where nationalism and even hostility to Poland had developed considerably in the previous century,[70] was for some directly opposed to the Wilsonian doctrine of self-determination and the ethnic state. And in actual fact Poland was soon to wage an aggressive war against Lithuania. But Conrad only reluctantly admits, "Charges of aggression are certain to be made, especially as related to the small states formed of the territories of the Old Republic." But he immediately dismisses the reality of charges inconsistent with his idealized view of Poland and his belief in the indissoluble organic union of the entire nation.

Already there are innuendoes, threats, hints thrown out, and even awful instances fabricated out of inadequate materials, but it is his-

[70]    Halecki, pp. 270-71, 282-84.

torically unthinkable that the Poland of the future, with its sacred tradition of freedom and its hereditary sense of respect for the rights of individuals and States, would seek its prosperity in aggressive action or in moral violence against that part of its once fellow citizens who are Ruthenians or Lithuanians.[71]

The second part of this last sentence is simply not true.

Using the familiar organic metaphor of romantic nationalism, Conrad celebrates the fourteenth-century Jagellonian Union which joined Poland to the Lithuanian and the Ruthenian lands as an "organic living thing capable of growth and development".[72] Once established, he insists, the Jagellonian Union remained firm.

Even after Poland lost its independence this alliance and this union remained firm in spirit and fidelity. All the national movements towards liberation were initiated in the name of the whole mass of people inhabiting the limits of the Old Republic.[73]

Like the romantic historians and poets of Poland, Conrad idealizes the national past. In describing the role of the masses he attributes what seem to be anachronistic motives to the Jagellonian Union.

The slowly-matured view of the economical and social necessities and, before all, the ripening moral sense of the masses were the motives that induced the forty-three representatives of Lithuanian and Ruthenian provinces, led by their paramount prince, to enter into a political combination unique in the history of the world, a spontaneous and complete union of sovereign States choosing deliberately the way of peace.[74]

The anachronism about "the ripening moral sense of the masses" may rise from Conrad's recollection of one of the favorite ideas of Joachim Lelewel, a friend of Mickiewicz and the romantic historian of Poland, whose histories for school children were widely read in Poland in the latter half of the nineteenth century. Liberty, equality, and fraternity, according to Lelewel, were not foreign

---

[71] "The Crime of Partition", *Notes on Life and Letters*, p. 133. Retinger points out that this essay is based on two of his own books which he published in France during the war (pp. 173-74).

[72] *Notes on Life and Letters*, p. 120.

[73] *Ibid.*, p. 121.

[74] *Notes on Life and Letters*, p. 120.

imports or recent developments but were treasures embedded deep
in the Polish national character. Lelewel further theorized about
the classless democracy of pre-Christian Poland about which, in
actual fact, very little is known.[75] Conrad's account here is vague
and extravagant. Any conventional brief account would include
the historical fact that the Jagellonian Union was accomplished
by a royal marriage uniting the Queen of Poland with the Grand
Duke of Lithuania. And the peaceful union of England and Scot-
land suggests that the union was not so "unique" as Conrad insists.

Conrad's concern for Polish rights in the East, the home for
many generations of the Korzeniowskis as well as the Bobrowskis,
recalls similar concerns of his father. In 1855, Apollo Korzeniowski tried to persuade the Poles to support the Ukranian peasants'
rebellion,[76] and later was active in fomenting demonstrations on
days celebrating the union of Poland and her eastern territories; [77]
and during his trial he was accused of writing a seditious pamphlet, *The Union of Poland and Lithuania*.[78]

Conrad's ideas concerning the perfect union of all peoples and
classes within the nation have much in common with the romantic
patriotism of other countries. But Conrad goes beyond this and
touches on national Messianism, the doctrine at the heart of Polish romantic nationalism. Like the Polish romantics, he works
through an interpretation of history. In the second half of the
eighteenth century, he says, Poland and France were the two
centers of liberal ideas on the continent. Russia and the two auto-
cratic powers of central Europe, Prussia and Austria, were forced
to choose which of these dangerous centers of forbidden ideas
they were to crush first. Russia, seeing also an opportunity for
westward expansion, led the way, and the others followed with
some reluctance in the partitioning of Poland.

The only States which dreaded the contamination of the new principles and had enough power to combat it were Prussia, Austria, and

---

[75] Ignacy Chrzanowski, "Joachim Lelewel", *Great Men and Women of
Poland*, p. 88.
[76] Aubry, *The Sea Dreamer*, p. 22.
[77] Baines, pp. 10-11.
[78] Aubry, *The Sea Dreamer*, p. 25.

Russia, and they had another centre of forbidden ideas to deal with in defenseless Poland, unprotected by nature, and offering an immediate satisfaction to their cupidity. They made their choice, and the untold sufferings of a nation which would not die was the price exacted by fate for the triumph of revolutionary ideals.

Thus even a crime may become a moral agent by the lapse of time and the course of history.[79]

In unmistakeable terms he says:

It may be truly said that the destruction of Poland secured the safety of the French Revolution. For when in 1795 the crime was consummated, the Revolution had turned the corner and was in a state to defend itself against the forces of reaction.[80]

This is, of course, Polish Messianism. The religious metaphor is absent – although we should notice the word *consummated* –, but the notion that Poland suffered and died politically that freedom might live elsewhere is an idea confined only to Poles and was a favorite one between the two insurrections. In this essay, for the first time Conrad defends the libertarian ideals of Polish nationalism. "Prince Roman", for example, had emphasized the aristocratic virtues of Polish patriotism. Here Conrad defends Polish nationalism largely as its adherents presented it, not as he had redefined it.

The facts hardly bear out this romantic patriotic interpretation imposed upon them. It is truer to say that the French Revolution secured the safety of the partitions of Poland, for the second and third partitions were undertaken by Russia only after she was sure that Prussia and Austria were so engaged with France that they must permit what a treaty with Poland bound them to prevent. Prussia and Austria consented to the final two partitionings only because they could not afford to go to war with Russia at a time when they were menaced by revolutionary France.[81] Conrad

---

[79] *Notes on Life and Letters*, pp. 117-18. Here, of course, I disagree with Mrs. Hay. She cites an analysis by two Polish scholars of Conrad's five reasons for Poland's right to exist and then comments: "Utterly lacking in Conrad's essays, however, is the romantic's generative myth for the rebirth of Poland" (p. 79).

[80] *Notes on Life and Letters*, p. 117.

[81] I am indebted to Mr. Gene Follis for this interpretation of the connection between the French Revolution and the last two partitions of Poland.

represents their actions as the result of Frederick of Prussia's delight in duplicity and betrayal, and Austria's inability to do otherwise. Conrad's view of the mutual benefits of the friendship between France and Poland is a characteristic Polish notion. Poles in the nineteenth century worshipped Napoleon and mistakenly trusted France to come to the aid of the insurrections. The notion that Poland and France were Europe's twin beacons of freedom and together would regenerate the world recalls the messianic expectation of Jules Michelet and Mickiewicz when they both lectured at the Collège de France in the 1840's.[82]

Although many of the ideas in this essay are inconsistent with Conrad's earlier pessimism and skepticism, he manages to harmonize his commitment to romantic nationalism with his earlier positions and, in one case, is able simply to apply to Poland an idea he had once used in praising Great Britain. Because the religious cast of Polish Messianism suggests divine intervention interrupting the processes of history, Conrad is able to evade the contradictions between his romantic nationalism and his disbelief in progress. The recent re-establishment of the Polish state Conrad calls a "miraculous rebirth".[83] The phrase is useful for Conrad. Although it represents his closest point of contact with Messianic doctrine, it allows him to escape commitment to another nineteenth-century idea which he had specifically rejected. Polish Messianism, in seeing ultimate benevolent purpose in history and in awaiting confidently a better future in which ideals will be realized, is related to the nineteenth-century faith in progress.[84] In "An Outpost of Progress", "Heart of Darkness", and *Nostromo*

[82] Kohn, *Prophets and Peoples*, p. 54. Victor Hugo, in 1846, also linked the two nations. "The French people", he said, were "civilization's missionary in Europe; the Polish people its knight". Quoted by Kohn, *Pan-Slavism: Its History and Ideology*, p. 30.

[83] *Notes on Life and Letters*, p. 129.

[84] "Messianism passed from Judaism into the thought of Western humanity. It accompanied the struggle of heretical sects and oppressed classes for the realization of their dreams and aspirations; it lent its form and symbols to the obscure longing of millions; it ended by being clothed in the garments of the philosophy of rationalism and modern science. As a secular idea of progress and of a new order, it dominates political and social aspirations today, deprived of its religious forms but retaining its religious fervor." Kohn, *The Idea of Nationalism*, p. 43.

Conrad had made it clear that he had no faith in inevitable beneficent progress (the belief that material progress brings spiritual
improvement) and that he entertained considerable skepticism
about man's ability to will a better future. In "Poland Revisted"
Conrad had pointed scornfully to the ugliness of steam cargo vessels and destructiveness of modern war as examples of progress.
"Miraculous rebirth" must mean then beneficent chance. Like
the word *sacred*, found often in his later works and in this essay
in the phrase "sacred tradition of freedom", the word *miraculous*
is a term of approbation, vaguely religious in connotation. Conrad's disbelief in progress and his quasi-Messianic patriotism meet
uneasily in a single passage.

Thus even a crime [the partitions] may become a moral agent by
the lapse of time and the course of history. Progress leaves its dead
by the way, for progress is only a great adventure as its leaders and
chiefs know very well in their hearts. It is a march into an undis-
covered country and in such an enterprise the victims do not count.[85]

The language of the passage recalls the fate of the infamous El-
dorado Exploring Expedition of "Heart of Darkness", and from
*Lord Jim* the sentence about stragglers from the ranks: "The
spirit of the land, as becomes the ruler of great enterprises, is careless of innumerable lives." [86] The drift in this passage seems to be
to disassociate "progress" from the idea that Poland's death
meant liberty's life in Europe, and associate it with the "emotional oratory of Freedom" elsewhere in Europe which offered nothing but words to Poland. The sentences on progress by means of
crime are followed immediately by this:

As an emotional outlet for the oratory of freedom it was convenient
enough to remember the Crime now and then: The Crime being the
murder of a State and the carving of its body into three pieces. There
was really nothing to do but to drop a few tears and a few flowers of
rhetoric upon the grave.[87]

Poland was a victim of progress, but refused to die completely. Its
refusal to die and its future resurrection are due to its own inner

---

85    *Notes on Life and Letters*, p. 118.
86    *Lord Jim*, p. 283.
87    *Notes on Life and Letters*, p. 118.

vitality almost in spite of the processes of world history. Thus
Conrad manages to reconcile opposites. By demonstrating that
what others have called progress is simply beneficent chance, he
reconciles his old skepticism with his new commitment to ideas
which always had a strong attraction for him and which now demanded his loyalty in unequivocal terms.

Elsewhere in the essay, Conrad again contrives to reconcile his
superficial skepticism with a tenet of romantic nationalism. In
admitting the possibility of Poland's ultimate disappearance at
one point in the essay, Conrad seems to deny one of the basic
beliefs of nationalism – the permanence of the nation, with its
pre-determined role in history and its character derived from pre-
historic times and carried biologically in the blood stream or
transcendentally in the "spirit" of the nation.[88] Conrad's apparent
denial, however, is merely a matter of intellectual caution, not a
genuine rejection. Furthermore, the permanence of the national
character is not one of the romantic doctrines to which he sur-
rendered only in his later years. He had earlier expressed it
unambiguously in reference to Great Britain, whose national history, despite imperialism, did not pose difficult problems for him.

The final section of *The Mirror of the Sea*, "The Heroic Age"
(1906), concludes with a highly rhetorical apostrophe to the
"national spirit, which, superior in its force and continuity to
good and evil fortune, can alone give us the feeling of an invinci-
ble power against the fates".[89] One suspects, however, that Conrad
did not in 1906 wholly believe his fulsome tributes to Britain, to
"The Faithful River", and to Lord Nelson. Rather he was af-
firming his loyalty to Britain and composing a piece for the Nelson
centennial. The final paragraph, praising the national spirit, is
even more romantic than Conrad's later Polish essays and contradicts the political skepticism of "Heart of Darkness" and
*Nostromo*.

Like a subtle and mysterious elixer poured into the perishable clay
of successive generations, it grows in truth, splendour, and potency
with the march of ages. In its incorruptible flow all round the globe

---

[88]  Kohn, *The Idea of Nationalism*, p. 13.
[89]  *The Mirror of the Sea*, p. 194.

of the earth it preserves from decay and forgetfulness of death the greatness of our great men, and amongst them the passionate and gentle greatness of Nelson, the nature of whose genius was, on the faith of a brave seaman and distinguished admiral, such as to "exalt the glory of our nation".[90]

Conrad here does not simply appeal to ideals with an heroic example from the national past. The national spirit is a beneficent reality, independent of the efforts of individuals, a bulwark against the particularly Conradian evil, "forgetfulness of death".

In "The Crime of Partition", however, Conrad accepts the idea of a permanent national character somewhat less lyrically.

Polish loyalty will be rooted in something much more solid and enduring, in something that could never be called eternal, but which is, in fact, life-enduring. It will be rooted in the national temperament, which is about the only thing on earth that can be trusted. Men may deteriorate, they may improve too, but they don't change. Misfortune is a hard school which may either mature or spoil a national character, but it may be reasonably advanced that the long course of adversity of the most cruel kind has not injured the fundamental characteristics of the Polish nation which has proved its vitality against the most demoralizing odds. The various phases of the Polish sense of self-preservation struggling amongst the menacing forces and the no less threatening chaos of the neighbouring Powers should be judged impartially.[91]

Conrad's rejection of "eternal" for "life-enduring" is a hedge by which he rejects the overtly religious basis and associations of nationalism. He accepts the existence of some permanent unchangeable reality at the base of the national character. To put faith in this idea, even with the metaphysics carefully excluded, is a mark of romantic nationalism.

"The Crime of Partition" was not the last public statement Conrad made for Poland. In 1920, he cabled a message for the use of a committee in Washington attempting to arrange a loan for the Polish government, which would finance the aggressive wars against Russia and Lithuania. The appeal to one democracy to aid

---

[90]  *Ibid.*
[91]  *Notes on Life and Letters*, p. 129.

another democracy in the name of common ideals may seem surprising from a man who for most of his life had disliked democracy. But a patriot devoted to the cause of Poland, as Mickiewicz had long ago pointed out, did not question the form of government in the newborn nation. Devotion trusted that the laws of the new nation would be just and perfect. The rhythm and rhetoric of this telegram are reminiscent, as Albert Guerard points out,[92] of the manifesto or proclamation. The first sentence runs:

For Poles the sense of duty and the imperishable feeling of nationality preserved in the hearts and defended by the hands of their immediate ancestors in open struggles against the might of three powers and in indomitable defense of crushing oppression for more than a hundred years is sufficient inducement to assist in reconstructing the independent dignity and usefulness of the reborn republic, investing generously in honour of the unconquered dead in testimony of their own national faith and for the peace and happiness of future generations.[93]

The impassioned rhetoric recalls Conrad's distrust of rhetoric in "Heart of Darkness", his skillful use of its characteristics for the corrupt judge's defense in "Prince Roman", and his ironic description of the decrees of confiscation of the San Tomé silver mine in *Nostromo*. The form of the telegram merely confirms Conrad's surrender to a deceitful rhetoric he had earlier distrusted.

Thus during World War I and its aftermath, Conrad discharged his patriotic debt to Poland by lending his support to her struggles for independence and for her former territories. He had at last fulfilled the demand which his father instilled into him. He was able to do so readily, not only because the demands of the political situation were urgent, but because, having made peace between the Korzeniowski and Bobrowski forces in his mind, he felt that the duty "only to be a Pole" perfectly agreed with the "duty according to circumstances and time". His enthusiastic espousal of romantic nationalism reveals how thorough was Conrad's inner reconciliation.

---

[92] Guerard, *Conrad the Novelist*, pp. 4-5.
[93] Telegram (April 26, 1920), *Joseph Conrad, Life and Letters*, II, p. 239.

### III

Although Conrad did not make national loyalty a major theme of his great fiction, he put into *Lord Jim* a brief but revealing passage about Jim's relation to his homeland.[94] We can better understand this passage after having studied Conrad's later reconciliation with romantic nationalism because in these pages of *Lord Jim* the ideas which Conrad presented more or less overtly in "Prince Roman" and his Polish essays operate as assumptions in the mind of Marlow. The later patriotic writings are thus related to *Lord Jim* in the same way that *The Shadow Line* is. Like *The Shadow Line*, they expound in clear, simple, and optimistic language, ideas which in *Lord Jim* exist in more complex, less optimistic form in the mind of the narrator. Moreover, comparing the style and tone of this passage with his later expressions of patriotism reveals his intellectual and artistic decline.

National loyalty is discussed in *Lord Jim* in a strange and beautiful passage of about three pages in which Marlow meditates on the meaning of the homeland and what it expects of those who wander from it. Marlow takes up several ideas familiar from romantic nationalism: a man although far from home must render an account of his doings to his native land; a nation has an eternal, unchangeable spirit which strengthens its people; a man draws his faith from his native land just as grass draws its life from the earth. Marlow, of course, does not insist that these are undoubted truths; he romantically invokes his feelings as proof of their reality, while showing his own skepticism. Not at all a digression, the passage is related directly to the heart of the book, because in it Marlow uses national sentiment as a means of exploring his relationship with Jim, and national loyalty as an introduction to the idea of the solidarity of mankind.

Marlow works into the subject gradually. He wants to see Jim, now successful in Patusan, once more before returning home – a reasonable desire in view of the distance between Britain and the East. Insightful about his motives in retrospect, he says:

---

[94]   *Lord Jim*, pp. 221-24.

I was about to go home for a time; and it may be I desired, more than I was aware myself, to dispose of him – to dispose of him, you understand – before I left. I was going home, and he had come to me from there, with his miserable trouble and his shadowy claim, like a man panting under a burden in a mist.

Out of Marlow's conventional fellow-feeling toward a countryman far from home grows another statement of the kinship between Jim and Marlow, of Marlow's troubled identification with Jim.

Moving fully into the subject of national loyalty, Marlow discusses both his own and Jim's relationship to their homeland:

And then, I repeat, I was going home – to that home distant enough for all its hearthstones to be like one hearthstone, by which the humblest of us has the right to sit. We wander in our thousands over the face of the earth, the illustrious and the obscure, earning beyond the seas our fame, our money, or only a crust of bread; but it seems to me that for each of us going home must be like going to render an account. We return to face our superiors, our kindred, our friends – those whom we obey, and those whom we love; but even they who have neither, the most free, lonely, irresponsible and bereft of ties, – even those for whom home holds no dear face, no familiar voice, – even they have to meet the spirit that dwells within the land, under its sky, in its air, in its valleys, and on its rises, in its fields, in its waters and its trees – a mute friend, judge, and inspirer. Say what you like, to get its joy, to breathe its peace, to face its truth, one must return with a clear consciousness.

Sensing that his audience may be unconvinced, Marlow says, "All of this may seem to you sheer sentimentalism", and he defends his idea of the nation inspiring and judging its sons. "Very few of us have the will or the capacity to look consciously under the surface of familiar emotions", he says and lists the familiar emotions: "The girls we love, the men we look up to, the tenderness, the friendships, the opportunities, the pleasures." He hints that behind these familiar emotions, and perhaps uniting them, is a large pervasive feeling for the homeland. At the least, he means that these familiar emotions and associations taken together make up the general sentiment for the native land. "But the fact remains", he says, still arguing against the charge of sheer sentimentalism, "that you must touch your reward with clean hands, lest it turn to dead leaves, to thorns, in your grasp". Twice he has asserted that the homeland demands a clear conscience, that a man with a bad conscience will feel the reality of its claims. His argument is romantic. National loyalty may be sheer sentimentalism when considered abstractly, but all of us feel its power.

The word *reward* serves as a pivot in the course of his argument. Earlier he had said that *even* those who do not return to claim a reward in the form of family, friends, and a place in an ordered society feel the claim of the spirit of the land as they experience the landscape. Now he specifically relates the people who are alone in life to the moral demands of the homeland.

I think it is the lonely, without a fireside or an affection they may call their own, those who return not to a dwelling but to the land itself, to meet its disembodied, eternal, and unchangeable spirit – it is those who understand best its severity, its saving power, the grace of its secular right to our fidelity, to our obedience.

This sentence unites the language and ideas underlying Conrad's two psychological antipathies: his uncle's concept of practical moral and professional duty and his father's concept of quasi-religious patriotic duty. Like the seaman's code of professional duty, the homeland serves the function of moral restraint. Not merely providing a set of ideals, the homeland also inspires people to live up to the ideals, for it commands "fidelity" and "obedience" and supplies a "saving power". Although nothing is said about the exile's service to the distant fatherland, the passage contains the language and sentiment of romantic nationalism. Conrad communicates the moral functions of the homeland through the religious metaphors from the literature of Polish Messianism: "saving power" and "grace" and "fidelity".

In the middle of the sentence, however, is the word "secular", a Conradian term always difficult to interpret. Since the spirit of the land is "eternal", the simple denotation of "secular" must be "lasting from age to age". But a complex of other contradictory meanings is also present. The word here connotes temporal, worldly, and non-religious, terms which thus qualify the romantic idea of the nation. Conrad is intellectually dishonest in "The Crime of Partition" where he replaces the untenable romantic epithet for the nation, "eternal", with the equivocal "life-enduring". In this sentence in *Lord Jim* where "secular" seems to replace "sacred" and "eternal", Marlow is neither dishonest nor even confused. Rather, he expresses his complex relationship to a sentiment whose objective reality cannot be proved, but whose existence seems, or at times he wants to seem, very real. At this point in these few pages Conrad's underlying anxieties about his Polish inheritance which produced the novel come to the surface.

Marlow argues with his hearers for the reality of national sentiment by asserting first the gulf between those who "feel" and those who do not.

Yes! few of us understand, but we all feel it though, and I say *all* without exception, because those who do not feel do not count. Each blade of grass has its spot on earth whence it draws its life, its strength; and so is man rooted to the land from which he draws his faith together with his life.

The metaphor of man as a natural growth rooted in his native landscape is familiar from romantic nationalism. Marlow does not so much assert a dubious fact of nature as he opposes the idea of Stein, who (in the previous chapter) had said of man: "Why should he run about here and there making a great noise about himself, talking about the stars, disturbing blades of grass?" In Stein's view, man contrasts with "Nature – the balance of colossal forces. Every star is so – and every blade of grass stands *so* – and the mighty Kosmos in perfect equilibrium produces – this." [95] "This magnificent butterfly finds a little heap of dirt and sits still on it; but man he will never on his heap of mud keep still." [96] To a man of the spiritual and moral stature of Jim, Marlow, or Stein, there is no real choice between sitting contentedly without illusions or ideals on a "heap of dirt" and submitting to the destructive element – attempting to live up to one's conception of oneself. Only reprehensible, "realistic" characters like the opportunist Chester advise being satisfied with the "heap of dirt". Marlow, however, seeks in the homeland a refuge or source of identification more sure than Stein's destructive element, the egoistic dream of greatness.

[95] *Ibid.*, p. 208.
[96] *Ibid.*, p. 213.

Without notice, Marlow shifts characteristically from himself to Jim in connection with the same problem, but he is still concerned with the reality of national sentiment.

> I don't know how much Jim understood; but I know he felt confusedly but powerfully, the demands of some such truth or some such illusion – I don't care how you call it, there is so little difference, and the difference means so little. The thing is that in virtue of his feeling he mattered. He would never go home now.

At the suggestion he return home, Marlow explains, Jim seemed to imagine something "unbearable ... revolting". Even not being able to return to the home he had betrayed had its value. Jim "mattered" because he felt he could not go back. Marlow emphasizes the impossibility of Jim's ever returning to *England*, rather than simply to his own home.

Marlow ends the meditation as he began it: by alluding to his own return home. In contrast to what he has just implied, he now rejects any connection between his returning to England and his responsibility for Jim.

> ... I do not mean to imply that I figure to myself the spirit of the land uprising above the white cliffs of Dover, to ask me what I – returning with no bones broken, so to speak – had done with my very young brother.

The reader might expect that Marlow will reject this vague and preposterous image in favor of a more subtle or realistic statement of how the spirit of the land demands to know if Marlow has truly been his brother's keeper. But Marlow's line of argument is different because he is beginning to move away from the subject of national sentiment which up to this point he has been defending so intensely. No one, he says, would inquire after Jim nor will Marlow actually feel that he has to account for Jim. He relates to the spirit of the land the probable lack of inquiry about Jim.

> The spirit of the land, as becomes the ruler of great enterprises, is careless of innumerable lives. Woe to the stragglers! We exist only in so far as we hang together. He had straggled in a way; he had not hung on; but he was aware of it with an intensity that made him touching.

By the end of this section, Marlow moves away from the idea that
he and Jim are bound to one another because they are brothers
from the same native land and even abandons the notion that it is
common nationality that requires and sanctions his intense interest in Jim. Their native land is not interested in stragglers. For
the moment he modestly asserts his interest in Jim as an unexceptional emotional reaction to youth in distress and a perfectly
conventional kindness: "I happened to be handy, and I happened
to be touched. That's all there is to it. I was concerned as to the
way he would go out." Marlow briefly insists on the casualness of
his interest. But as he continues he again reveals his deeper involvement. His argument turns from the nation, whose claims he
feels and which seems to be the largest loyalty Jim can recognize,
to his own profounder idea of the solidarity of mankind.

> It would have hurt me if, for instance, he had taken to drink ...
> You know the awful jaunty bearing of the scarecrows coming to you
> from a decent past, the rasping careless voice, the half-adverted im-
> pudent glances – those meetings more trying to a man who believes
> in the solidarity of our lives than the sight of an impenitent deathbed
> to a priest.

Conrad has had Marlow employ the loyalties and human relationships of romantic nationalism as a way of exploring the meaning
of Jim's betrayal on the *Patna* and the relationship between the
two men. Like the consideration of the missing bond of profession,
Marlow's meditation on the bond of the homeland adds emotional
intensity to the novel. Although romantic nationalistic sentiments
are finally abandoned in most particulars, they remain one of
Marlow's attempts to get at the meaning of Jim and of their relationship, and as an ideal neither wholly real nor wholly illusory.

Conrad's concept of the solidarity of mankind, the moral community, probably stems from his insight into his father's national
faith. Like partitioned Poland, the moral community has no real
existence or future except that which human faith and will can
give it. Poland in the last century was somewhere between a truth
and an illusion, and when "understood" by foreign observers
often appeared no more than "sheer sentimentalism". Poles who
cooperated with the partitioning powers at home or lived com-

fortably abroad ignoring their country's fate were obviously more in touch with reality than their compatriots who continued to believe and struggle. Thus the patriots felt contempt for those indifferent Poles who undermined their faith. Mickiewicz or Conrad's father, whose poetry romantically divides mankind into "men of feeling" and "swine",[97] might well have asserted like Marlow, "Those who do not feel do not count."

This passage is superior to Conrad's other evocations of the national spirit. In *The Mirror of the Sea*, the prose is oratorical, confident, and unconvincing. In the patriotic essays, of course, Conrad simply asserts the truth of the ideas of romantic nationalism. In "Prince Roman", the narrator approaches something like Marlow's involvement with the sentiment of loyalty to the nation, but the connection between the Polish narrator and the hero, a man who is tempted to betray his country, is not very clear, and the perfect simplicity of Prince Roman excludes very much examination of his loyalty. The narrator and his friends argue with some convincing emotion, but their vehemence occasionally suggests Conrad's private disbelief or indifference. In *Lord Jim*, however, Conrad impresses the reader with the passion of Marlow's arguments in favor of a source of moral strength and the meaning of life, arguments which he carries on against his own innate skepticism as well as his listeners' doubts. In *Lord Jim* the truth or falsity of the claims of romantic nationalism are largely bypassed. Conrad uses these claims to reveal matters both more individual and more universal than the nation. The great strength of *Lord Jim* lies in the fact that Conrad was able to transform his personal guilt about deserting Poland into a universal moral problem.

## IV

In 1919 Conrad finally ended his long silence about his father. The same year in which, with "The Crime of Partition" he embraced Polish nationalism without reservation, he also made an

---

[97]   Hay, p. 39.

open and direct defense of Apollo Korzeniowski. Conrad had fulfilled the debt, which, long ago, when his father lay dying, he had tried to renounce. In his Author's Note for the re-issue of *A Personal Record*, from whose pages Korzeniowski is largely absent, Conrad alters his father's character so that his revolutionary characteristics disappear, leaving only his patriotic faith; and the differences between Apollo Korzeniowski and Tadeusz Bobrowski become distinctions between Poles and their enemies. Furthermore, he attempts to show that his uncle had made an innocent mistake in criticizing his father. But he says much of this in such pompous and repetitious language that one suspects that he had not altogether freed himself from his embarrassment about his father's career nor wholly believed what he was saying.

Korzeniowski, as Conrad presents him in the Author's Note, is different from the man one finds in the critical remarks of Bobrowski and in his own correspondence. Conrad selects and interprets facts in order to harmonize the conflicts in his own mind over his father's career. Denying Apollo Korzeniowski's political and social liberalism, which made him part of a contentious and violent faction within Poland, Conrad insists that his father was not a "revolutionist" but a patriot, devoted to the spirit of his nation.

One of the most sympathetic of my critics tried to account for certain characteristics of my work by the fact of my being, in his own words, "the son of a revolutionist". No epithet could be more inapplicable to a man with such a strong sense of responsibility in the region of ideas and action and so indifferent to the promptings of personal ambition as my father. Why the description "revolutionary" should have been applied all through Europe to the Polish risings of 1831 and 1863 I really cannot understand. These risings were pure revolts against foreign domination. The Russians themselves called them "rebellions", which, from their point of view, was the exact truth. Amongst the men concerned in the preliminaries of the 1863 movement my father was no more revolutionary than the others, in the sense of working for the subversion of any social or political scheme of existence. He was simply a patriot in the sense of a man who believing in the spirituality of a national existence could not bear to see that spirit enslaved.[98]

[98] *A Personal Record*, pp. vii-viii.

The paragraph simply juggles words. With semantic naiveté, Conrad discusses his father's life in terms of the mutually exclusive categories of "revolution", "rising", "rebellion", and "patriot". Conrad evidently was not psychologically prepared to make a more convincing case by pointing out the distinctions between individual revolutionists or the contrasts between revolutionary patriotism of the early nineteenth century and the later international anarchist, socialist, and communist movements. For Conrad the word *revolutionist* denominates an evil category which by definition includes total irresponsibility and selfish ambition. If his father was to receive his full approval – the only kind of approval which Conrad could award to matters of great importance to himself in his later years – Apollo Korzeniowski must be removed from that category.

The remainder of the discussion of Korzeniowski completes this austere official portrait. He mentions the public funeral attended by thousands who wished to pay tribute "not to the man but to the Idea".[99] For Conrad, of course, the "Idea" was an ideal commanding men's loyalty without ministering to their egoism. Like Prince Roman, Apollo Korzeniowski is praised both as an individual and the follower of an impeccable cause. Conrad also mentions Korzeniowski's recently revived fame as a translator of "Shakespeare, Victor Hugo, and Alfred de Vigny, to whose drama *Chatterton*, translated by himself, he had written an eloquent preface defending the poet's deep humanity and his ideal of noble stoicism".[100] The preface to *Chatterton*, from which Conrad perhaps derived his defense of his father as a patriot and not a revolutionist, is here alluded to simply to associate Korzeniowski with rational austerity. Conrad avoids referring to his father's self-defense perhaps because the mere existence of such argument suggests that there was some truth to the charge of social revolutionary sentiments. Throughout this Author's Note, Conrad majestically, diplomatically, and graciously clarifies and explains. Real debates do no exist, even those long ago between his father and his critics.

---

[99]   *Ibid.*, p. viii.
[100]   *Ibid.*, p. ix.

All this might answer those friendly contemporary critics who had found hereditary revolutionary elements in Conrad's writing, but Conrad was not satisfied until he had also closed the basic division in his nature caused by the opposition of his father and his uncle. His method is devious. Just before his elaborate explanation that his father was not a revolutionist, Conrad politely discounts attempts to find Slavic elements in his writing. First he asserts Poland's affinity with Italy and France and then contrasts Polish and, by implication, Russian views of society.

An impartial view of humanity with a special regard for the rights of the unprivileged of this earth, not on any mystic ground but on the ground of simple fellowship and honorable reciprocity of services was the dominant characteristic of the mental and moral atmosphere of the houses which sheltered my hazardous childhood: − matters of calm and deep conviction both lasting and consistent, and removed as far as possible from that humanitarianism that seems to be merely a matter of crazy nerves or a morbid conscience.[101]

One of those "houses which sheltered my hazardous childhood" was, of course, Tadeusz Bobrowski's estate, and the paragraph sums up his social views and, one might surmise, his practice as a landlord. He supported serf emancipation, seeing it as a necessary first step in a general reform of the state.[102]

Conrad's diction in this passage reveals assumptions behind his portrayal of the Polish social idea exemplified by his uncle. "Unprivileged" is a Conradian term substituting for the customary humanitarian term "under-privileged". The change of prefix and the addition of "the rights of the unprivileged" evokes a stable and happy society with well-defined classes. Conrad's dislike of Tolstoy lurks in the background of these remarks. The terms, "mystic ground", "crazy nerves", and "morbid conscience" make up a Slavic Russian figure on which Conrad concentrates his scornful rejection of social reform and humanitarianism. He is, as Gustave Morf points out, portraying revolutionists and reformers as so wholly reprehensible as to prove that his father was

---

[101]  *Ibid.*, p. vii.
[102]  Letter to Mrs. John Galsworthy (Nov. 2, 1905), *Joseph Conrad, Life and Letters*, II, p. 28.

not one of them.[103] The figure of Tadeusz Bobrowski is not called up here in his usual position of contrast with Apollo Korzeniowski, but in contrast with morbid Slavic humanitarianism. As in "Prince Roman", an internal disagreement in Poland is treated as a hostile foreign criticism of an all Polish virtue.

Although Conrad has suggested that Apollo Korzeniowski and Tadeusz Bobrowski were very much alike, largely for the benefit of friendly English and American critics unfamiliar with Polish history or his father's biography, he had not yet solved the remaining problem of his uncle's overt criticism of his father. Conrad found a release from his dilemma in some books recently published in Poland. In fact, he says, these books permitted the idealized portrait of his father to be made public in this Note.

The political side of his life was being recalled too; for some men of his time, his co-workers in the task of keeping the national spirit firm in the hope of an independent future, had been in their old age publishing their memoirs, where the part he played was for the first time publicly disclosed to the world. I learned then of things in his life I never knew before, things which outside the group of the initiated could have been known by no living being except my mother. It was thus from a volume of posthumous memoirs dealing with those bitter years I learned the fact that the first inception of the secret National Committee intended primarily to organize moral resistance to the augmented pressure of Russianism arose on my father's initiative, and that its first meetings were held in our Warsaw house. . . .[104]

Those recently published memoirs demonstrate to Conrad's satisfaction, or are made to demonstrate, that Tadeusz Bobrowski had been mistaken about his brother-in-law's political activities, but that because of the necessary secrecy surrounding all patriotic activities during a time of oppression, he could not be blamed for this honest mistake. Apollo Korzeniowski was not planning armed resistance; he was planning purely moral resistance. The redundant insistence in phrases like "publicly disclosed to the whole world", "things I never knew before", and "to no living being except my mother" suggest that Conrad had not altogether convinced himself by his ingenious reasoning. Not only does Conrad

103 Morf, pp. 39-40.
104 *A Personal Record*, pp. ix-x.

embrace and accept both father and uncle in this note, but his description of his father's real activities among that "group of the initiated" that excluded Bobrowski recalls Bobrowski's own analysis of the plight of Poland struggling to keep her identity in the years after 1863. Both the refashioned Korzeniowski of this note and the real Bobrowski agreed about the importance of keeping the sense of national individuality alive until independence should be possible at some undetermined date in the future.

Conrad's long silence about his father proved useful. Having never committed himself to criticism of Apollo Korzeniowski except for, apparently, a few guarded remarks to Ford, Garnett, and Retinger, he was able without publicly contradicting himself to present his father in a way consonant with the peaceful and undisturbed maturity he now saw as his own nature. This Author's Note finally concludes Conrad's disturbing but productive sense of his relationship to his father and his uncle. His critical disapproval of his father's romanticism coupled with his awareness of its psychological pull was fruitful for literature. Even the early stages of his acceptance of romanticism during which he remained partially aware of its dangers were still potentially productive. But after he had fully accepted his father and discharged his debt to his fatherland, he had lost that inner tension responsible for his creativity. He could write little more than poor imitations of his best work and unconvincing sentimental stories, or could grope toward new basic concerns in areas formerly peripheral.

This Author's Note closes with a sentence both defensive and sentimental in which mother, father, and uncle are put beyond analysis or criticism.

And now, having been again evoked in answer to the words of a friendly critic, these Shades may be allowed to return to their place of rest where their forms in life linger yet, dim yet poignant, and awaiting the moment when their haunting reality, their last trace on earth, shall pass for ever with me out of the world.[105]

Kurtz too in "Heart of Darkness" was a shade of "haunting reality", but his importance was not asserted to be of a wholly private, sentimentally indulgent nature.

[105]  *Ibid.*, p. x.

IV

## THE OLD MAN OF THE SEA

When the tension in Conrad's mind between Apollo Korzeniowski and Tadeusz Bobrowski relaxed and when Conrad felt that he had discharged his patriotic debt to Poland, his attitudes underwent profound changes damaging to his artistry. Conrad lost, for the most part, that productive balance of contrary attractions. The old fruitful conflict between drives and controls, between sympathy and judgment, was replaced by a sterile opposition between conscious, often forced, attitudes and unconscious disbelief or indifference. His concern with moral responsibility was superseded by excuses and forgiveness. The later Conrad explains tolerantly in the Author's Note to *Chance*, "And it is only for their intentions that men can be held responsible. The ultimate effects of whatever they do are far beyond their control." [1]

Conrad's inner reconciliation and, later, his sense that he had paid his patriotic debt to Poland were accompanied by changes in his personality which the conditions of his life, after the popularity of *Chance* in 1913, increasingly fostered. Encouraged by his belated popularity and, later, by the patriotic demands of World War I, Conrad began to think of himself no longer as a craftsman skeptical of popular taste and popular values but rather in the public role of a skillful literary entertainer and old seaman-patriot. Identifying himself with his public, he tolerantly rejoiced, he said, in the intellectual limitations he shared with his readers; he insisted that he accepted their conventional values; and he assured them that he never offended against the scruples of literary gentility. Especially anxious to be accepted as an expert seaman and

[1] *Chance*, p. x.

patriot, he defensively asserted his authority about sea life, often when he was only partially acquainted with his subject. The picture of sea life which he presented in these later sea essays, many of which praise the British merchant fleet for their wartime service, differs considerably from his earlier views; he invariably insists on the unquestioned virtues of seamen, sentimentalizing his earlier realistic conception of their weaknesses as well as their strengths.

The essentially virtuous seamen of his later novels no longer need their profession as a bulwark against evil. Similarly, Conrad no longer needs his own professional technique to explore complex moral and psychological issues. In *Chance* and two short stories written at the same time, Conrad displays his technique ostentiously but irrelevantly, merely to celebrate the virtues of seamen and deprecate the vices of shore people. In his last novels, the reconciliation of the Korzeniowski and Bobrowski heritages and his acceptance of romantic nationalism had more damaging results.

The heroes, all self-portraits to some degree, lack genuine inner conflict and too obviously represent Conrad's conception of himself as though his own inner struggles had never existed or had been of little importance. The hero of *The Arrow of Gold* has almost no character at all; the hero of *The Rover* is obviously a facile self-justification of Conrad's desertion of his fatherland; and the hero of *Suspense* represents an easy compromise of both heritages. The political material in these novels, like the political ideas of the Polish essays, is highly simplified; and it is, moreover, badly integrated with the heroes' lives and characters. The concept of profession and the spiritual father, once a check in Conrad's mind against political folly, are reduced in *The Arrow of Gold* to mere picturesque decorations, and in *The Rover* they are too easily harmonized with and made subservient to political ends. Only in the fragment *Suspense*, which portrays more genuine political conflict than the others, are the spiritual father and politics united convincingly in a single character. The figure of the spiritual father especially is invoked in a strange and beautiful symbolic passage.

I

The popularity of his books, beginning with *Chance* in 1913, greatly affected Conrad's conception of himself by making of him a public figure. He had always agreed with Henry James about the ills of newspapers, but he rarely before had faced reporters flattering him with a request for an interview. He had once even refused to have his picture taken for advertisements of his work and obstinately declined to see visitors. But increasingly after 1910, he held open house to a procession of admirers, for the most part of much lower intellectual and literary stature than the group which earlier gathered about him. In his earlier days Conrad had enjoyed associating his skeptical view of democracy with a disdain for popularity. But when the reading public of two large democracies clamored for his works, he found withdrawal impossible and realized only too well that the sensitive coterie had not supported him financially. His popularity forced him into a relationship with his vast reading public.

He attempted to fashion a new opinion of the public which he formerly deprecated sardonically, but he succeeded only in debasing his old belief in the solidarity of mankind. Increasingly after 1913 he celebrated the values and attainments of ordinary people. Undoubtedly the men on the *Narcissus*, in the book which most fully dramatizes the older ideal, were not of exceptional intelligence, but Conrad did not need to raise the issue there. However, when Conrad came to consider the solidarity of his readers, the issue of intelligence became rather important. Especially was it important when he considered that he had been misunderstood for years. He solved the problem by deciding that intelligence was of little account. In "Geography and Some Explorers", he rejoiced in the stupidity he shared with the majority of mankind. The essay opens inauspiciously:

It is safe to say that for the majority of mankind the superiority of geography over geometry lies in the appeal of its figures. It may be an effect of the incorrigible frivolity inherent in human nature, but most of us will agree that a map is more fascinating to look at than a figure in a treatise on conic sections – at any rate for the simple minds which are all the equipment of the majority of the dwellers on this earth.[2]

This cheap, good-natured appeal to his readers in no way adequately introduces the account of some of his major interests and adventures. He firmly believed that limited intelligence was adequate and that what lay outside its range was probably false. In his later essays he often contrasted simple beliefs and feelings with "subtle dialectics" which invariably try to destroy ideals and the basis for moral action.[3] Leonardo Da Vinci's idea of the necessity of work "has a simplicity and a truth which no amount of subtle comment can destroy".[4] The simplicity of an idea usually guaranteed its truth and value. His praise of simple steadfast seamen like Singleton and MacWhirr had hardened into anti-intellectualism.

In *Victory* (1914) and *The Rover* (1922) Conrad dramatized his anti-intellectualism. The incisive skeptical intelligence of Axel Heyst destroys all values and sympathies until he learns, although too late, about life's true values from a simple girl. The contrast between Heyst and Lena unintentionally parodies the familiar opposition between discursive reason and intuition. The romantic who emphasizes feeling, intuition, and faith usually assumes that these are the primary qualities of a rich and intelligent sensibility receptive to widely varied experiences. Lena's faith is the residue of brief childhood attendance at a dissenters' Sunday School, and her intuition is only the woman's intuition of a mind ordinary to begin with and dulled by misfortune. In his short story of 1902, "Amy Foster", Conrad had more plausibly shown the limitations of a warm-hearted but stupid woman facing the unfamiliar.

In the love plot of *The Rover* Conrad repeats the same situation. Lieutenant Réal, a pessimistic rationalist, is converted to life by his love for a girl in a state of total shock. Conrad had once realized the dangers of an attraction to the stupid ("A Smile of Fortune") and had shown that although pity and love are often confused, they are contrary emotions. But when his desire to iden-

---

[2]  *Last Essays*, p. 1.
[3]  "Well Done", *Notes on Life and Letters*, p. 183.
[4]  "Tradition", *ibid.*, p. 194.

tify himself with ordinary humanity grew strong, what had once been, in *Lord Jim* and "Heart of Darkness", an intelligent skepticism about the limits of rationality now became anti-intellectualism. He lost a fruitful area of fictional exploration by exaggerating and making rigid an attitude.

Not only did the older Conrad glory in mental mediocrity, but he also liked to emphasize that he shared his readers' conventional values. The Author's Note to *Chance* (1920) explains that its popularity justified his belief in the solidarity of mankind.

> The general public responded largely, more largely perhaps than to any other book of mine, in the only way the general public can respond, that is by buying a certain number of copies. This gave me a considerable amount of pleasure, because what I always feared most was drifting unconsciously into the position of a writer for a limited coterie; a position which would have been odious to me as throwing a doubt on the soundness of my belief in the solidarity of all mankind in simple ideas and in sincere emotions. Regarded as a manifestation of criticism (for it would be outrageous to deny to the general public the possession of a critical mind) the reception was very satisfactory. I saw that I had managed to please a certain number of minds busy attending to their own very real affairs.[5]

One would hardly think that this was written by the same man who resisted Fisher Unwin's attempt to interest him in writing for a popular market and who often damned the imperceptive reading public and who once declared that he was satisfied in obtaining the appreciation of a few elite spirits.[6] Moreover, Conrad here essentially equates a big sale with literary value. His satisfaction that busy people had favored his books with their valuable time is merely pathetic. And his pose of reluctant frankness about the money the book earned hardly covers his embarrassment. He then explains that although the book has no moral purpose, the morality inherent in the book is purely conventional.

> It may have happened to me to sin against taste now and then, but apparently I have never sinned against the basic feelings and elementary convictions which make life possible to the mass of mankind

---

[5] *Chance*, pp. x-xi.
[6] Letter to the Baroness de Brunnow (Feb. 10, 1897), *Lettres Françaises*, p. 32.

and, by establishing a standard of judgment, set their idealism free to look for plainer ways, for higher feelings, for deeper purposes.[7]

Conrad speaks rather generally here, but one suspects that "Heart of Darkness" does sin against these basic feelings and elementary convictions. The statement reveals that by 1920 Conrad had cut himself off from any further analysis of the place of illusion in life and that he considered his books harmless entertainment. At the most he claims for himself the social function of a Tennyson or Longfellow, confirming the public in their common values and optimism while vaguely encouraging morality and progress.

Despite confessing occasional sins against taste in this Author's Note, Conrad throughout his other Author's Notes (written between 1917 and 1920) defends himself anxiously to his large body of readers against charges of coarseness, brutality, or cynicism in his early work. "My intention in writing 'Falk' was not to shock anybody." [8] Disturbed that a lady had found *Lord Jim* "morbid", Conrad insisted that Jim "is not the product of coldly perverted thinking".[9] Of the anarchists in *Under Western Eyes* he wrote: "Nobody is exhibited as a monster here", but lest anyone in 1920 think he had gone soft on Russian revolutionists, he added that two of them in his novel are "the apes of a sinister jungle".[10] After describing Nostromo as free "from his class-conventions and all settled modes of thinking", Conrad had to defend himself immediately: "This is not a side snarl at conventions." [11] He confessed that he had been considerably abused for the gratuitous cruelty of "Freya of the Seven Isles", and evidently the result of this criticism was that Freya became a story "which I cannot recall and would not recall if I could".[12] He took special pains to point out that the charge of "false realism" in "The Planter of Malata" was not justified. "The distinguished critic was accusing me simply of having sought to evade a happy ending out of a sort

---

[7]  *Chance*, p. xii.
[8]  *Typhoon and Other Stories*, p. vii.
[9]  *Lord Jim*, p. ix.
[10]  *Under Western Eyes*, p. ix.
[11]  *Nostromo*, p. xxi.
[12]  *'Twixt Land and Sea*, p. x.

of moral cowardice, lest I should be condemned as a superficially sentimental person." [13] Conrad reveals considerable relief at finding that this charge comes out of a misunderstanding of the characters. His defense of himself goes so far that he even abandons his favorite idea that fiction must contain truth and says evasively that the primary intention of this story was "mainly aesthetic; an essay in description and narrative around a given psychological situation".

Of all his books *The Secret Agent* brought forth the most elaborate defense against "false realism".

I have always had a propensity to justify my action. Not to defend. To justify. Not to insist that I was right but simply to explain that there was no perverse intention, no secret scorn for the natural sensibilities of mankind at the bottom of my impulses.[14]

Admitting that the world may not be interested in his motives, however guileless, and that in writing the book he was "under no necessity to deal with that subject", he nevertheless continues his extensive justification:

But the thought of elaborating mere ugliness in order to shock, or even to surprise my readers by a change of front has never entered my head. In making this statement I expect to be believed, not only on the evidence of my general character but also for the reason, which anybody can see, that the whole treatment of the tale, its inspiring indignation and underlying pity and contempt, prove my detachment from the squalor and sordidness which lie simply in the outward circumstances of the setting.[15]

These defenses of his work are largely true, and possibly Conrad had to distinguish himself from the esthetic decadents who confused his concern about moral evil with their obsession with the black arts,[16] and perhaps also from the naturalists who seemed to glory in the squalor of their material and the toughness of their attitudes. Had he been such a naturalist Doubleday would not have become his American publisher, for Mrs. Doubleday, the "Flor-

---

[13]   *Ibid.*, p. vii.
[14]   *Ibid.*, p. viii.
[15]   *Ibid.*
[16]   Arthur Symons, *Notes on Joseph Conrad* (London, Myers, 1925), pp. 7-8.

ence" of Conrad's letters, had suppressed *Sister Carrie*. In an age when the confident spokesmen of a genteel literary public were quick to strike out against any work of literature which seemed "strong" or indecent, Conrad may be justified in protecting himself against charges throwing a false emphasis on his books. But he was not always obsessed with the essential gentility of his work. In 1895 he wrote for his first novel a preface which attacks genteel feminine disapproval of the harsh, unpleasant, and "decivilized" material which he wrote about in *Almayer's Folly*. He contrasts the "common mortals" throughout the world about whom he writes and with whom he sympathizes with "the charming and graceful phantoms that move about in our mud and smoke and are softly luminous with the radiance of all our virtues; that are possessed of all refinements, of all sensibilities, of all wisdom – but, being only phantoms, possess no heart".[17] Undoubtedly when in his later Author's Notes he asserted that his works did not offend the conventions of ordinary humanity, he thought he was again identifying himself with "common mortals". But the emphasis on the inoffensive quality of his works betrays only his desire to be accepted by his middle-class readers. In 1897 he warned a friend that his mother might find *The Nigger of the 'Narcissus'* too frank in language,[18] and he complained to Garnett that his squeamish publisher had insisted that he remove the *bloody*'s from the text.[19]

Conrad was never important in the revolt against Victorian inhibitions, but when, late in his career, he introduced his work to the public, he hastened eagerly to assure them that he had never criticized a restrictive social code. Furthermore, in these Author's Notes he seems unaware of the obvious social criticism and satire of some of his work. He does not mention his attacks on imperial-

[17]  *Almayer's Folly*, p. viii. In his essay on Daudet (1898) Conrad repeated this contrast: "... Alphonse Daudet, a man as naively clear, honest, and vibrating as the sunshine of his native land; that regrettably undiscriminating sunshine which matures grapes and pumpkins alike, and cannot, of course, obtain the commendation of the very select who look at life under a parasol" (*Notes on Life and Letters*, p. 21).
[18]  Letter to Edward Sanderson (Wednesday, May 1897), *Joseph Conrad, Life and Letters*, I, pp. 204-05.
[19]  *Garnett Letters* (Oct. 11, 1897), p. 113.

ism and capitalism in works like "Heart of Darkness" and *Nostromo* and never refers to the strong anti-bourgeois and anti-business strain in his work between 1910 and 1913 ("The Partner", 1910; *Chance*, 1911; "A Smile of Fortune", 1912; "The Planter of Malata", 1913). Significantly, his defenses of his gentility as well as his genteel evasions about social criticism in his writing refer only to his early work. Except for clearing up the unimportant misunderstanding about "The Planter of Malata", Conrad felt that he did not have to defend any novels later than *Under Western Eyes* (1909) or stories later than "Freya of the Seven Isles" (1912). By that time the rift between Conrad and conventional society was closing and there were no charges of sordidness or morbidity which he had to answer.

In addition to defending himself against charges of violating the code of literary gentility in his earlier works, the older Conrad was very anxious to be accepted as an authority on the merchant service and the sea. This anxiety is especially noticeable in the patriotic essays about the activities of the British Navy and merchant fleet during the First World War, essays which he probably felt patriotically constrained to compose. However, in other contemporary writing about the sea, the same anxiety is perceptible. In these later essays he does not always trust the persuasiveness of what he has to say about his subject and usually interrupts his thought to cite his own specific qualifications as an expert. The interruptions usually occur in essays discussing subjects somewhat removed from Conrad's own experiences at sea over twenty years earlier or about which Conrad was less informed than he liked. In "Tradition", a 1917 essay lauding the merchant fleet's wartime performance of duty, he says unctuously:

Allowed to share in this work and in this tradition for something like twenty years, I am bold enough to think that perhaps I am not altogether unworthy to speak of it. It was the sphere not only of my activity, but, I may safely say, also my affections; but after such a close connection it is very difficult to avoid bringing in one's own personality.[20]

[20]  *Notes on Life and Letters*, pp. 197-98.

In "Confidence", another newspaper paean to the greatness of the British Merchant Service, he asserts, at first, a little more modestly: "I am speaking now naturally of the sea, as a man who has lived on it many years..." [21] However, Conrad may have thought this simple statement too unemphatic, for two pages later he again establishes his authority by reminding the reader that he served in the British merchant marine: "I may permit myself to speak of it in these terms because as a matter of fact it was on that very symbol [the Red ensign of the British merchant fleet] that I founded my life..." [22]

In "The Unlighted Coast", an essay written for the Admiralty, Conrad praises naval defense operations: "I know that praise often is but more or less conscious impertinence. But after all this is seamen's work, and half a lifetime at sea may perhaps justify me in expressing the highest possible sense..." [23] In 1919 a Liverpool ship owner asked Conrad to write a memorandum on fitting out a training ship. Although the request was clearly made to an old experienced seaman, Conrad nevertheless insists on his authority twice in his answer. He first speaks of his qualifications in the style of a legal document:

I must premise here that in all that I am going to say I will be drawing on my own experience as a seaman trained to his duties under the British flag and, in regard to the performance of such duties, having a good record for more than sixteen years of sea life both in sail and steam. [24]

A page later he insists again:

I beg the gentlemen concerned with this scheme to understand that I am not speaking as a literary person indulging his fancy but as the usual sort of Merchant Service officer who has served in all sorts of ships and draws upon his ordinary experience. [25]

Not all of Conrad's assertions about his experience as a basis for authority are pompous or superfluous. In some of his later writing

---

[21] *Ibid.*, p. 202.
[22] *Ibid.*, p. 204.
[23] *Last Essays*, p. 50.
[24] *Ibid.*, p. 67.
[25] *Ibid.*, p. 68.

about the sea he recovered the modest tone of quiet authority which marks *The Mirror of the Sea*. Like *The Mirror of the Sea* these essays present solid information and personal experience. Before he had fully conceived of himself as Britain's old seaman-patriot, he referred to his own experience in two essays on sea disasters: the sinking of the *Titanic* and the mid-ocean collision of the *Empress of Ireland* with the *Storstad*. Because he argues there with honest indignation, his assertions of twenty years of experience do not have the editorial pomposity of the wartime and post-war marine essays. In those essays of 1912 and 1914 Conrad has his eye on the subject rather than on himself, and he can show the relevance of his own sea experiences. He argues with unembarrassed sincerity for the use of a cork fender to cushion a ship during a collision:

I have followed the sea for more than twenty years; I have seen collisions; I have been involved in a collision myself; and I do believe that in the case under consideration this little thing would have made all that enormous difference – the difference between considerable damage and an appalling disaster.[26]

In "Well Done",[27] a 1918 essay on the merchant seaman's code of duty, which we might expect to be as pompous and self-assertive as the other contemporary sea essays, Conrad refers to his own authority with modest confidence because there he is discussing his own experiences. Conrad's patriotic essay of 1921, "The Dover Patrol", might also be expected to include an assertion of authority. And since Conrad in this essay does not discuss his own experiences, we might expect such an assertion to be pompous and defensive. But such is not the case, because, as the essay reveals, Conrad had thorough and detailed knowledge of the mission and accomplishments of the Dover Patrol. Living on the south coast of England, Conrad had seen the Dover Patrol in action during the war. Like any writer, Conrad wrote better about the things he knew. Perhaps he felt patriotically constrained to write the inferior essays even though he realized his ignorance of naval and merchant marine activities. By 1921 he had taken the time to be-

[26]   *Notes on Life and Letters*, pp. 254-55.
[27]   *Ibid.*, pp. 179-83.

come fully informed about his subject, so that between the old seaman-patriot and the knowledge he ought to have there was no embarrassing gap to be filled up with windy rhetoric supported by justifications of the author's authority.

Even before Conrad felt that patriotism demanded the clear confident voice of a popular author, he reacted strongly to any questioning of his authority. His 1914 essay on the protection of ocean liners (inspired by the *Storstad-Empress of Ireland* collision) aroused criticism which he answered angrily in a letter to the *Daily Mail*.

As I fully expected, this morning's post brought me not a few letters on the subject of that article of mine in the *Illustrated London News*. And they are very much what I expected them to be.

I shall address my reply to Captain Littlehales since obviously he can speak with authority, and speaks in his own name, not under a pseudonym. And also for the reason that it is no use talking to men who tell you to shut your head for a confounded fool. They are not likely to listen to you.[28]

Conrad has obviously lost the modest confidence and honest indignation of the essay he is now driven to defend. Again in 1914 Conrad was annoyed and embarrassed when the captain of the North Sea steamship on which the Conrads were travelling did not acknowledge him as a fellow seaman well versed in the craft.[29]

The older Conrad, who saw himself as an inoffensive popular novelist and an elder seaman-patriot obliged to raise his voice from time to time in favor of his country, his old profession and his Polish homeland, altered some of his views about the life and character of seamen. The strength of Conrad's earlier ideal of of profession lay in its function as a bulwark against unreason and evil. When Conrad no longer felt their menace, one of the prime

---

[28] *Ibid.*, p. 256. Mrs. Conrad pointed out that "in later years . . . his clear judgment would often be obscured by some little hurt to his personal pride – some trifle he would obstinately regard as injurious to the dignity of · Joseph Conrad – which impelled him to write a long letter of flowery remonstrance or furious protest. . . ." (*Joseph Conrad as I Knew Him*, pp. 3-4).

[29] Retinger, pp. 148-49. Conrad revenged himself in "Poland Revisited" by portraying the captain as a simple-minded Germanophile (*Notes on Life and Letters*, p. 159).

motives for his devotion to profession disappeared. He saw the unendangered virtues of professional seamen as secure and unquestioned possessions, demanding only adequate public advertisement.

In this later writing Conrad, in contradiction to his earlier views, insists that seamen, despite minor flaws, are irreprehensible, that crime does not exist among them, and that their duty is based on their love of their ships, not, as he had earlier believed, on their commitment to austere professional ideals. Because their virtues are so secure, Conrad is no longer concerned with the corrupting effects of egoism. Despite this confidence, however, in every one of his late essays about the sea, Conrad emphasizes repeatedly that merchant seamen performed their duty in spite of contrary predictions and great difficulties. This insistence may betray Conrad's lack of total conviction.

In these pieces Conrad does not admit the possibility of criticizing seamen and in fact apologizes in "Well Done", the essay which most thoroughly expresses his later view of seamen, for having suggested in The Nigger of the 'Narcissus' that seamen can be in any way reprovable.

I have written of them with all the truth that was in me, and with all the impartiality of which I was capable. Let me not be misunderstood in this statement. Affection can be very exacting, and can easily miss fairness on the critical side.[30]

In order to make British seamen appear human Conrad admits to their possessing a few faults but quickly minimizes these and even blames them on the temporary corruptions of shore life.

But I repeat that I claim no particular morality for seamen. I will admit without difficulty that I have found among them the usual defects of mankind, characters not quite straight, uncertain tempers, vacillating wills, capriciousness, small meannesses – all these coming out mostly on the contact with the shore; and all rather naive, peculiar, a little fantastic.[31]

Genuine crime does not exist among them. In "Well Done", he tells of the single thief in his sea experience. The story of the thief

[30]    "Well Done", Notes on Life and Letters, pp. 182-83.
[31]    Ibid., p. 185.

who stole the captain's watch out of sheer audacity rather than criminal greed[32] is amusing and illustrates its point. But when Conrad insists that there is no crime aboard British merchant vessels, he contradicts the profound concern throughout his best work with men who violate the seamen's code of duty. *The Nigger of the 'Narcissus'* tells of theft and mutiny. *Lord Jim* recounts a criminal dereliction of duty at sea. In *The Shadow Line* Conrad wrote about a mad captain who sought to destroy his ship and crew. "The Secret Sharer" concerns a ship captain's concealment of a murderer. Perhaps by 1918 Conrad had forgotten how seriously he had emphasized crime in his earlier work. One would hardly recognize "The Secret Sharer" from his description of it in the 1923 preface to a volume of his short stories: "The second story deals with what may be called the *"esprit de corps"*, the deep fellowship of two young seamen meeting for the first time." [33]

When in his later fiction Conrad needed a seaman to commit a crime, he wrote about a man who has become such a hopeless derelict that he is scarcely human. In "The Partner" (1910) the villain who wrecks a ship for a price and who murders the captain is a disgraced steamship officer who, ashore, drinks and lives off a woman. For *The Rescue* (1920) Conrad portrayed Jörgensen, a corpse-like man whose crimes do not indict seamen in general.

In "Well Done" Conrad has a good deal to say about the fatuousness of the love of adventure for its own sake and man's need for a sense of immediate duty which will act as a feeling of "impalpable constraint".[34] But although these statements sound very much like his earlier sentiments, he discovers new, easier motives for seamen to perform their duty. Conrad says that seamen perform their duties faithfully because they love their ships. In *The Mirror of the Sea* he had said that duty arises from the perfect love of the craft, or the love of the fine art of seamanship which goes beyond mere efficiency and technical perfection. In the earlier work, of course, he is talking largely about ships' officers, especially captains. In the later he is writing about the ordinary

[32] *Ibid.*
[33] "Preface to *The Shorter Tales*", *Last Essays*, p. 145.
[34] *Notes on Life and Letters*, pp. 190-91.

seamen's performance of duty, and perhaps this difference should be allowed to qualify any criticism of a decline in standards. But by the time he composed "Well Done" the popular sentiments of a democratic age had demanded his loyalty, and he was probably not prepared to repeat that the men of the *Narcissus* would not have done their duty at all had not the captain and first mate given them examples of courage and later outfaced their mutiny.

For the older Conrad the problem of egoism lost much of its acuteness. Earlier he had deprecated the man who exercised his profession for his own sake rather than for the perfect love of the craft which serves as a means of self-control and a way of fulfilling social commitments. In *The Mirror of the Sea*, for example, Conrad criticizes the shipmaster who commands his ship with all the finesse of an artist, but solely for the sake of his own vanity.[35] But after he had reconciled the divisive force in his life, he no longer insisted on the love of the craft as a form of self-control. His Captain Davidson in "Because of the Dollars", for example, has no need of self-restraint because of his perfect innate goodness. When Conrad came to complete *The Rescue*, according to Thomas Moser, he removed from his portrayal of Captain Lingard all those elements of egoism motivating him to command his ship merely to satisfy his vanity.[36]

## II

Conrad's own early technical achievements in prose resulted from his perfect love of the craft. But after the inner division between Conrad's Bobrowski and Korzeniowski heritages had closed, Conrad, like the seamen he once criticized, displayed technique simply for its own sake. No longer concerned with technique as a means of investigating complex psychological and moral questions, Conrad, the professional man, the novelist, could frankly exult in his own skill and the admiration of his audience.

In the first novel and the first story written after his serious

---

[35]   *The Mirror of the Sea*, p. 34.
[36]   Moser, pp. 146-48.

illness in 1910 (*Chance* and "The Partner") as well as in a short story written immediately after *Chance* ("The Inn of the Two Witches"), Conrad emphasizes complicated technique, often indeed drawing attention to his skill by direct references in the prose. The complex narrative devices of this fiction are not closely related to the material – the connection between the narrators and their stories is often rather distant, – but one can see a connection between the meretricious technique and the presentation in these stories of virtuous and attractive seamen, professionals menaced only by unscrupulous shore people, especially businessmen. This contrast is a hardened form of his earlier fruitful opposition of the two which had called forth an elaborate technique for adequate exposition. By means of intricate narrative methods Conrad had explored the seaman Lord Jim and the businessman Gould in *Nostromo*. But because the sailors and businessmen of the later works are neither psychologically complex nor ethically significant, Conrad's technique became an irresponsible exhibition. Using clever methods, Conrad described from a secure distance his business scoundrels and weaklings menacing honest ship captains.

In "The Partner" Conrad fails wholly to integrate the narrative machinery with the story and its meaning. The first person narrator, an author vacationing at a small seaside town in southern England, and bored with the rain, strikes up an acquaintance with "an imposing old ruffian" [37] who, although he looks as though he had had many adventures in the dark parts of the earth, gives some indication of never having left England. Conrad leads the reader to think that the story will primarily concern the mysterious old man. However, the old man, instead of speaking of his adventures, gives the writer a long account of a ship grounded for insurance money and the accidental murder of its captain, a story that has almost nothing to do with its teller. As though he were making a final important revelation, the writer concludes with a rhetorical flourish which reveals the identity of the old man: "the most imposing old ruffian that ever followed the unromantic trade of

[37]  *Within the Tides*, p. 90.

master stevedore in the port of London".[38] Conrad has carefully accredited the stevedore-narrator as an acquaintance of the major actors in the story, a confidant of one of them, and (a partially credible device borrowed from *Lord Jim*) a confidant of the clergyman who heard the deathbed confession of the villain. The stevedore, nevertheless, is related to his narrative merely by his disgust with the false story that the local tour boatmen tell about the shipwreck on the rocks and his desire to clear the dead captain, who had given him his first job, of a false charge of suicide. He hopes that the writer will compose the story and thus clear the captain's memory.

Out of this hope comes the stevedore's naive interest in the craft of fiction which he discusses with the writer. The writer is an even less satisfactory medium for this story although before the story itself begins Conrad skillfully uses his conversation with the old man to mock his own professional competence. The writer sketches a Conradian sea story much like *Typhoon*, to be called "In the Channel". The legend of the wreck provides him, he says, with "a hint, enabling me to see these rocks, this gale they speak of, the heavy seas, etc. etc. in relation to mankind. The struggle against natural forces and the effect of the issue on at least one, say, exalted –." [39] The writer counters the stevedore's contemptuous description of the dangerous rocks, "like plums in a slice of cold pudding",[40] with a short unspoken prose poem that concludes "a symphony in grey and black – a Whistler".[41] The stevedore is rather short with the writer's grandiose descriptions and his theory of fiction. In a passage satirically reminiscent of Ford and Conrad's fictional theories, the writer says of accidents: "An accident has its backward and forward connections, which, if they could be set forth –." [42] The stevedore interrupts him from time to time to ask him if he could produce a certain effect in the story.

38    *Ibid.*, p. 128.
39    *Ibid.*, p. 91.
40    *Ibid.*
41    *Ibid.*, p. 92.
42    *Ibid.*

"You'll mind that this was long before Cloete came into it at all," he muttered, warningly.

"Yes. I will mind," I said. "We generally say: some years passed. That's soon done." [43]

The writer has to assure his informant that he can describe the women in the story and the character of the business adventurer.

All this is amusingly done, and the central story itself is very competently told in short sentences and fragments in the present tense. But there is a cleavage between the frame, the idle conversation of a rather shallow professional author, and the serious story of an insurance swindle ending in murder and madness. Furthermore, Conrad is confused concerning his writer, who comments wittily about the techniques he would employ to write the story. Conrad aims partly at an ironic effect at the writer's expense: the writer is so absorbed in his craft that his professional reaction to the story is inhuman; his conventions of story-telling blind him to the effect of the story. But in the last two paragraphs Conrad presents two contradictory aspects of his narrator. The writer begins his final comment on the story he has just heard by saying:

As the vindication of Captain Harry from the charge of suicide seemed to be his only object, I did not thank him very effusively for his material. And then it was not worth many thanks in any case.

Conrad intends this passage to reveal the writer's callousness, but the subsequent paragraph attempts another type of irony. The writer speaks here apparently with his own conscious irony to show he perceives the business chicanery underlying the life of ships.

For it is too startling even to think of such things happening in our respectable Channel in full view, so to speak, of the luxurious continental traffic to Switzerland and Monte Carlo. This story to be acceptable should have been transposed to somewhere in the South Seas. But it would have been too much trouble to cook it for the consumption of magazine readers. So here it is raw, so to speak – just as it was told to me – but unfortunately robbed of the striking effect of the narrator; the most imposing old ruffian that ever fol-

43 *Ibid.*, p. 96.

lowed the unromantic trade of master stevedore in the port of London.[44]

With far too heavy a hand, the narrator ironically taunts any of his readers who are so naive as to be ignorant of murder and swindles near home. Conrad's writer does not apologize convincingly for the story's lack of striking effect and its rawness, because, in fact, Conrad himself is merely calling attention to the clever way he has told the story.

Similarly, one remembers *Chance* particularly for its brilliant method. Yet here again Conrad did not employ the technique organically, and because he did not integrate his method with the material and its meaning, the technique claims our attention. This meretricious technique again accompanies a highly simplified view of character and ethics.

Not wholly satisfactory as narrative devices, *Chance*'s two chief narrators, Charles Marlow and Charles Powell, exemplify the older Conrad's view of profession. These two seamen enjoy the same kind of exclusive pride in their profession which the writer in "The Partner" displayed, and they express attitudes much like Conrad's own in the patriotic sea essays. In the opening scene Marlow meets Mr. Powell, and they discuss the superiority of seamen, disciplined and responsible, to the entire shore gang. They exult in the exclusive advantages of their profession. Powell says:

"And the thought that I was done with the earth for many months to come made me feel very quiet and self-contained as it were. Sailors will understand what I mean."

Marlow nodded. "It is a strictly professional feeling", he commented. "But other professions or trades know nothing of it. It is only this calling whose primary appeal lies in the suggestion of restless adventure which holds out that deep sensation to those who embrace it. It is difficult to define I admit."

"I should call it the peace of the sea", said Mr. Charles Powell in an earnest tone but looking at us as though he expected to be met by a laugh of derision and were half prepared to salve his reputation for common sense by joining in it. But neither of us laughed at Mr. Charles Powell. . . . He was lucky in his audience.

"A very good name", said Marlow looking at him approvingly.

---

[44] *Ibid.*, p. 128.

A sailor finds a deep feeling of security in the exercise of his calling. The exacting life of the sea has this advantage over the life of the earth, that its claims are simple and cannot be evaded.

"Gospel truth", assented Mr. Powell. "No! they cannot be evaded." [45]

Conrad's first person narrator comments respectfully on the friendship sprung up between the two seamen.

But I have observed that profane men living in ships, like the holy men gathered in monasteries, develop traits of profound resemblance. This must be because the service of the sea and the service of a temple are both detached from the vanities and errors of a world which follows no severe rule. The men of the sea understand each other very well in their view of earthly things, for simplicity is a good counsellor and isolation not a bad educator. A turn of mind composed of innocence and scepticism is common to them all, with the addition of an unexpected insight into motives, as of disinterested lookers-on at a game. [46]

For Conrad, who was once aware of subtle differences, these are rather broad generalizations. He will admit no adverse criticism of sea life. Isolation, one of his deepest concerns earlier, is casually praised as an educator. Innocence and skepticism, which he once saw ambivalently, unite to make all seamen innocent of evil, but skeptical enough to cope with it. For seamen innocence can no longer be ignorance, nor skepticism a power capable of immobilizing the will. Conrad's old metaphor of the strength and security possible in a religious brotherhood becomes a bald statement of unshakeable confidence in the life of a sailor. In short, Conrad assumed that what he once regarded as the ideal possibilities of the sea were unquestioned realities. In the world evoked by this passage, the *Narcissus* and *Patna* are impossibilities.

The novelist as superior professionalist also makes his presence felt in this book. Not the least of the novel's clever effects is the theme of chance. Because Marlow often insists upon the sheer chance of trivial events so happening as to bring about vast consequences, the reader realizes that Conrad means not only to underline the operation of chance in life, but also to advertise the skill-

---

[45]   *Chance*, pp. 31-32.
[46]   *Ibid.*, pp. 32-33.

ful novelist's ability to contrive events as he pleases and still have his story accepted by his readers.

Found not merely in a single scene, Conrad's simplified view of seamen and writers appears detrimentally in the method of narration. Marlow does not function with complete success as the narrator, because by the time Conrad wrote *Chance*, he was unable to dramatize the disturbing bond of weakness that gives *Lord Jim* its depth and significance. *Chance*'s Marlow has only a tenuous relationship to the other characters and to the significance of the story. Indeed Conrad illustrates his theme of chance by the unpredictable accidents by which Marlow meets the major characters and thus hears their stories. Characteristically, Marlow begins his narration with "All I knew of him was an accident called Fyne".[47] Meeting the Fynes and Flora by chance on vacation and accidentally running into Powell in a restaurant and later up an obscure creek in the Thames estuary illustrate the sheer fortuity of Marlow's even knowing the whole story, but make him rather distant and unconcerned. The narrator of *Under Western Eyes* had also been fairly aloof from the characters, but although he narrates from a position of secure judgment, the book as a whole, as Albert Guerard points out,[48] creates more disturbing sympathy than appears in its narrator. In addition, part of that novel is supposed to be the journal of its hero Razumov, an intelligent man who can express his own situation; the actors in *Chance* are not capable of seeing themselves objectively or articulating their problems. Marlow alone from his position of security can give the significance of the story.

Not only does Marlow's lack of involvement reduce his value as a narrator, but it also makes of him a character far less impressive in his own right than the mature Marlow of *Lord Jim* and the *Youth* volume. Critics like Hewitt, Moser, and Guerard have pointed out the differences between the earlier and later Marlow. He is a lesser creation, less intelligent. His manner, Guerard says, "has become urban, polite, jocular, chatty, feminine and vulgarly

---

[47]   *Ibid.*, p. 36.
[48]   Guerard, p. 244.

'literary' ".[49] Marlow's lack of involvement from time to time makes him seem an inquisitive busybody. "Our friend", the narrator says of him, "knows something of every ship. He seems to have gone about the seas prying into things considerably." [50] A few pages later the narrator defends the "respectable faculty of curiosity",[51] and Marlow himself once explains his curiosity and tendency to analyze by saying that he had long ago caught this disposition from a "puzzle-headed chief mate" who was also "an accomplished practical seaman".[52] Perhaps Conrad included these passages to justify Marlow's avid interest in others which is necessary for the novel. Conrad has given Marlow plenty of time to indulge his curiosity. In *Chance* he has retired – apparently with a good deal of money and a fourteen ton yacht – and spends his time cruising and peering into the lives of others. In the retrospective parts of the narrative taking place while Marlow is still a ship captain, he is on a long vacation away from the sea. The close connection between Marlow's character and his profession with the stories he tells in the earlier fiction is absent from *Chance*.

At times Marlow resembles Mary Worth of the comic strips, kindly and sentimental, interfering in the love-lives of younger people. The isolation and stoic detachment of the earlier Marlow give way to the social irrelevance of the late Marlow. Essentially unconcerned with the lives of the major characters, and no longer apparently concerned with the conduct of his own life, Marlow can be sentimental and ironic by turns. His feelings have become matters for his own indulgence and amusement.

Not only as a disappointing revival of a famous character established in earlier fiction does Marlow resemble Conan Doyle's Sherlock Holmes. The single friendly auditor who visits Marlow in his snug bachelor quarters, accompanies him on a journey out of London, admires his sagacity, and objects to his cynicism – which is largely bogus – recalls Holmes's confidant Dr. Watson. Marlow does not use heroin, as the old Holmes did before the

---

[49]   *Ibid.*, p. 269.
[50]   *Chance*, p. 35.
[51]   *Ibid.*, p. 40.
[52]   *Ibid.*, p. 102.

conventional Dr. Watson broke him of the habit – with something of the same results as Conrad's curing Marlow of his old
pessimism – but his insistence on his own powers of psychological
penetration recall the detective's spectacular cleverness. Holmes is
made memorable to readers by is eccentricities, and Conrad,
employing a narrator whose warm-hearted views make him indistinguishable from the mass of mankind, is forced to give Marlow some eccentricities in order to give him individuality. On a
day of fine weather, for example, the leisured vacationing Marlow
loves to sit at a window with a book on his knees. To go outdoors
is to waste the day, and he invites the Fynes to tea at the farm-
house where he rents a room rather than spoil a summer's day
with a walk. The earlier Marlow did not need to cultivate oddities
in order to appear an exceptional man. Henry James's epithet,
"the preposterous master-mariner" almost applies to the narrator
of *Chance*.

Suddenly and briefly, however, Marlow takes on an added interest in a unique passage which is unfortunately unrelated to the
book. The first person narrator comments on Marlow's long, mysterious absence from the sea.

From year to year he dwelt on land as a bird rests on the branch of
a tree, so tense with the power of brusque flight into its true element
that it is incomprehensible why it should sit still minute after minute.
The sea is the sailor's true element, and Marlow, lingering on shore,
was to me an object of incredulous commiseration like a bird, which,
secretly, should have lost its faith in the high virtue of flying.[53]

The passage contains Tadeusz Bobrowski's metaphor of the bird
on the branch in a new context suggesting involuntary desertion
of the sea and a destructive powerlessness. This interesting passage touches on some of Conrad's deepest concerns, but we hear
no more about Marlow's relation to the sea he has left. The narrator's phrase, "the subtly provisional character of Marlow's long
sojourn amongst us" [54] is merely an irrelevant echo of "Youth"
and "Heart of Darkness", not the beginning of an exploration of
an aspect of Marlow's character.

[53]  *Ibid.*, pp. 33-34.
[54]  *Ibid.*, p. 34.

As a narrative foil to the subtle and perceptive Marlow, Conrad has created the simple and straightforward ship's officer, Charles Powell. Despite considerable interest as a character and some value as a narrator, Powell is far less satisfactory as a medium for the story than Marlow. In the long opening chapter of the novel, Conrad has Powell tell how he obtained his first job. Although worthy to stand with Conrad's best writing because of its vivid portrayal of the young man attempting to get his start in life, this account is irrelevant to the major concerns of the book. Powell, uninvolved with the fate of the major characters, is merely a narrative device. And he is an inefficient one. With ignorant bewilderment, Powell gropes his way through mysterious clues in the second half of the book to information already revealed to the reader in the first part of the novel. The naive narrator (or point of view character) can be a brilliant technical device in works like *Benito Cereno* or *The Ambassadors* where, because of skillful presentation of information, an alert reader is just a step ahead of the narrator in interpreting details, and in which the education or obtuseness of the narrator provides the outline for the action. Powell's simplicity and ignorance appear useful to the story largely in only one respect: his bewildered and obscure fear of Flora's possessive, crazed father communicates an important emotion to the reader. Usually, however, Powell is merely a coarse medium for the story, and a passage intended to point up his contrast with Marlow makes his simplicity look like stupidity. Of Marlow, Powell says, "He's the sort that's always chasing some notion or other round and round his head just for the fun of the thing." [55] The contrast between Marlow and Powell remains just a contrast, not the plan of a narrative method germane to the novel. Their shared egoistic professionalism unites them to their author and distracts from the story they are telling. *Chance*'s complicated technique, as Henry James observed with his metaphor of five airplanes flying above the same patch of earth and darkening it with their combined shadows, obscures the subject matter.[56]

In the introduction to "The Inn of the Two Witches" (1913),

---

[55] *Ibid.*, p. 33.
[56] Henry James, *Notes on Novelists* (New York, Scribners, 1914), p. 348.

another story contrasting stalwart and virtuous seamen with mur-
derous shore people, Conrad calls attention to his own narrative
skill and suggests his superiority as a skillful novelist to Ford
Madox Ford, with whom he had quarrelled four years earlier and
whom he satirizes in "The Planter of Malata", also written in
1913. Conrad draws particular attention to the dullness of the old
manuscript from which he says he drew the story, asserts that the
loss of many of its pages is no misfortune, and even apologizes
ingenuously for the obviousness of the title. Of the manuscript he
says:

Oh, but it was a dull-faced MS., each line resembling every other
line in their close-set and regular order. It was like the drone of a
monotonous voice. A treatise on sugar-refining (the dreariest subject I can think of) could have given a more lively appearance. "In
A. D. 1813, I was twenty-two years old", he begins earnestly and
goes on with every appearance of calm, horrible industry.[57]

Conrad tells the story which follows with a great deal of skillfully
managed suspense and terror and thus invites the reader's gratitude
for having so improved upon the original. Conrad's emphasis on
the dullness of the manuscript and his discussion of the point of
view from which it was written suggests that Conrad intends an
oblique attack on Ford Madox Ford whose manuscript *Seraphina*
they jointly turned into the exciting adventure story *Romance*. In
the introduction to "The Inn of the Two Witches", Conrad discusses at some length the attitudes of the sixty year old author of
the manuscript toward the adventures of his youth which he is
recounting. This distinctly recalls Ford's attempt to write *Seraphina* from the point of view of a sixty-two year old man looking
back dimly on his extremely exciting youthful adventures.[58] Since
Ford himself confessed that his original treatment of the story
was "of incredible thinness ... like the whisper of a nonageneri-
an",[59] and that it was Conrad who had insisted on a more vivid
treatment, it seems probable that Conrad is saying here that he

[57]   *Within the Tides*, pp. 131-56.
[58]   Ford, *Joseph Conrad, A Personal Remembrance*, p. 23.
[59]   *Ibid.*, p. 6.

made Ford's dull account of potentially exciting material into a fascinating story.[60]

Conrad had always employed unusual narrative techniques, but in his earlier stories he made technique functional rather than an irrelevant display created for its own sake. This is as true of stories aimed at a popular market like "Gaspar Ruiz" and "An Anarchist" as it is of his serious fiction. The technique in his early works does not call attention to itself. One forgets that "Amy Foster" is partly narrated in reverse order or that the first chapter of *A Personal Record* is composed of two circles of time looping progressively farther into the past. "The Partner", *Chance*, and "The Inn of the Two Witches", however, make their strongest impression through their clever narration and Conrad's insistence on his technical skill.

### III

The professionalism marring Conrad's later writing is not the only attitude to act detrimentally on the content and form of his work. His acceptance of romantic nationalism has similar results. While professionalism is the deterioration of his early ideal of profession, that control encouraged by Tadeusz Bobrowski for the vagaries of a romantic temperament and the dangers of lofty idealism, romantic nationalism represents the uncritical acceptance of many of the political principles of Apollo Korzeniowski. Profession was a safeguard against the misleading excesses of romantic politics. Professionalism exists comfortable with romantic politics throughout many of his later novels. Conrad replaced the mature complexities

---

[60] *Within the Tides*, p. 132. "The Inn of the Two Witches" contains several other links with *Romance* and, thus, Ford's *Seraphina*. Each story tells of the perilous adventures of a young Englishman among Spanish-speaking people. Reference to two British seamen in the short story as "heretics" irrelevantly echoes the incident in *Romance* in which an aroused Cuban mob threatens John Kemp because he is a heretic. One of the characters in the short story is named Cuba Tom because he had once walked across Cuba. Conrad accounts this way for the enlisted seaman's necessary knowledge of Spanish, but this allusion to the setting of *Romance* seems a choice arbitrary enough to be a link.

of his three great political novels, *Nostromo*, *The Secret Agent*, and *Under Western Eyes*, with the simplified and confused politics of his Polish essays. In the later fiction, Conrad alternates between disdain for the internal politics of a nation and a belief in loyal sacrifice for the nation menaced by a foreign power. Indifference to internal politics is inherent in romantic nationalism which emphasizes natural and unchanging uniformity of all people throughout the nation.

In his last years Conrad turned again to politics and history as material for novels. *The Arrow of Gold*, *The Rover*, and *Suspense* have backgrounds of Spain, France, and Italy at moments of political crisis. Unlike the earlier political novels, these do not deal with contemporary or very recent material. But although removed in time and immediate historical significance, they contain far more undisguised biographical material. *The Arrow of Gold* is, of course, almost pure autobiography, drawn from Conrad's adventures in the Carlist war. As much of *Suspense* as Conrad finished before he died shows that he repeated the personal contents of *The Arrow of Gold*. *The Rover* is almost certainly a sentimental and justifying self-portrait of the old seaman whose sacrifice of his own life for young lovers and his country's safety allays any doubts which his leaving many years before may have raised about his loyalty. In themselves these books are neither very good historical fiction nor perceptive autobiography. What they reveal unconsciously or inadvertently about Conrad himself is, however, of considerable interest. These three books reflect Conrad's late simplified attitudes and confused ideas about political problems and, in the portrayal of the hero, an unconvincing union of Bobrowski and Korzeniowski traits of character as well as Conrad's desire to justify his life. The protagonists of these books are among his least satisfactory characters. Moreover, there is usually very little real connection between the political material and the character of the hero. For the most part Conrad also presents unsatisfactorily in these novels the figure of the spiritual father and his influence. Dominic Cervoni himself is a character in *The Arrow of Gold*, but he has no perceptible effect on the hero. The hero of *The Rover*, also based on Cervoni, meets an old apprentice, but the brief conflict of loyalties arising from this meeting is quickly solved for the benefit of all, and Conrad wrings a little easy pathos from the situation in which the younger man does not recognize his spiritual father of many years before. In *Suspense*, however, a credible character based on Cervoni is apparently to exert a healthful influence on the hero, and in one brief impressive passage, Conrad describes a symbolic vision of the communion between spiritual father and son.

A list of the contents of *The Arrow of Gold* suggests that it belongs with Conrad's finest novels, presenting like some of them significant political and historical material and depicting in the hero, as well as in one other character, aspects of Conrad's own personality. But Conrad presents both the political and autobiographical material unconvincingly or, at best, fragmentarily. In the "First Note" to the novel he announces that the complexities of political history have nothing to do with his story. In the narrative itself, he portrays politics as merely ludicrous reactionary conservatism and dismisses other political ideas as cafe conversation. Furthermore, he is unable to integrate the political material with the central characters; the heroine has only nominal reasons for supporting revolution, and there is no connection between the hero's passion for her and the politics it involves him in. The material which Conrad drew from his own personality and his Polish background is also unsatisfactory. The hero is supposedly a self-portrait of the youthful Conrad in Marseilles, but because the characterization lacks the inner conflicts and vitality of the original, it remains a mere empty figure. Conrad has in fact specifically rejected his own chief conflict, his disturbed relation to his fatherland. Although Conrad has portrayed himself more effectively in Captain Blunt, Blunt drops from the novel before its climax, immediately after a potentially significant scene which suggests the theme of the psychological double.

Conrad, who had demonstrated his great ability to turn political and historical material to fictional use, had a potentially interesting subject for a novel in the attempt of Don Carlos, pretender to the Spanish throne, to overthrow the reigning king during the 1870's. But early in *The Arrow of Gold*, in the "First Note",

Conrad reveals that he is not interested in a serious presentation of the Carlists. He comments blithely on what the historians will say of them.

It is perhaps the last instance of a Pretender's adventure for a Crown that History will have to record with the usual grave moral disapproval tinged by a shamefaced regret for the departing romance. Historians are very much like other people.[61]

If one ignores the tone of mocking deprecation, one finds Conrad rejecting precisely the combination of romantic emotional attraction and rational moral disapproval that underlies much of his good political fiction. Furthermore, he insists, "History had nothing to do with this tale".

Not only does Conrad reject any serious portrayal of the Carlists, but in the picture of them that he does give he omits the nationalism which historically was an important part of their appeal to their supporters. His portrayal of the Carlists is an exaggerated satire on political conservatism. One suspects that he removed nationalism from this picture because when he was writing the novel which is unsympathetic to the Carlists he was also writing his highly patriotic essays about Poland and the British merchant fleet, the chief sentiment of which of course is nationalism. The real Don Carlos appealed for loyalty with the battle cry, "God, Fatherland, and King".[62] In the novel his appeal is merely that of Altar and Throne, which by the 1870's was an anachronism; and Conrad presents the Carlists working only for the church and the true king. Although the Basques supported the historical Don Carlos because he promised them a measure of independence and Conrad makes Rita (the heroine of the novel), her sister, uncle, and the villain Ortega Basques, he almost wholly excludes any reference to the cause of Basque nationalism. He touches it very slightly in only one passage in which Rita's uncle, a priest, says that "the people were all for God, their lawful King and their old privileges".[63]

---

[61]  *The Arrow of Gold*, p. 4.
[62]  Allen, p. 71.
[63]  *The Arrow of Gold*, p. 114.

Not only does Conrad anachronistically reduce the Carlist cause to Altar and Throne, but he caricatures those two. He sees in the church only gloomy superstition and fanaticism and says that the cause of the "true king" Carlos is indistinguishable from the cause of the ruling king Alphonso. The political insight may be accurate, but as it is used, it harms the book. Unlike Stendhal in *The Red and the Black* showing in detail the essential likeness of two opposing parties, Conrad's narrator expresses the idea in a single remark. It reveals his political indifference, not his perceptiveness.

Other political material is treated even more fragmentarily. Jerry Allen shows that in Marseilles the young Conrad first experienced the clash of widely varying political opinions. In the novel, however, Conrad alludes vaguely to this experience as conversation overheard in cafes. Conrad avoids presenting any political opposition out of which he could have created dramatic conflict, except in one obscure scene in which an excessively civilized and artificial Parisian journalist styling himself a Republican and a Red attacks the heroine's interest in a reactionary cause. But following the scene the journalist and his ideas disappear from the book.

As this incident suggests, the chief shortcoming of all this political material in the novel is that it has only a nominal connection with the major characters. Conrad never makes clear Rita's motives for aiding Don Carlos. Perhaps he was working too close to reality, and in evading the fact that Rita was the mistress of the Pretender, he destroyed her chief motive. Although the hero aids the Carlists because of his passion for Rita, Conrad is unable to make the kind of significant connection between the hero's love and his political activities he had made in *Nostromo*. In that novel Martin Decoud irresponsibly joins a revolt because he has fallen in love with a girl of strong political idealism, and his love story becomes inherently political. But George in *The Arrow of Gold* makes it clear that the Carlist cause has no meaning for him, and even his direct involvement with its failures and successes is rather unreal to him. His ship sinks, but he passes this disaster off hastily.

Unconnected with his intensely political environment, George is also an unimpressive character in other respects. Conrad's own inner reconciliation between his father and his uncle resulted in an empty self-portrait. The characterization is empty because it is a portrait of the youthful Conrad without his inner conflict about Poland and his alternating melancholy and zest for experience which arose from the tension between his double heritage. George only faintly resembles the youthful Conrad or the self-portraits in his fiction, Marlow, Decoud, Razumov, the captain of "The Secret Sharer", characterizations conceived when Conrad felt the contrary attractions of his heritage. Had Conrad been able to present his own character with any kind of depth and accuracy in *The Arrow of Gold*, that novel could have been one of his most profound psychological studies. In his Marseilles days Conrad was undergoing formative experiences. His actions represented a rebellion against both his uncle's counsel of a settled profession and narrowly circumscribed duty and his father's transcendental patriotism. They simultaneously manifested the Korzeniowski temperament and, in his ultimate initiation into the craft of the sea, a carrying out of his uncle's precepts. But George, although clearly far from home, lacks any sense of exile or tie to his fatherland, and, in fact, Conrad never tells the reader where George comes from or anything about his background. Conrad's initiation into the craft of the sea is also bypassed; Dominic Cervoni, his spiritual father, appears as a picturesque Mediterranean seafarer, and his wisdom is reduced to some commonplaces about women. Near the end of the novel George refers to his love of the sea and his profession, but this is only a reference.

Unable to depict the truly significant aspects of his character as a young man, Conrad attempted vainly to show how George was "initiated into the life of passion", but the result, whether based on actual experience or not, is not a character but mere long-winded love rhetoric or, as Virginia Woolf suggested, the "dreams of a charming boy over the photograph of an actress".[64] How Conrad might have developed George at a time when he still

[64] Virginia Woolf, "Mr. Conrad, A Conversation", *The Captain's Death-bed* (London, The Hogarth Press, 1950), p. 81.

felt the contradictions of his father's and his uncle's influences is suggested by the hero of *The Sisters*, the 1896 fragment which later became the basis of *The Arrow of Gold*. Unconvincingly and far too conceptually portrayed, Stephen had at least two interesting characteristics. He is self-exiled from Russia, to which he feels obscurely he can never return; his skepticism, artistic temperament, and wanderlust isolate him from his dead parents and his practical brother. He searches compulsively for the meaning of life.

George is not the development of this potentially interesting character, but resembles what twenty years earlier Conrad regarded as a hero consciously constructed for public popularity. In *Romance* Conrad and Ford attempted to put together a pot boiler. The result was a brilliantly written, utterly insignificant book. *Romance* serves as a warning of what Conrad was capable when his full creative talent was not engaged in his work. The hero John Kemp is a handsome and brave young Englishman who goes through an incredible sequence of adventures and finally, after nearly being hanged, settles down to happy domesticity. He manages easily to be both a romantic wanderer and lover and also a worthy scion of solid country gentry. Except for an inability to let his numerous enemies die in anything but a fair encounter, he lacks all distinguishing marks of character.

In the "First Note" to *The Arrow of Gold*, Conrad indicates that he realized the differences between George and the compelling heroes of his best fiction by suggesting that the novel might have been written in the form of George's defense of his life of wandering to someone who remained faithfully at home. Such a device reminiscent of Marlow's attempts to explain himself to an audience could have made M. George a fully developed character, completely convincing to the reader. The supposed editor of George's autobiographical manuscript explains that George wrote it for a woman from whom he had parted as a youth, but who had written him years later. In her letters she shows disapproval of his leaving home.

I have been hearing of you lately. I know where life has brought you. You certainly selected your own road. But to us, left behind, it always looked as if you had struck out into a pathless desert. But you have turned up again; and though we may never see each other, my memory welcomes you and I confess to you I should like to know the incidents on the road which has led you to where you are now.[65]

One may recall how Marlow realized that no one at home would ever inquire after Jim. Despite the friendly tone of the request, the letter clearly demands a justification of his life. The particular character of this woman to whom George must account for himself is important. In the manuscript of *The Arrow of Gold* Conrad described her more thoroughly as a woman of "great austerity of feeling and conviction". "The moral centre of a group of young people ... she had the power of an exalted character." [66] Similarities between the woman described in the cancelled passage and the Polish girl who Conrad said in his Author's Note to *Nostromo* was his model for Antonia Avellanos show that the austere convictions which made her a moral force were patriotic: "She was an uncompromising Puritan of patriotism." [67] She represents the political ideals of Apollo Korzeniowski according to which George must explain his conduct.

Conrad only alludes to this approach to the story. Although George writes this woman that she may not understand and that she may be shocked, his self-justifying appeal is cut short by the "editor", who explains: "In the form in which it [his manuscript] is presented here it has been pruned of all allusions to their common past, of all asides, disquisitions and explanations addressed directly to the friend of his childhood." [68] In short, it has been pruned of characteristics which we associate with Conrad's best prose. Conrad even insists that self-justification and moral evaluation will not be a part of the novel.

Neither is the moral justification or condemnation of conduct aimed at here. If anything, it is perhaps a little sympathy that the writer expects for his buried youth, as he lives it over at the end of his insignificant course on this earth.[69]

[65]    *The Arrow of Gold*, p. 3.
[66]    Quoted in Aubry, *The Sea Dreamer*, p. 287.
[67]    *Nostromo*, p. xxiv.
[68]    *The Arrow of Gold*, p. 4.
[69]    *Ibid.*, pp. 4-5.

Unable to portray himself in the narrator and to employ a method of composition characteristic of his best work, Conrad nevertheless portrays one subsidiary character sucessfully by drawing on his Polish background and his own personality. The outward resemblances between Captain John Blunt and Conrad's background are obvious. As a southern veteran of the American Civil War living in France, Blunt, like many Poles, is an aristocratic exile of a defeated but sacred lost cause. As a gentleman living by his sword and quick to react to any affront to his honor, even to challenging a rival to a duel, John Blunt recalls the familiar type of the Polish aristocrat and perhaps also Conrad's uncle Stefan Bobrowski. One of Conrad's shrewd insights into Blunt's pride may recall the haughty and irresponsible aristocracy of Poland.

It was the perfect pride of Republician aristocracy, which has no gradations and knows no limit, and, as if created by the grace of God, thinks it ennobles everything it touches: people, ideas, even passing tastes.[70]

In the same passage Blunt's mother describes her son in a way that suggests Apollo Korzeniowski's sufferings arising from the differences between his ideals and reality: "He suffers from a profound discord between the necessary reactions to life and even the impulses of nature and the lofty idealism of his feelings." Blunt describes himself many times as an *Américain, Catholique, et gentilhomme*, words which recall the inscription that the five year old Conrad wrote on the back of a photograph of himself taken in Russia: "To my dear grandmother who helped me send cakes to my poor father in prison – Pole, Catholic, gentleman." [71]

Not only the Polish background which he had exploited so successfully in other fiction goes to make up the character of John Blunt, but Conrad put something of himself into him. H. G. Wells's cruel caricature of Conrad's conception of himself – "a romantic adventurous un-mercenary intensely artistic European gentleman carrying an exquisite code of unblemished honour through a universe of baseness" [72] – could be applied in large part to Blunt,

---

[70] *Ibid.*, p. 185.
[71] Aubry, *Joseph Conrad, Life and Letters*, I, p. 8.
[72] H. G. Wells, *Experiment in Autobiography* (New York, Macmillan, 1934), p. 530.

whose mother becomes very angry at the hint that her son is a mercenary soldier.[73] Blunt's avoiding the American "Yankee" consul in Marseilles recalls Conrad's life-long avoidance of Russians and his failure in Marseilles to apply to the Russian consul for permission to go to sea.[74] Perhaps his long-delayed naturalization came from his reluctance to visit a Russian consul. Conrad's own aristocratic manner alternating between graciousness and aloofness and his passion as a young ship's officer for elegant clothes are also characteristic of Blunt, and both share a taste for fine food. Conrad may have borrowed for Blunt's attendance upon Doña Rita his own distant and correct courtship of Eugenie Renouf in Mauritius. Captain Conrad was thirty in 1888, the age he gives to Captain Blunt,[75] and each, the last member of an old aristocratic family, was attempting to settle his life permanently in a place far from his origins and somewhat arbitrarily chosen. Neither courtship succeeds. Conrad gave up the command of the *Otago* rather than return to Mauritius, and Blunt Challenges his rival to a duel. The rigidity of Blunt's character and his quickness to sense hostility also recall the young ship's officer known to his colleagues as the "Russian Count".[76]

The great potentialities for Conrad of a novel in which both the hero and his rival are modelled on Conrad himself should have been enormous, but unfortunately they are not realized. Had Conrad been able to develop the theme of the affinities between George and Blunt, *The Arrow of Gold* would have been another of Conrad's profound stories of identification with the psychological double, a lower, reprehensible self potentially in the hero. Conrad even recognized this possibility in his material and once suggested it. During one scene the affinities between Blunt and Conrad's avatar M. George promise to come directly into the book, but after brief presentation they are rejected. The scene has many analogues throughout Conrad's fiction. In it, as in the pirate Brown's appeal to Jim in *Lord Jim* or in the appeal of Legatt to

[73] *The Arrow of Gold*, p. 176.
[74] Letter from Tadeusz Bobrowski to Stefan Buszczynski (March 24, 1879), quoted in Guerard, p. 304.
[75] *The Arrow of Gold*, p. 172.
[76] Aubry, *The Sea Dreamer*, p. 140.

the young captain in "The Secret Sharer", sympathy and aid are requested in the name of common qualities, experiences, and backgrounds. In this scene Mrs. Blunt is attempting to persuade George to go away and leave Rita and her fortune free for her son. She appeals first by asking sympathy for her son in almost the same words in which Conrad had defended himself against the charge of deserting Poland in *A Personal Record*. Explaining that she and her son are aristocratic exiles "ruined in a most righteous cause", she says, "a chivalrous young American may offer his life for a remote ideal which may yet belong to his familial tradition".[77] In his own defense Conrad had said: "The fidelity to a special tradition may last through the events of an unrelated existence." [78] Significantly, George reacts by thinking of Blunt according to the formula which described Apollo Korzeniowski: "*Américain, Catholique, et gentilhomme*". He then answers her assertion that "a young man of good connection and distinguished relations must settle down some day, dispose of his life" by denying any knowledge "about those necessities. I have broken away for ever from those things." But Mrs. Blunt, like Jim appealing to Marlow, or Gentleman Brown appealing to Jim when he realizes that he has found a soft spot to exploit, continues to insist on their affinities.

I am aware that you are very much younger, but the similitudes of opinions, origins and perhaps at bottom, faintly of character, of a chivalrous devotion – no, you must be able to understand him in a measure. He is infinitely scrupulous and recklessly brave.[79]

George's suppressed anger, however Jamesian in expression, betrays the effect of her statement: "I listened deferentially to the end yet with every nerve in my body tingling in hostile response to the Blunt vibration, which seemed to have got into my very hair." But the hostile response is forgotten, and we hear no more of the disturbing affinity between the two men. The final duel over Rita, which comes as a surprise since Blunt has been absent for many pages, might have been more interesting had George

[77] *The Arrow of Gold*, p. 175.
[78] *A Personal Record*, p. 36.
[79] *The Arrow of Gold*, p. 175.

realized he was fighting against a man very like himself. If Conrad had developed Blunt as a double for George, a lower self potentially in the young man, George would have become more than a stick figure.

*The Arrow of Gold* is an empty and unconvincing love story with a number of potentially interesting digressions. In turning his back on political history, moral evaluation, the theme of self-justification, for the most part the method of indirect narration, and the theme of identification with the double, Conrad turned his back on what made him a great novelist. One can almost say that *The Arrow of Gold* is an insignificant novel because Conrad so intended it. And this occurred because the tensions of his inner life had gone slack.

In *The Arrow of Gold* Conrad had asserted only once that George was guiltless and deserving of sympathy; in *The Rover* he went much farther in justifying his hero and thus himself. Jean Peyrol in *The Rover* is a sentimental portrayal of the older Conrad's conception of himself. Like *Chance*'s Powell and Marlow, Peyrol, having retired from the sea and having purchased a yacht, still prides himself on his profession and feels fairly contemptuous of shore people. Beneath a surface skepticism he is wholly conventional in approving true love and patriotism. Through this character Conrad tried to show that he has solved most of the profound problems arising from his inner conflict. Unsolved, these same problems had given rise to some of his best writing. Thus *The Rover* is neither a very profound nor compelling book.

In *The Rover* Conrad raises the problem of the hero's desertion of the fatherland, but Peyrol easily rejects the charge as false, proves his patriotism by self-sacrifice, and finally is praised by a trio representing moral and patriotic authority. In proving Peyrol's loyalty, Conrad seems to have drawn on his own brief but highly satisfying tour of duty with the Royal Navy during World War I. Not only a patriot, but also a professional, Pyerol is based partly on Dominic Cervoni, but Cervoni's lawlessness has been considerably softened and sentimentalized, and Peyrol discerns an easy solution to his conflicting loyalties between his country and his profession. The political content of the novel is highly simplified;

revolutionary fanaticism is reduced to mere caricature, revolutionary ideas are vulgarized and made compatible with Peyrol's presumptuous interfering with others; simple patriotism is lauded as the only political virtue necessary.

The chief issue raised in *The Rover*, as critics have recognized, is desertion or apparent desertion of the fatherland, but it is decisively settled. Conrad was probably thinking of his own leaving of Czarist-dominated Poland when he has Peyrol defend himself against the charge of deserting France and, apparently, the royalist French navy by saying, "If there was anything of the sort it was in the time of kings and aristocrats." [80] Peyrol also refuses to acknowledge the validity of the charge that he had deserted the republican French navy after returning to France with a prize ship. Peyrol is frequently accused of deserting France, but he refuses to be defensive or disturbed about it. Conrad is so determined to justify his hero that he merely makes him slightly annoyed at false charges. Conrad thoroughly dissipates the charge of desertion at the end of the book where Peyrol's patriotic sacrifice receives praise from figures who represent moral and patriotic authority to Conrad. As in *Lord Jim*, the most telling accusation of Peyrol's failure of duty had come from a wounded French naval officer who has not prospered in the service, a threadbare, one-eyed captain who recalls the austerely moral French lieutenant. Furthermore, after Peyrol has redeemed his reputation, another wounded naval officer, actually a French lieutenant for most of the book, sets his approval on the old man: "But the only certain thing we can say of him is that he was not a bad Frenchman." [81] Lieutenant Réal's wound, inflicted at Trafalgar, has left no visible scar, but Conrad has compensated for that by having a cripple second the officer's praise with "Everything's in that". Conrad suggests obscurely that the woman to whom M. George had justified his life would also approve of Peyrol's sacrifice. He may merely be borrowing a picturesque detail from his 1917 Author's Note to *Nostromo* when he describes old Catherine entering the church very slim and erect to pray for Peyrol. But this recalls his descrip-

---

[80] *The Rover*, p. 4.
[81] *Ibid.*, p. 286.

tion of Antonia, grown old and white-haired, praying in the cathedral for three dead patriots and "going out serenely ... with her upright carriage".[82] If the link between two women is significant, then Conrad has also given Peyrol the approval of a figure closely related to the austerely patriotic Polish girl of his youth who had criticized his desertion of the fatherland. Finally even his nation's enemies render homage to Peyrol much as Conrad's mother had "compelled the admiration even of our foes".[83] The death of Peyrol, Albert Guerard points out,[84] recalls the moving scene at the end of *A Personal Record* which tells how Conrad first saw a British ship and heard the voice of a British seaman. Captain Vincent, the British commander, praises his brave old opponent Peyrol to Lord Nelson, an embodiment to Conrad in *The Rover* as in *The Mirror of the Sea* of heroic British sea patriotism. Nelson then lauds Peyrol by identifying with him: "I have hardly enough breath in my body to carry me from day to day ... But I am like that white-headed man you admire so much, Vincent, I will stick to my task till perhaps some shot from the enemy puts an end to everything." [85]

*The Rover* also reflects Conrad's wartime experiences of which he was very proud. Deeply upset by World War I, he worried that he was unable to do anything – although he once considered becoming a stevedore [86] – and even took satisfaction in giving his older son to the war. He visited naval installations, evidently in preparation for his patriotic essays. He also spent two weeks on the North Sea aboard a sailing vessel which had been disguised as a Norwegian trader and fitted out with anti-submarine guns. Both this episode in Conrad's biography and *The Rover* tell of an old man, a civilian, serving his country aboard a vessel disguised to hide her true mission. The country's acceptance of that service and of the old man who proves himself neither too old nor too foreign to serve runs as a source of satisfaction through *The Rover*

[82]   *Nostromo*, p. xxiv.
[83]   *A Personal Record*, p. 29.
[84]   Guerard, p. 287.
[85]   *The Rover*, pp. 275-76.
[86]   Letter to J. B. Pinker (Thursday, 1917), *Joseph Conrad, Life and Letters*, II, p. 185.

and Conrad's last essays. In the 1917 essay "Flight", Conrad records with pleasure that at a Royal Navy Air Station he "was made to feel very much at home by the nicest lot of quietly interesting young men it had ever been my good fortune to meet". "Those dear boys did not seem to notice my age – fifty-eight if a day – nor my infirmities – a gouty subject for years." [87]

Although Peyrol is primarily a sentimental self-portrait, he shares with Conrad's first sea mentor, Dominic Cervoni, some characteristics which had once troubled Conrad. In *The Rover* he softens them. Cervoni's contempt for law and his smuggling are reflected in Peyrol's years of piracy, but the career of crime is removed to the eastern seas where it somehow does not matter much. Dominic Cervoni's scorn for upper class conventions and beliefs dwindles into Peyrol's dislike of officers and his suspicion of officialdom, sentiments compatible nonetheless with a fairly humble knowing his place. Cervoni's profound cynicism and skepticism becomes superficial. Conrad had made Cervoni's fictional avatar, Nostromo, a more compelling character, capable of real crime. Nostromo keeps for himself a fortune which falls into his hands, and he becomes isolated and morally ruined. When Peyrol, however, keeps for himself the treasure he discovered aboard his prize ship, no disaster results.

That plunder had never burdened his conscience. It had merely on occasion oppressed his body; and if it had at all affected his spirits it was not by its secrecy but by its mere weight, which was inconvenient, irritating, and towards the end of a day altogether insupportable. [88]

Indeed, rather than ruining Peyrol's moral character, the weight of his stolen gold improves it.

It made a free-limbed, deep-breathing sailor-man feel like a mere overloaded animal, thus extending whatever there was of compassion in Peyrol's nature towards the four-footed beasts that carry men's burdens on the earth. [89]

Nothing significant ever comes of Peyrol's gold; he hides it in a well where it is discovered years after his death and properly turn-

[87] *Notes on Life and Letters*, p. 210.
[88] *The Rover*, pp. 34-35.
[89] *Ibid.*, p. 35.

ed over to the government by the patriotic French naval officer, Lieutenant Réal.

Like Cervoni and his pupil Conrad, Peyrol is a member of the professional brotherhood of the sea. Conrad makes a good deal of Peyrol's membership in the "Brotherhod of the Coast", a large pirate organization in the eastern seas to which he had to belong in order to survive. Although the accusers of Peyrol stress the lawlessness of this organization, it had taught him his craft and the sense of loyalty. At one point the opposition of craft and country promises to bring a difficult moral choice into the novel. Peyrol has captured a British seaman exploring the French coast. He recognizes Sam Symons as a former Brother of the Coast, indeed as a man for whom he had long ago served as spiritual father. For a moment he is faced by the choice of either remaining loyal to France by turning his friend over to the authorities or remaining loyal to his professional brotherhood by letting the man escape possibly with danger to France. This is a moral dilemma worthy of *Under Western Eyes* or "The Secret Sharer". Peyrol, however, solves the problem without betraying either of his loyalties. By giving the English seaman false information and allowing him to escape to his ship, he easily remains loyal to the brotherhood and simultaneously serves France. Conrad depicted this situation mainly because it was an opportunity for ironic pathos. The English seaman never recognizes his old spiritual father, and he complains humorously when he is ordered to steer the dead Peyrol's captured boat.

Politically, the novel merely advocates patriotism, and it simplifies and vulgarizes other political ideas and problems. Conrad only tentatively explores the problem of revolution. The novel disapproves of the reign of terror, and, through its two heroes, Peyrol and Réal, shows skepticism about revolutionary oratory. This combination of surface idealism and underlying terrorism produces no Kurtz-like revolutionist in the character of Citizen Scevola. Conrad later said that he did not even intend Scevola to be a serious portrait of the revolutionary mentality, but in making him stupid, a product purely of mob frenzy, a *sans-culotte* drinker of blood, Conrad created, as he was forced to agree with Garnett, "a scarecrow of the revolution". He admitted that he had avoided portaying a formidable revolutionist as an opponent for Peyrol.[90] A portrait of a real revolutionist would have introduced a political dimension into the book threatening its patriotic simplicity. Conrad insisted to Garnett that Lieutenant Réal was the doctrinaire revolutionist in the book, but Réal fills this role only by mildly remarking on the return of the priests and Napoleon's desire to be emperor. Like the old Garibaldino in *Nostromo* who bitterly regrets the corruption of the idea of a free and united Italy by the "accursed Piedmontese race of kings and ministers",[91] a doctrinaire revolutionist would surely be disillusioned by the growth of Napoleon's strength, but old Peyrol easily reconciles the ideas of the revolution and Napoleonic power. "Equality – yes. But no body of men ever accomplished anything without a chief." [92] Of Napoleon's ambition to be crowned Peyrol comments: "I have heard no talk of an emperor. But what does it matter? Under one name or another a chief can be no more than a chief, and that general whom they have been calling consul is a good chief – nobody can deny that." [93] Peyrol easily explains the other two revolutionary ideals: "Liberty – to hold your own in the world if you could" – a defense of little more than jungle economics; and fraternity, "the claim of the brotherhood was a claim for help against the outside world" [94] – the ethics of a pirate gang. Even granting that these ideas come from a simple old man, one must admit that Peyrol's political and social philosophy is a corruption of revolutionary ideals. Peyrol's interpreting these ideals in terms of his own experience and deciding that they were not new resembles the idea of Joachim Lelewel, the Polish romantic historian, that liberty, fraternity, and equality were treasures buried deep in the Polish national character.[95] Sure of his position in the natural political hierarchy, Peyrol does not hesitate to dispense with the lives of his inferiors. We may approve of Peyrol's forcing the mad

[90]   *Garnett Letters* (Dec. 4, 1923), pp. 298-300.
[91]   *Nostromo*, pp. 23-24.
[92]   *The Rover*, p. 132.
[93]   *Ibid.*, p. 77.
[94]   *Ibid.*, p. 132.
[95]   Chrzanowski, p. 88.

and homicidal Scevola to accompany him on the boat to certain death, but we may wonder at his presuming to take his friend Michel also to his death. He does not inform the simple-minded old man in advance about the perils of the trip. Peyrol feels that Michel would not know what to do with himself without Peyrols' commanding companionship and is thus better off dead. Never before had Conrad so praised benevolent meddling.

Aside from the facile reconciliation of liberty, equality, and fraternity with the power of the self-appointed hero, the novel expresses one political idea: loyalty to one's native land is more important than understanding and taking part in its inner political conflicts, which are thus best ignored. Conrad's simple acceptance of romantic nationalism excludes any subtle treatment of the historical material.

In its initial conception Conrad's fragmentary last novel, *Suspense*, was probably a better book than either *The Arrow of Gold* or *The Rover*. Both the personal and political history in the novel are given more complete treatment than they receive in either of the other books. Conrad seems even determined to deal at some length with his basic concerns. *The Arrow of Gold* had been straight autobiography and fragmentarily glimpsed politics with most of the significance of both removed or repressed. *The Rover* took up the problem of desertion, but in a character so simple and direct that the charge is unfounded. At last in *Suspense*, which he had been considering since 1907 and had actually begun immediately after *The Arrow of Gold*, Conrad took up his own youthful wandering and love-affair in a setting of international political intrigue, derived from his considerable reading in the Napoleonic period.

But again, so far as we can tell from the fragment, Conrad failed for the most part to make significant either the character of his hero and that of other persons, or the political material in the novel. Apparently considering the presentation of a father-son relationship, Conrad has modelled the hero's father, as well as one aspect of another character, on his own father, but because by the time he wrote *Suspense* he conceived of his father as a rather austere and aristocratic republican patriot, he merely made ineffectual and inconsistent what had been in his source, *The Memoirs of the Countess De Boigne*, a vividly eccentric English nobleman. Any possibility of conflict between father and son is quickly passed over. The hero himself is an unconvincing author-projection of a young man whose inner turmoil cannot be taken very seriously. Politically, the novel seems somewhat more significant; but, despite providing considerable information about the forces of European politics in 1815, legitimism, Bonapartism, and liberal nationalism, Conrad involves his hero only superficially with the political scene. Drawing heavily on the countess' memoirs, Conrad was able to integrate the political concerns of two other characters with their personal lives. With only one character does Conrad manage to present significant personal and political material. Although presented briefly, the character of Attilio combines political loyalties drawn from Conrad's romantic Polish background – nationalism, revolution, liberalism, and hopes of success with Napoleon's help – and the profession of the sea. In a single efficient paragraph Conrad sketches Attilio's life, showing how his experiences naturally resulted in his taking part in the underground politics of liberal nationalism. In two short impressive passages Attilio appears persuasively in the roles of spiritual father and son. The force of the presentation of Attilio reveals that deeper than the older Conrad's exhaustion and inner reconciliation of his later years his old conflicts still continued and still were able, at rare moments, to inspire his fiction.

Conrad seems determined to consider the relations between the hero and his family, a matter almost wholly absent from *The Arrow of Gold* and *The Rover* in which heroes and heroines have been orphaned early in his life. In those two novels Conrad raised serious problems only to solve them easily or evade them. Likewise, in depicting the character of Cosmo's father and his relationship to his son, Conrad approaches one of his basic disturbances only to dissipate it. Cosmo's father, Sir Charles Latham, after a romantic youth, retired to his Yorkshire estate, having become slightly cynical. He feels distant from his only son. Conrad follows the Countess's memoirs rather closely in this portrayal, but he emphasizes certain traits and alters his original so that Sir

Charles resembles in part Apollo Korzeniowski as Conrad had come to see him in his later years. This process unnecessarily sentimentalizes the strange man described by the Countess. The historical Sir John's love of nature becomes the fictional Sir Charles's affection for his Yorkshire estate and a taste for sunset viewing. His domestic tyranny becomes a restrained disappointment with his commonplace wife. His belief in "all the prejudices and claims of the English as to their supremacy over all other nations" [96] becomes a pompous, supposedly mature patriotism. Conrad has replaced the Countess's phrase "entertained all prejudices" with his own more approving "fidelity to national prejudices".[97] Sir John Legard had no liking for society. Following the Countess, Conrad says that Sir Charles "despised the fashionable world",[98] but then Conrad violates the consistency of his character by also attributing to him a taste for society. Attempting, nevertheless, to give a unified personality to Sir Charles, Conrad insists that his brilliant entry into French society was not a result of the usual social qualities.

In those last days before the Revolution *le chevalier* Latham obtained a great social recognition in Paris and Versailles amongst the very best people not so much by his brilliance as by the depth of his character and the largeness of his ideas.[99]

Although Conrad, concerned with his plot, may only wish to motivate Sir Charles's entry into French society where he met the heroine's family, this inconsistent trait may also reflect his attempt to re-model his original after an idealized version of Apollo Korzeniowski. Sir Charles receives his apotheosis as another character praises him in terms reminiscent both of Apollo Korzeniowski's personality and his politics,

In the austerity of his convictions your father was more like a republican of ancient times ... Your father understood every kind of fidelity. The world had never known him and it will never know

---

[96]    *Memoirs of the Comtesse De Boigne*, ed. Charles Nicoullaud (London, Heinemann, 1907-08), I, p. 92.
[97]    *Suspense*, p. 20.
[98]    *Ibid.*
[99]    *Ibid.*, p. 18.

him now . . . He was a scornful man . . . Yes. *Un grand dédaigneux.* But one accepted it from him as one would not from another man, because one felt that it was not the result of mean grievances or disappointed hopes.[100]

Cosmo is glad to hear his father praised. The speaker, although a convinced royalist, also resembles Apollo Korzeniowski. He freely confesses to a charge which had been brought against Korzeniowski. "All I could offer to my Princes was my life, my toil, the sacrifice of my deepest feelings as husband and father. I don't say this to boast. I could not have done otherwise." [101] But although his daughter has married a wealthy and brutal boor to save her parents from poverty, the Marquis is apparently absolved from neglect. Higher loyalties had called him, and the question of conflicting claims is resolved under the heading of sacrifice.

Some of this material in *Suspense* resembles not only Apollo Korzeniowski but also the fictional presentation of Charles Gould and his father in *Nostromo*. Cosmo, like Charles Gould, has seen little of his father because he has been away at school and college. However, Conrad is careful to show that Cosmo is not alienated from his father nor that Sir Charles has influenced his son adversely. Although Sir Charles had not approved of Cosmo's joining the cavalry to fight in the Peninsular War – Sir Charles appears to be a "little Englander" – on his son's return they shake hands for a full minute in the great hall of the family castle. This aspect of Cosmo's isolation turns out to be a simple, rather normal, and uninteresting distance between a young man and his father.

Cosmo at first appears to be an interesting character divided by contradictory impulses: an honest attempt by Conrad to deal with serious problems in fiction. But like Peyrol he is a creation of Conrad's wishes. As an author-projection, Cosmo unites the romantic wanderlust, melancholy, and, apparently, the romantic politics of the Korzeniowskis with the Bobrowskis' stability and financial security. The Lathams are country gentry, complete even to faithful old family retainers. A projection of the young Conrad in

---

[100]    *Ibid.*, p. 99.
[101]    *Ibid.*, pp. 99-100.

Marseilles, Cosmo resembles Stephen in *The Sisters* more than he does the featureless George of *The Arrow of Gold*, but he is neither an exile from his country nor a deserter; he is simply taking the grand tour. Cosmo is a youthful world-weary romantic, oppressed by the ambiguity of experience, the lack of meaning in life, and the beginnings of a hopeless love affair. Conrad expresses Cosmo's romantic weariness and despair in ways that lead some recent critics to suspect the portrayal of Cosmo reflects Conrad's own semi-invalid state while he was writing the novel. Unfinished as the novel is, Conrad has left a few hints of Cosmo's future psychological development. Cosmo once asserts that reason is his only guide, and Conrad tells us that for Cosmo and his father "the world appraised by reason preserved a mysterious complexity and a dual character".[102] Like Heyst, another man brought by reason only to the senselessness of existence, Cosmo would probably have been converted from reason to sentiment which, as Conrad pointed out in "Prince Roman" and almost every succeeding work, perceives the uncomplicated values on which a man may confidently base his life. Never before in his writing had Conrad tried to include so much of his father's outlook, his uncle's stability, and his own personality in one character, and never before had he asserted that all those contrary elements could be combined without inner strain. Cosmo's character is both superficial and unconvincing.

The politics of the novel are somewhat more interesting than its hero. Furthermore, Conrad tries to make the politics organic. *The Arrow of Gold* suffered from George's self-important lack of involvement with the fragmentarily revealed political life. In *Suspense* Conrad genuinely tries to integrate the political background with the lives of his characters. They are all given clear political affinities or relations to the political forces of the time, and they all have an opinion of Napoleon.

Conrad has put three political forces into his novel and has for the most part indicated both their admirable and reprehensible qualities. Cosmo usually makes the judgment, but he seems only superficially concerned. The first political force, re-established

[102]   *Ibid.*, p. 38.

conservatism, arouses Cosmo's admiration in the character of the Marquis, an incorruptible man of sterling principles. But Cosmo also sees the hypocrisy and corruption of revived conservatism. He avoids Vienna on his grand tour because he dislikes what the Congress is doing. (Among other things the Congress of Vienna made the Czar the hereditary king of Poland.) And he realizes the futility of reaction:

Cosmo ... felt ... totally estranged from the ideas those people were expressing to each other. He could not possibly be in sympathy with the fears and hopes, strictly personal, and with the royalist-legitimist enthusiasms of these advocates of an order of things that had been buried for a quarter of a century and now was paraded like a rouged and powdered corpse putting on a swagger of life and revenge.[103]

This is a common estimate of the reactionary party of 1815. Although in outline Conrad agrees with Stendhal, his political opinion does not express a similar deep personal involvement.

Toward Napoleon, however, Conrad's political view, seen largely through Cosmo, has more genuine ambivalence. Fascinated by Napoleon, Cosmo gathers many eye witness accounts and opinions of him in preparation for his own visit to Elba. However, he "had adopted neither of the contrasted views of Napoleon Emperor entertained by his contemporaries".[104] When Cosmo proclaims that Napoleon seems the only man among a lot of scarecrows, an English friend objects by pointing out Napoleon's betrayal of liberty and his undying hostility to England. Cosmo's utter assurance that Napoleon can never threaten England gives him the security from which he can view Napoleon and continental politics. Unfortunately this security finally reduces Cosmo's fascination to mere interest. Conrad's sources in historical research are only too evident in one passage in which Cosmo recounts what the English traveller Wycherly had said of his own visit to Elba; Cosmo's account concludes: "He told me he is going to publish a pamphlet about his visit." [105]

The third political force portrayed in the fragment is the briefly presented liberal nationalism, and here too Cosmo is superficially

[103]  *Ibid.*, p. 114.
[104]  *Ibid.*, p. 38.
[105]  *Ibid.*, p. 107.

involved. Italian patriots have joined the Bonapartists in plotting
to liberate Napoleon so that he might unite Italy and reign over it.
This plan probably appealed to Conrad because it resembled Polish
hopes for liberation and re-unification by Napoleon. Cantelucci,
the patriotic innkeeper, admits that he worships Napoleon because
of the "idea", a favorite Conradian term for a compelling and
unselfish ideal. After Cosmo becomes involved with the patriots
by accident, he decides to join them, and the fragment ends with
his secretly leaving Genoa for Elba. But Cosmo expresses no commitment to liberal nationalism and indeed once wonders why he
does not simply leave the conspirators.

   Although the novel is unfinished one can predict what will become of Cosmo and his involvement with three forces of continental politics. After arriving in Elba, Cosmo might have seen
Napoleon and been disillusioned when he realized that the Bonapartists were using the patriots only for Napoleon's return to
France, not in the cause of Italian nationalism. With a little
wrenching of chronology Conrad could have Cosmo meet (or at
least hear of) Countess Maria Waleska, Napoleon's Polish mistress who visited him at Elba disguised as his wife. Faithful to the
end, though betrayed and without hope, the Polish noblewoman
might well be a touching and authentic means for Cosmo to learn
that the patriots had been mistaken in trusting their hopes to one
man. One might predict that Cosmo, after being extricated from
his Elban adventure, will probably arrive at Waterloo in time to
distinguish himself in Wellington's cavalry. Unlike the events in
*Lord Jim*, Cosmo's success at his second chance will thoroughly
compensate for any tampering with the safety of Europe.

   Two characters taken directly from the Countess's memoirs
show more interesting political ambivalence than the unengaged
Cosmo. Although Dr. Martel appears in only a few passages in
the memoirs and in a few pages of the novel, he is more compelling both as a character and a source of ideas than his usual auditor Cosmo. An English physician, Martel (his real name was
Marshall) combined his professional life with wonderful adventures amidst political upheavals. He had aided the oppressed
Neopolitan Jacobins who, he insists to Cosmo, were men of posi-

tions, attainments, and intelligence, not mere populace.[106] In 1815 he is working with the Bonapartists, who want to release Napoleon from Elba, as well as spying for the king of France. According to Conrad's source, he informed the Marquis of the plot to release Napoleon from Elba, a piece of information which, if the French government had taken advantage of it, would have prevented the Hundred Days.[107] A secret agent like Verloc or Razumov, but also a mature and skeptical man, and a professional man of compassion, he recalls characters in some of Conrad's best work, but one suspects that if Conrad had finished the book this man who unites so many Conradian virtues and who functions as a source of auctorial opinion will be too generously permitted to take all sides of a conflict for the ultimate good and may even help extricate Cosmo from an Elban conspiracy.

The Countess herself is the best drawn major character in the novel although Conrad has done little more than efficiently summarize the story of her marriage and her political opinions from the memoirs. For her own preservation she must conduct herself circumspectly both personally and politically. Although one may have reservations about Adele's passionate exclamation of the familiar tag about the returned Bourbons' having learned nothing and forgotten nothing, her position as a French liberal patriot, as the wife of a Bonapartist, and as the daughter and confidante of a royalist ambassador make her a character in which personal life and political life are integrated. What would happen to her if the novel were finished is not clear. Perhaps her Bonapartist husband (a wealthy peasant upstart and opportunist who torments his young wife) would be killed or executed, leaving her free to marry Cosmo who, tired of European political adventures would retire to his Yorkshire estate, much as the hero and heroine of *Romance* retired into happy domesticity.[108]

---

[106]  *Ibid.,* p. 67.
[107]  *Memoirs of the Comtesse De Boigne,* II, pp. 27-28.
[108]  If, however, Conrad sticks to his source, then Adele will, of course, not marry Cosmo; and Conrad's substantial hint that she is Cosmo's half sister will effectively stop their romance. In that case Cosmo may, as Guerard suggests, tame and marry the Count's unruly niece although the general snobbishness of the book and its hero make that unlikely.

One character is both significant and original with Conrad. Based on Dominic Cervoni, Attilio unites two underlying concerns: nation and profession. Unlike the sentimental combination of the two in the portrait of old Peyrol in *The Rover*, Conrad's depiction of Attilio in the few pages devoted to him commands the reader's respect. Conrad does not attempt to excuse Attilio's shortcomings by rising sophisticatedly above moral concerns as he had tried to do in *The Arrow of Gold* or by putting all his lawlessness safely into the past and in far off places as he had done in *The Rover*. Attilio's revolutionary patriotism does not receive Conrad's full approval. Near the end of the fragment Conrad sketches in his history in which for the first time in the book political opinions become a part of personality rather than detached judgments or opinions determined somewhat mechanically by a character's position.

Attilio was a native of a tiny white townlet on the eastern shore of the Gulf of Genoa. His people were all small cultivators and fishermen. Their name was Pieschi, from whose blood came the well-known conspirator against the power of the Dorias and in the days of the Republic. Of this fact Attilio had heard only lately (Cantelucci had told him) with a certain satisfaction. In his early youth, spent on the coast of the South American continent, he had heard much talk of a subversive kind and had become familiar with the idea of revolt looked upon as an assertion of manly dignity and the spiritual aim of life. He had come back to his country about six months before and, beholding the aged faces of some of his people in the unchanged surroundings, it seemed to him that it was his own life that had been very long, though he was only about thirty. Being a relation of Cantelucci he found himself very soon in touch with the humbler members of secret societies, survivals of the revolutionary epoch, stirred up by the downfall of the Empire and inspired by grandiose ideas, by the hatred of the Austrian invaders bringing back with them the old tyrannical superstitions of religion and the oppression of privileged classes. Like the polite innkeeper he believed in the absolute equality of all men. He respected all religions but despised the priests who preached submission and perceived nothing extravagant in the formation of an Italian empire (of which he had the first hint from the irritable old cobbler, the uncle of Cecchina) since there was a great man – a great Emperor – to put at its head very close at hand. The great thing was to keep him safe from the attempts of all these kings and princes now engaged in plotting against his life in Vienna – till the hour of action came. No small task, for the world outside the ranks of the people was full of his enemies.[109]

Despite Conrad's awareness of the shortcomings of Attilio's politics, he has softened the cynicism, political indifference, and personal anarchism of the real Cervoni by the addition of revolutionary nationalist ideals. Attilio's crew of insurrectionist boatmen is made up of men resembling a professional band which had Conrad's unequivocal approval, the Marseilles Pilots' Association. The connection is slight but real. In the insurgents' boat in *Suspense* as in the pilots' boat described in *A Personal Record* is a very feeble old man. These two old men are linked by the fact that the old man in Marseilles recalled from his distant childhood the return of Napoleon from Elba.[110] Conrad continues his elevation of Attilio by another parallel with his experiences with the Marseilles pilots. Attilio's command, "Take care", breaking the silence as they prepare to board the ship that will carry them to Elba recalls even more directly than the ringing English command of "steady" during the death scene of Peyrol, the first words of English ever addressed to Conrad, "Look out there".

Attilio appears most significantly in a passage near the beginning of the book. The dream-like prose describes a young man's recognition of his spiritual father. Soon after meeting Cosmo accidentally, Attilio recounts an incident of his youth. He describes the wisdom of an old man he had known.

"The wisdom of a great plain as level almost as the sea", said the other [Attilio] gravely. "His voice was as unexpected when I heard it as your own, signore. The evening shadows had closed about me just after I had seen to the west, on the edge of the world as it were, a lion miss his spring on a bounding deer. They went away into the glow and vanished. It was as though I had dreamed. When I turned round there was the old man behind me no farther away than half the width of this platform. He only smiled at my startled looks. His long silver locks stirred in the breeze. He had been watching me, it seems, from folds of ground and from amongst reed beds for nearly

109   *Suspense*, pp. 256-57.
110   *A Personal Record*, p. 106.

half a day, wondering what I might be at. I had come ashore to wander on the plain. I like to be alone sometimes. My ship was anchored in a bight of this deserted coast a good many miles away, too many to walk back in the dark for a stranger like me. So I spent the night in that old man's ranch, a hut of grass and reeds, near a little piece of water peopled by a multitude of birds. He treated me as if I had been his son. We talked till dawn and when the sun rose I did not go back to my ship. What I had on board of my own was not of much value, and there was certainly no one there to address me as "my son" in that particular tone – you know what I mean signore.[111]

Because the passage is unrelated to its context, we can interpret it only by referring to the single other aspect of *Suspense* to which it is related – Attilio as an incipient spiritual father to Cosmo – and to related aspects in Conrad's other writing. This vision of the spiritual father is somewhat mysteriously linked to Cosmo's friendship with Atillio by the description of the sunset. The sunset in Atillio's narrative in which the cruelty of nature is halted contrasts with the Genoa sunset when Cosmo first meets Attilio: "The dark red streak on the western sky left by the retreating sun like a long gash inflicted on the suffering body of the universe." The image, crudely obvious as it is, resembles the ominous sunsets at the opening of "Heart of Darkness', and, more specifically, before the hero's death in *Lord Jim*: "The sky over Patusan was blood-red, immense, streaming like an open vein." [112] Although the meaning of these two contrasting sunsets in *Suspense* is not clear, except perhaps as a prediction of better things for Cosmo once he has met Attilio, it does provide a link between the Attilio-hermit relationship and the Cosmo-Attilio relationship. More significantly Cosmo's voyage with Attilio is linked to Attilio's desertion of his ship in order to stay with the hermit. Like the wisdom to be gained in the heart of darkness, the hermit's wisdom must be paid for by a risk. This episode of Attilio's youth prefigures Cosmo's leaving the security of the city and his nominal commitments to established political order for his voyage with Attilio, which, despite its lawlessness, is going to have a beneficial effect upon him.

[111]   *Suspense*, p. 6.
[112]   *Lord Jim*, p. 413.

Outside of the fragment there are other clues in Conrad's writing to the meaning of the passage. That Attilio is meant to figure as Cosmo's spiritual father is suggested by his affinities in one respect with Captain Cook, the eighteenth-century explorer whom Conrad had admired greatly since childhood. Attilio's lonely self-communion as he walks along the deserted shore after leaving his ship has a significant analogue in the description of Captain Cook in an autobiographical essay nearly contemporary with *Suspense*. Conrad concludes "Geography and Some Explorers" by describing Captain Cook nearing the end of a successful voyage of exploration and walking alone on a desert island.[113] Captain Cook's purity of spirit, his selfless devotion to scientific geography and his profession, are invoked in the essay as the inspiration and justification for Conrad's own sea adventures. The essay's reiterated phrase, "son of the soil", links Captain Cook and Conrad: both are men who would not be expected to go to sea. In Conrad's imagination Captain Cook served as a spiritual father.

Most significantly, the paragraph in *Suspense* reflects those parts of *Nostromo* dealing with a spiritual father and son. Nostromo, a Genoese seaman like Attilio, is persuaded to desert his ship in order to try shore life in a South American port by an old man, the Italian patriot Giorgio Viola, who speaks of him as his son. Viola had himself long before deserted a trading vessel in Montevideo to join Garibaldi. Just as he had created Viola's worship of Garibaldi to stand behind his paternal interest in Nostromo, Conrad probably intended Attilio's relationship with the hermit to prefigure and sanction his relationship with Cosmo. Attilio's political opinions, which Conrad describes later in the book, are almost identical with those liberal nationalistic views with which Viola indoctrinates Nostromo. Attilio, however, seems to have learned these ideas not from the hermit, but somewhere else on the coast of South America. Conrad portrays a more complex relationship in *Nostromo*, but the relationship evoked in *Suspense* is not simplified to mere sentimental idealism. It remains an authentic vision of the ideal of the spiritual father.

Once again in *Suspense* Conrad refers to the hermit. At the end

113 *Last Essays*, p. 21.

of the fragment Cosmo and Attilio express their profound friendship, which seems to them bound up with their good fortune. This moving passage late in the fragment follows a passage in which Cosmo expresses wonder whether any man is a free agent.

"Tell me, Attilio", Cosmo questioned, not widely but in a quiet, almost confidental tone, and laying his hand for the first time on the shoulder of that man only a little older than himself. "Tell me, what am I doing here?"

Attilio, the wanderer of the seas along the southern shores of the earth and the pupil of the hermit of the plains that lie under the constellation of the southern sky, smiled in the dark, a faint friendly gleam of white teeth in an over-shadowed face. But all the answer he made was:

"Who would dare say now that our stars have not come together?" [114]

This scene in which Cosmo recognizes Attilio as a spiritual father may very well reflect an interchange between Conrad and Dominic Cervoni as well as Conrad's affection for Edward Garnett which seems, according to Conrad's letters and Garnett's reminiscences, to have grown very strong during the last year of Conrad's life.[115]

This explanation surely does not exhaust the significance of Attilio's account of the old man on the deserted beach, a passage in which Conrad wrote more persuasive prose than appears anywhere else in the novel. He has gone beyond the personality of the tolerant and tired old seaman-patriot to create this vision of the spiritual father. Compared with it, the balanced textbook views of political history, adroit borrowings from the Countess de Boigne, and Cosmo's *Weltschmerz* reveal themselves even more as the uninspired and unoriginal efforts of an author driven by exhaustion to imitating himself and to leaning heavily on sources.

Throughout his later works, from *Chance* and "Prince Roman" to *Suspense* and "Geography and Some Explorers" there are brief flashes of authentic Conrad. One can recall the account of Prince Roman's refusal to betray his country, Marlow's inexpli-

---

[114]  *Suspense*, p. 273.
[115]  *Garnett Letters*, pp. 28, 294, 97, 300-01.

cable desertion of the sea in *Chance* and the portrait of the brutal poet, Heyst's infidelity to his father's memory in *Victory*, almost all of *The Shadow Line*, Mrs. Blunt's appeal to M. George in *The Arrow of Gold* and her son's rigid compulsion to be an aristocrat, Conrad's tender and guilty memories of his father in "Poland Revisited", the grip of his native soil on the returned Rover, Conrad's memory in "Geography and Some Explorers" of having found the desert island in the Torres Strait where Captain Cook had meditated on the sand, and in *Suspense* the vision of the spiritual father and the burgeoning friendship of Attilio and Cosmo. We cannot include in this list the occasional abstract statements about initiation, egoism, or duty which recall the assumptions of his earlier, better work. Rather, we must include the unexpected images, the surprising episodes, or penetrating question of a narrator which reveal that beneath the serene and often insincere masks of the older Conrad lay the eternal conflict between Korzeniowski and Bobrowski, the unappeasable and unfair guilt over deserting the fatherland, the driving need to discover the spiritual father, and the reassuring moments of quiet communion between spiritual father and son.

# BIBLIOGRAPHY

## BOOKS

Allen, Jerry, *The Thunder and the Sunshine: A Biography of Joseph Conrad* (New York, G. P. Putnam's Sons, 1958).

Aubry, G. Jean-, *Joseph Conrad, Life and Letters*, 2 vols. (Garden City, New York, Doubleday Page, 1927).

——, *The Sea Dreamer: A Definitive Biography of Joseph Conrad*, Translated by Helen Sebba (Garden City, New York, Doubleday, 1957).

Baines, Jocelyn, *Joseph Conrad: A Critical Biography* (New York, McGraw-Hill, 1960).

Boigne, Adelaide, Comtesse de, *Memoirs of the Comtesse De Boigne*, edited by Charles Nicoullaud, 3 vols. (London, Heinemann, 1907-1908).

Bradbrook, M. C., *Joseph Conrad* (Cambridge, Cambridge University Press, 1942).

Bullock, W. H., *Polish Experiences during the Insurrection of 1863-64* (London, Macmillan, 1864).

Chrzanowski, Ignacy, "Joachim Lelewel", *Great Men and Women of Poland*, edited by Stephen Mizwa (New York, Macmillan, 1942).

Coates, W. P. and Zelda, *Six Centuries of Russo-Polish Relations* (London, Lawrence and Wishart, 1948).

Conrad, Jessie, *Joseph Conrad As I Knew Him* (Garden City, New York, Doubleday Page, 1926).

——, *Joseph Conrad and his Circle* (New York, E. P. Dutton, 1935).

Conrad, Joseph, *Collected Edition of the Works of Joseph Conrad* (London, J. M. Dent and Sons, 1948-1955).

——, *Conrad to a Friend: 150 Selected Letters from Joseph Conrad to Richard Curle*, edited by Richard Curle (London, Sampson Low, Marston and Co., 1928).

——, *Letters from Conrad: 1895 to 1924*, edited by Edward Garnett (Indianapolis, Bobbs-Merrill, 1928).

——, *Letters of Joseph Conrad to Marguerite Poradowska: 1890-1920*, translated from the French and edited by John A. Gee and Paul J. Sturm (New Haven, Yale University Press, 1940).

——, *Joseph Conrad: Letters to William Blackwood and David S. Meldrum*, edited by William Blackburn (Durham, North Carolina, Duke University Press, 1958).

Conrad, Joseph, *Lettres Françaises*, with an introduction and notes by G. Jean-Aubry (Paris, Gallimard, 1929).

——, *The Sisters*, Introduction by Ford Madox Ford (New York, Crosby Gaige, 1928).

Curle, Richard, *The Last Twelve Years of Joseph Conrad* (London, Sampson Low, Marston and Co., 1928).

Dostoevsky, Fyodor, *The Idiot*, translated by Constance Garnett (New York, Macmillan, 1922).

Dyboski, Roman, "Joseph Conrad", *Great Men and Women of Poland*, edited by Stephen Mizwa (New York, Macmillan, 1942).

——, *Periods of Polish Literary History* (London, Oxford University Press, 1923).

Edwards, H. Sutherland, *The Private History of a Polish Insurrection*, 2 vols. (London, Saunders, Otley, and Co., 1865).

Ford, Ford Madox, *Joseph Conrad: A Personal Remembrance* (Boston, Little Brown, 1924).

Galsworthy, John, *Castles in Spain and Other Screeds* (New York, Scribners, 1927).

——, *Letters from John Galsworthy: 1900-1932*, edited by Edward Garnett (London, Jonathan Cape, 1934).

Garnett, David, *The Golden Echo* (London, Chatto and Windus, 1953).

Guerard, Albert, *Conrad the Novelist* (Cambridge, Mass., Harvard University Press, 1958).

Gurko, Leo, *Joseph Conrad: Giant in Exile* (New York, Macmillan, 1962).

Halecki, Oscar, *A History of Poland* (New York, Roy Publisher, 1956).

Hay, Eloise Knapp, *The Political Novels of Joseph Conrad* (Chicago, University of Chicago Press, 1963).

Herndon, Richard, "The Collaboration of Joseph Conrad with Ford Madox Ford", Unpublished Ph.D. dissertation, Department of English, Stanford University (1957).

Hewitt, Douglas, *Conrad: A Reassessment* (Cambridge, Bowes and Bowes, 1952).

Homans, George C., *The Human Group* (New York, Harcourt Brace, 1950).

Howe, Irving, *Politics and the Novel* (New York, Meridian Books, 1957).

James, Henry, *Notes on Novelists* (New York, Scribners, 1914).

Kohn, Hans, *The Idea of Nationalism: A Study in Its Origins and Background* (New York, Macmillan, 1944).

——, *Pan-Slavism: Its History and Ideology* (Notre Dame, Indiana, University of Notre Dame Press, 1953).

——, *Prophets and Peoples: Studies in Nineteenth Century Nationalism* (New York, Macmillan, 1946).

Krasinski, Zygmunt, *Iridion*, translated by Florence Noyes (London, Oxford University Press, 1927).

Krazewski, Joseph, *The Jew*, translated by Linda Da Kowalewska (New York, Dodd Mead, 1890).

Krutch, Joseph Wood, *Five Masters* (New York, Jonathan Cape and Harrison Smith, 1930).

Krzyzanowski, Julian, *Polish Romantic Literature* (New York, E. P. Dutton, 1931).

Krzyzanowski, Ludwik (ed.), *Joseph Conrad: Centennial Essays* (New York, The Polish Institute of Arts and Sciences in America, 1960).

Leavis, F. R., *The Great Tradition* (Garden City, New York, Doubleday, 1954).

Lesser, Simon O., *Fiction and the Unconscious* (Boston, Beacon Press, 1957).

Lord, Robert H., *The Second Partition of Poland* (Cambridge, Mass., Harvard University Press, 1915).

Mansfield, Katherine, *Novels and Novelists* (New York, Knopf, 1930).

Megroz, R. L., *Joseph Conrad's Mind and Method: A Study of Personality in Art* (London, Faber and Faber, 1931).

——, *A Talk with Joseph Conrad and A Criticism of His Mind and Method* (London, Elkin Mathews, 1926).

Mencken, H. L., *A Book of Prefaces* (Garden City, New York, Garden City Publishing Co., 1927).

Mickiewicz, Adam, *Pan Tadeusz*, translated by George Rapall Noyes (London, Everyman's Library, 1930).

——, *Poems by Adam Mickiewicz*, translated by various hands and edited by George Rapall Noyes (New York, Polish Institute of Arts and Sciences in America, 1944).

——, *Selected Poetry and Prose*, edited by Stanislaw Helsztynski (Warsaw, Polonia Publishing House, 1955).

Mizwa, Stephen, "Joseph Pilsudski", *Great Men and Women of Poland*, edited by Stephen Mizwa (New York, Macmillan, 1942).

Morf, Gustav, *The Polish Heritage of Joseph Conrad* (London, Sampson Low, Marston and Co., 1930).

Moser, Thomas, *Joseph Conrad: Achievement and Decline* (Cambridge, Mass., Harvard University Press, 1957).

Mosse, W. E., *Alexander II and the Modernization of Russia* (New York, Macmillan, 1958).

Najder, Zdzisław, *Conrad's Polish Background, Letters to and from Polish Friends* (London, Oxford University Press, 1964).

Retinger, J. H., *Conrad and His Contemporaries* (New York, Roy Publishers, 1943).

Slowacki, Juljusz, *Anhelli*, translated by Dorothea Prall Radin with an introduction and notes by George Rapall Noyes (London, Allen and Unwin, 1930).

Sutherland, J. G., *At Sea with Joseph Conrad* (London, Grant Richards, 1922).

Symons, Arthur, *Notes on Joseph Conrad* (London, Myers and Co., 1925).

Terlecki, Tymon Tadeusz Julian, "Polish Literature", *Encyclopedia Britannica*, 14th edition.

Visiak, E. H., *The Mirror of Conrad* (London, Werner Laurie, 1955).

Warren, Robert Penn, "Introduction" to *Nostromo* by Joseph Conrad (New York, The Modern Library, 1951).

Weintraub, Wiktor, *The Poetry of Adam Mickiewicz* (The Hague, Mouton, 1954).

Wells, H. G., *Experiment in Autobiography* (New York, Macmillan, 1934).

Wiley, Paul L., *Conrad's Measure of Man* (Madison, University of Wisconsin Press, 1954).

Woolf, Virginia, *The Captain's Deathbed* (London, The Hogarth Press, 1950).

Zoltowski, Adam, "Idealogical Developments in Polish Catholicism", *Church and Society: Catholic Social and Political Thought and Movements 1789-1950*, edited by Joseph N. Moody (New York, Arts Inc., 1953).

## ARTICLES

Benson, Carl, "Conrad's Two Stories of Initiation", *PMLA*, LXIX (March, 1954), pp. 46-56.

Conrad, Borys, "A Famous Father and His Son", *New York Times Book Review*, LXII (Dec. 1, 1957), pp. 7 & 74.

Conrad, Joseph, "Mr. Conrad Is not a Jew", *New Republic*, XIV (Aug 24. 1918), p. 109.

Cunninghame Graham, R. B., "*Inveni Portam* Joseph Conrad", *Saturday Review*, CXXXVIII (Aug. 16, 1924), pp. 162-63.

Dabrowska, Maria, "A Polish Press Interview with Joseph Conrad", *Poland* (American Edition), June, 1960, pp. 26-27. (A complete translation of the text of an interview conducted by Maria Dabrowski and published in the *Tygodnik Ilustrowany*, 1914, No. 16.)

Lovejoy, Arthur O., "The Meaning of Romanticism for the Historian of Ideas", *Journal of the History of Ideas*, II (1941), pp. 257-78.

Milosz, Czeslaw, "Joseph Conrad in Polish Eyes", *Atlantic Monthly*, CC (Nov., 1957), pp. 219-28.

# STUDIES IN ENGLISH LITERATURE

14. CHARLOTTE BRADFORD HUGHES: *John Crowne's "Sir Courtly Nice: A Critical Edition".* 1966. 183 pp. Cloth.     Gld. 23.—

16. BARBARA BARTHOLOMEW: *Fortuna and Natura: A Reading of Three Chaucer Narratives.* 1966. 112 pp. Cloth.     Gld. 17.—

17. GEORG B. FERGUSON: *John Fletcher: The Woman's Prize or The Tamer Tamed. A Critical Edition.* 1966. 223 pp. Cloth.
Gld. 24.—

18. EDWARD VASTA: *The Spiritual Basis of "Piers Plowman".* 1965. 143 pp. Cloth.     Gld. 18.—

19. WILLIAM B. TOOLE: *Shakespeare's Problem Plays: Studies in Form and Meaning.* 1966. 242 pp. Cloth.     Gld. 28.—

20. LOUISE BAUGHMAN MURDY: *Sound and Meaning in Dylan Thomas's Poetry.* 1966. 172 pp., 11 spectograms. Cloth.
Gld. 21.—

21. BEN H. SMITH: *Traditional Imagery of Charity in "Piers Plowman".* 1966. 106 pp. Cloth.     Gld. 14.—

22. OVERTON P. JAMES: *The Relation of Tristram Shandy to the Life of Sterne.* 1966. 174 pp. Cloth.     Gld. 21.—

25. BRADFORD B. BROUGHTON: *The Legends of King Richard I: Coeur de Lion: A Study of Sources and Variations to the Year 1600.* 1966. 161 pp. Cloth.     Gld. 20.—

26. WILLIAM M. WYNKOOP: *Three Children of the Universe: Emerson's View of Shakespeare, Bacon, and Milton.* 1966. 199 pp., portrait. Cloth.     Gld. 22.—

28. SOPHIA BLAYDES: *Christopher Smart as a Poet of His Time: A Re-Appraisal.* 1966. 182 pp. Cloth.     Gld. 24.—

31. ERIC LAGUARDIA: *Nature Redeemed: The Imitation of Order in Three Renaissance Poems.* 1966. 180 pp. Cloth.     Gld. 20.—

MOUTON & CO. — PUBLISHERS — THE HAGUE